TEACHER'S ANNOT...

Vocabulary Workshop
New Edition

Level G

Jerome Shostak

Series Consultants

Sylvia A. Rendón, Ph.D.
Coord., Secondary Reading
Cypress-Fairbanks I.S.D.
Houston, Texas

John Heath, Ph.D.
Department of Classics
Santa Clara University
Santa Clara, California

Mel H. Farberman
Director of English
  Language Arts, K–12
Bay Shore U.F.S.D.
Bay Shore, New York

Sadlier-Oxford
A Division of William H. Sadlier, Inc.

Reviewers

The publisher wishes to thank for their comments and suggestions the following teachers and administrators, who read portions of the series prior to publication.

Anne S. Crane
Clinician, English Education
Georgia State University
Atlanta, GA

Susan W. Keogh
Curriculum Coordinator
Lake Highland Preparatory
Orlando, FL

Mary Louise Ellena-Wygonik
English Teacher
Hampton High School
Allison Park, PA

Lisa Anne Pomi
Language Arts Chairperson
Woodside High School
Woodside, CA

Arlene A. Oraby
Dept. Chair (Ret.), English 6–12
Briarcliff Public Schools
Briarcliff Manor, NY

Susan Cotter McDonough
English Department Chair
Wakefield High School
Wakefield, MA

Sr. M. Francis Regis Trojano
Sisters of St. Joseph (CSJ)
Educational Consultant
Boston, MA

Keith Yost
Director of Humanities
Tomball Ind. School District
Tomball, TX

Patricia M. Stack
English Teacher
South Park School District
South Park, PA

Joy Vander Vliet
English Teacher
Council Rock High School
Newtown, PA

Karen Christine Solheim
English Teacher
Jefferson High School
Jefferson, GA

Printed in the United States of America.
ISBN: 0-8215-7122-2
7 8 9 RRDH 13 12 11

CONTENTS

Online Components and other resources
available at **www.vocabularyworkshop.com.**

INTRODUCTION

VOCABULARY WORKSHOP has for more than five decades been the leading program for systematic vocabulary development for grades 6–12. It has been proven a highly successful tool in helping students expand their vocabularies, improve their vocabulary skills, and prepare for the vocabulary strands of standardized tests.

This New Edition of VOCABULARY WORKSHOP preserves and improves upon those key elements of the program that have made it so effective *and* introduces important new features that make the series more comprehensive in scope and current in approach to vocabulary instruction, especially with respect to standardized testing.

Key Elements

- At each Level, a **word list** of 300 main entries, plus hundreds of synonyms, antonyms, and other related words

- Proven and effective **five-step approach to instruction**, leading students to mastery of word meanings and usage

- Excellent **preparation for the SAT, ACT**, and other standardized tests with strong correlations between word lists and words that frequently appear on the standardized tests, as well as practice in types and formats of exercises found on the standardized tests

- Frequent **review and assessment** both in Student Text and in supplementary programs

New Features

To address recent changes in such standardized tests as the SAT and the ACT, the New Edition of VOCABULARY WORKSHOP introduces two features designed to provide students with further opportunities to prepare for new challenges presented on these standardized tests and, at the same time, to apply and extend their vocabulary, reading, and writing skills. These new features appear in each of the Reviews.

- **Vocabulary for Comprehension**, a two-page feature, consists of a reading passage and a page of exercises that give students practice in the kinds of comprehension and vocabulary questions that appear on such standardized tests as the "new" SAT and the ACT.

- Following the Vocabulary for Comprehension exercises is a new feature called **Grammar in Context**. Referring to a grammar or usage topic illustrated in the preceding reading passage, Grammar in Context provides instruction and practice in a grammar or usage skill tested on the Writing section of the "new" SAT and on other standardized tests.

Other Features

Among the features that were introduced in the previous edition of the VOCABULARY WORKSHOP program and that have been carried over to the New Edition are the following:

- In the Units, an expanded **Definitions** section that includes synonyms, antonyms, and complete illustrative sentences for each part of speech for every taught word

- Also in the Units, **Vocabulary in Context**, a reading passage that provides examples of how Unit words are used in more fully developed contexts than simple sentences

- Instruction in and examples of key vocabulary **strategies**—using context and using word structure—for decoding word meanings

- In the Reviews, the **Building with Classical Roots** section, an exercise that acquaints students with Latin and Greek roots and provides a strategy for finding the meaning of words derived from these roots

- In the Cumulative Reviews, the **Enriching Your Vocabulary** section, designed to broaden and enhance students' understanding of the relationships, history, and origins of the words that make up the English language

- For all Levels, A–H, a **Test Generator** that adds a secure and customizable assessment option to the program, eliminating the risk of "secondhand" tests that may distort assessment results

ONLINE COMPONENTS
www.vocabularyworkshop.com

Now available at www.vocabularyworkshop.com

- For Levels A–F, an **Online Audio Program** with definitions, pronunciations, and examples of usage for all 300 key words per Level

- For all Levels, A–H, **SAT and ACT Practice Worksheets** for the Passage-based Reading, Grammar, and Timed Essay parts of these tests

- For all Levels, A–H, **Interactive Games and Puzzles** that extend and enrich the instruction and practice provided in the Student Texts.

For more information about the VOCABULARY WORKSHOP Online Components, see page T21.

OVERVIEW

"Pure Vocabulary" Approach: Systematic Vocabulary Instruction

The VOCABULARY WORKSHOP program focuses on words themselves, their meanings (both literal and figurative), their ranges of application (or usage), and their relationships to other words.

The approach is systematic in the sense that it begins with and builds upon a word list compiled to provide students with vocabulary they will encounter in their reading both in and out of the classroom. It is designed to provide students with the vocabulary skills they will need in order to achieve higher-level reading proficiency and to succeed at standardized tests.

The VOCABULARY WORKSHOP systematic approach differs from a literature-based approach in that each Unit begins with a thorough consideration of the words themselves rather than with a reading selection featuring words to be studied. (This is not to say that VOCABULARY WORKSHOP cannot be profitably used as a complement to a literature-based approach. See pages T30–T31 for suggestions on how this might be done.)

Rather than in the circumstantial context of literature, VOCABULARY WORKSHOP introduces and exemplifies vocabulary usage in varied and controlled contexts. These range from short phrases to full sentences to the Vocabulary in Context reading passages.

For effective study, the "pure vocabulary" approach also offers these advantages:

- It provides unlimited flexibility in the choice and placement of grade-appropriate material.

- It avoids the problem of trying to deal with a literary passage both as literature and as a vehicle for vocabulary instruction.

- It focuses more directly and completely on the words themselves, their meanings, their usage, and their relationships to other words.

- By economizing space, it allows a greater range of practice, reinforcement, and enhancement.

- It allows maximum coverage of a maximum number of key words.

One of the cornerstones of the VOCABULARY WORKSHOP approach is intensive practice through varied and abundant "hands-on" exercises. This method ensures that students are provided with:

- maximum exposure to different meanings of the key words studied;

- maximum coverage of the range of each key word through its appearance in many different contexts;

• fullest understanding of the key words' relationships to other words.

The aim of the pattern of intensive practice is to include the words in the students' active, daily-use vocabulary. This implies the ability to use a given word not only in its literal, or narrow, sense but also in a figurative way. Furthermore, it means that students will be able to use the word with confidence both as speakers and as writers.

Grade-Level Placements

The chart below shows the suggested grade placement for each Level of VOCABULARY WORKSHOP, depending on the overall ability of the student population involved.

In determining "proper" placement of a particular Level of VOCABULARY WORKSHOP in a given situation, the following considerations should be taken into account:

• Grade placements are based on actual teacher experience and recommendations throughout the long course of VOCABULARY WORKSHOP's history.

• Differences in grade are reflected not only in the "difficulty" of the words presented but also in the "maturity" of the sentences and other contexts in which those words are used.

• Grade levels indicated in the chart should not be taken in too literal or rigorous a sense. A certain amount of experimentation, as well as the use of the diagnostic materials provided in the program, will establish the "correct" placement of a particular Level in a given situation.

• The use of Level H with "above-average" students is designed to enhance preparation for the SAT and other college-entrance examinations.

Grade Placements			
"Average" Students		"Above-Average" Students	
Level	Grade	Level	Grade
A	6	A	5
B	7	B	6
C	8	C	7
D	9	D	8
E	10	E	9
F	11	F	10
G	12	G	11
		H	12

Word Lists

Each Student Text in the VOCABULARY WORKSHOP program for Levels A–H contains 300 words organized in 15 Units.

Criteria for Selection

The selection of words for the VOCABULARY WORKSHOP program is based on four major criteria:

- currency in and usefulness for present-day American oral or written communication;
- frequency on recognized vocabulary lists;
- applicability to standardized tests, especially the SAT;
- current grade-placement research.

General Sources

The lists of key words were developed from many sources:

- traditional, classic, and contemporary literature, including novels, short stories, essays, newspaper and magazine articles, plays, films, videos, and TV programs;
- spelling and vocabulary lists recognized as valid bases for teaching language skills at the middle and secondary levels;
- current subject-area textbooks, glossaries, and ancillary materials (especially for general, nontechnical terms).

Dictionary and Reference Sources

The following were the primary dictionary resources used for word (and definition) selection:

- *Webster's Third International Dictionary of the English Language* (unabridged)
- *Merriam-Webster's Collegiate Dictionary* (Ninth and Tenth editions)

Other supplementary dictionaries consulted included:

- *The American Heritage Dictionary of the English Language* (all four editions)
- *The Random House Dictionary of the English Language* (unabridged; both editions)
- *The Compact Edition of the Oxford English Dictionary*

Standard Word-Frequency Sources

Standard word-frequency studies were employed to evaluate and revise the words on the tentative lists. These included:

- *Primary*
  Dale-O'Rourke: *The Living Word Vocabulary*
  Carroll-Davies-Richman: *Word Frequency Book*

- *Supplementary*
  Harris-Jacobsen: *Basic Reading Vocabularies*
  Thorndike-Lorge: *The Teacher's Word Book of 30,000 Words*
  Zeno-Ivens-Millard-Duvvuri: *The Educator's Word Frequency Guide*

"Sliding-Scale" Placement

Each word list works on a sliding scale based on these principles:

- No word that Dale-O'Rourke indicates as known in a given grade is presented in that grade. Instead, where possible, it is presented 2 or 3 grades earlier.

- Each grade level contains a preponderance of words not known (according to Dale-O'Rourke) 2 or 3 grades later, with an admixture (in decreasing numbers) of words not known 4 or more grades later.

- The higher the grade, the larger the percentage of more difficult words contained on the word list. This was done to accommodate as many "SAT-type" words as possible in the key word lists for Grades 10–12.

PROGRAM COMPONENTS

This New Edition of VOCABULARY WORKSHOP, Levels A–H, consists of the following components:

Components of the VOCABULARY WORKSHOP Program

- **Student Texts,** 8 Levels (A–H)

- **Teacher's Annotated Editions,** 8 Levels (A–H)

- **Test Booklets**
  - Form A, 8 Levels (A–H)
  - Form B, 8 Levels (A–H)
  - Combined Answer Keys, 8 Levels (A–H)

- **Test Generator with *ExamView® Assessment Suite,*** 8 Levels (A–H)

- SAT-Type **TEST PREP Blackline Masters** (answers included), 8 Levels (A–H)

- **Online Audio Program**, 6 Levels (A–F) at **www.vocabularyworkshop.com**

- Online **SAT and ACT Practice Worksheets**, 8 Levels (A–H) at **www.vocabularyworkshop.com**

- Online **Interactive Games and Puzzles**, 8 Levels (A–H) at **www.vocabularyworkshop.com**

The components have been designed for use in an integrated year-long vocabulary program, as suggested in the chart on pages T23–T25.

The Student Texts

All eight Student Texts (Levels A–H) present 300 key words and are organized in the same way: 15 Units of 20 words each; 5 Reviews (following Units 3, 6, 9, 12, and 15); and 4 Cumulative Reviews. Preceding the first Unit is a section titled The Vocabulary of Vocabulary and a Diagnostic Test. Concluding each Student Text is a Final Mastery Test.

Vocabulary of Vocabulary (Student Text pages 7–17)

The purpose of this section is to familiarize students with some of the terms, concepts, and strategies that will be introduced and applied in the program. The practice exercises that accompany the discussions are meant to clarify and consolidate the concepts involved.

Some of these terms (for example, *synonyms* and *antonyms*) will already be familiar to most students. However, teachers should not hesitate to review these terms if doing so seems advisable, even at the upper levels of the program. Other, more complex concepts (such as analogies and context), however, may require more instruction and practice, both as preparation for related exercises and as review or reteaching for any students who have difficulty in successfully completing those exercises.

This is particularly true of analogies, which many students find especially challenging. One page of Vocabulary of Vocabulary is devoted to this important critical-thinking exercise so often found on standardized tests.

Diagnostic Test (Student Text pages 18–20)

A Diagnostic Test has been provided at the beginning of each Level as a means of assessing the students' overall vocabulary and test-taking skills. The Test covers a selection of key words introduced in the Level in question and is presented in the form of 50 synonym and antonym items.

Although the Diagnostic Test may be presented as a timed speed test, with the specific aim of determining how many items students can answer in 10 or 15 minutes, it is better used as an informal assessment and/or motivational device. Speed will come when confidence and vocabulary fluency have developed.

The Units

At the heart of the Student Texts—and of the VOCABULARY WORKSHOP program—are the 15 Units in which the 300 key words are introduced.

The work of each Unit is divided into a unique 5-part structure designed to give maximum coverage to each of the key words within the space available.

Structure of the Unit
(20 words)
1. Definitions
2. Completing the Sentence
3. Synonyms and Antonyms
4. Choosing the Right Word
5. Vocabulary in Context

The following descriptions of the individual exercises in a typical Unit of Levels A–H are designed to aid the teacher in using the text to maximum effect in the classroom.

1. DEFINITIONS

The first section of each Unit provides definitions, parts of speech, pronunciation, synonyms, antonyms, and illustrative sentences.

DEFINITIONS

The definitions provided are not of the dictionary type. They are, for the most part, relatively brief and simple. The intent is to give students a reasonably good "core" idea of what each word means, without extensive detail or secondary connotations.

Generally, only a single meaning of maximum usefulness is given the student. However, several meanings may be indicated if they are distinct, if they appear to be more or less equally useful, or if they will enable students to prepare for the vocabulary-in-context strand of the Critical Reading section of the new SAT.

PART OF SPEECH

The part of speech of each word is indicated at the beginning of the definition, using a simple set of abbreviations. When a word functions as several parts of speech, the appropriate abbreviation appears before the corresponding definition. (An explanation of the abbreviations used can be found on page 6 of each Student Text.)

PRONUNCIATION

With each word listing, the pronunciation is indicated by means of a simple set of diacritical marks presented at the beginning of every Student Text (page 6).

The practice has been to indicate only one pronunciation, even where alternate pronunciations are sanctioned by the dictionary. There are only a few exceptions to this—for example, when a word changes its pronunciation in accordance with its use as different parts of speech (ob´ ject and ob ject´).

Note that as they complete the first section of each Unit, students may utilize the **Online Audio Program** (Levels A–F only) for that Unit. Available at **www.vocabularyworkshop.com**, this program provides about four hours of spoken material per Student Text, including pronunciation. For further details about the Audio Program, see page T21.

SYNONYMS AND ANTONYMS

A list of synonyms and/or antonyms is given for each key word for which there is one or more of either. Some of these synonyms and antonyms will reappear in the Synonyms and Antonyms section (see page T13). By studying the given synonyms and antonyms, students will better understand the denotational family of words of which each key word is part; and by comparing specific usages of key words and their synonyms, students can better appreciate appropriate contexts for, and nuances in meaning and connotation represented by, these words.

Note that the lists of synonyms and antonyms are not meant to be exhaustive. Grade-level parameters have been taken into account; and obscure, archaic, and slang synonyms and antonyms have generally been avoided.

ILLUSTRATIVE SENTENCE

Concluding each key entry is an illustrative sentence including a blank space in which students must write the taught word. These sentences, although necessarily brief, provide a context that clarifies the meaning of each word and points up its idiomatic usage. By writing the word in such contextual settings, students begin to see how it can be used effectively in their own writing. Furthermore, the act of writing is in itself a form of reinforcement; and by writing the word, the student must focus attention on its spelling as well.

2. COMPLETING THE SENTENCE

The next activity, Completing the Sentence, is a simple completion exercise in which students are asked to choose and write the word that logically and meaningfully fits into a blank in a given sentence.

When using this activity in the classroom, the teacher should bear in mind the following considerations:

- The sentences in this activity call for the literal or direct (as opposed to the metaphorical or extended) meaning of the words involved. This is an easier usage for students to grasp and provides a good foundation for the more sophisticated contexts that appear in Choosing the Right Word.

- The sentences are designed so that one and only one of the words fits in the given blank. Selection of the proper word has been facilitated by the incorporation of context clues in each sentence.

- The words are to be used as the part of speech given in Definitions. The only exceptions are: Nouns given in the singular in Definitions may be plural in the sentences; verbs given in the base form in Definitions may be used in any tense or form (including participial) required by the sentence.

3. SYNONYMS AND ANTONYMS

In this section students are given phrases that include synonyms or antonyms as presented in the Definitions section and must choose the appropriate key word for each phrase. Each of the 20 key Unit words is covered once in either the Synonyms or the Antonyms part of the section. Besides reinforcing meanings, this exercise provides students with further examples of usage and context.

4. Choosing the Right Word

The fourth activity in each Unit is called Choosing the Right Word. In it students are asked to choose the member of a pair of words that more satisfactorily completes the sentence. At first appearance this exercise may seem an easier activity than Completing the Sentence. In fact, however:

- sentences in this activity are more mature linguistically and in subject matter;
- in many cases the words covered are used in a more figurative, extended, or abstract meaning;
- the part of speech or form of the key word has been changed (for example, from an adjective to an adverb) whenever convenient.

Accordingly, this activity is in reality more difficult than Completing the Sentence and requires real effort and a thorough understanding of the range of a word to complete successfully.

5. Vocabulary in Context

The fifth, and last, section of each Unit is an activity titled Vocabulary in Context. The activity is presented in the form of a reading passage, approximating a standardized-test format, into which a number of the key Unit words have been woven. Its purpose is threefold:

- to give further examples of usage for the selected words;
- to offer an opportunity to derive meaning from context;
- to provide practice in the sort of vocabulary exercises found on standardized tests.

With this activity, it may prove helpful to refer students, if necessary, to the section of Vocabulary of Vocabulary (see Student Text pages 7–17) that serves as an introduction to the strategies involved in studying vocabulary in context.

Follow-Up Activities

Once the work of the Unit is completed, you may find it useful to give a writing exercise in which students may apply and illustrate what they have learned about the words introduced in the Unit.

Writing Essays or Stories

Students might be invited to create their own brief essays or short stories and encouraged to use as many of the Unit's key words as is practical. (Students should, however, be discouraged from trying to "force" key words into their essays or stories indiscriminately, just for the sake of number alone. It is essential that students get in the habit of using these words correctly.) If they are to write essays, students might refer to the Vocabulary in Context passages as models.

WRITING SENTENCES

Depending on the ability level of individual students or of classes, you may prefer instead to administer a short writing exercise (5–10 items) such as the one shown below. This exercise is not so challenging as writing a story or essay but will give students an opportunity to "try out" some of the words they have learned and will provide the teacher with a means of assessing how well students have mastered the meaning and usage of these words.

Sample Writing Exercise (Level D)

Framing Sentences   *On the lines provided, write an **original** sentence that illustrates the meaning and use of each of the following words. Do **not** merely copy one of the sentences given in the Student Text.*

1. dilemma

_____

_____

_____

2. relinquish

_____

_____

_____

3. breach

_____

_____

_____

4. circumspect

_____

_____

_____

5. opinionated

_____

_____

_____

The Reviews

A Review follows every three Units. Every effort has been made to include all of the 60 key words at least once in the Review for the three corresponding Units.

Structure of the Review
1. Vocabulary for Comprehension
2. Grammar in Context
3. Two-Word Completions
4. Choosing the Right Meaning
5. Antonyms
6. Word Families
7. Word Associations
8. Building with Classical Roots

SAT Sections

The first four parts of each Review have been specially designed to meet the needs of students seriously preparing for the Critical Reading and the Writing sections of the SAT and similar standardized tests.

Vocabulary for Comprehension (Part 1)

This new feature is modeled on, and designed to help students prepare for, the Reading sections of standardized tests. Students first read a passage of expository or informational text and then answer vocabulary-in-context and comprehension questions relating to that text. An introduction to this feature may be found on pages 13–15 of the Student Text. It is recommended that students read this introduction and discuss it with their teacher before they undertake the Vocabulary for Comprehension exercises in the Reviews.

Grammar in Context (Part 2)

Also a new feature, Grammar in Context aims to provide review and practice in those grammar and usage skills most commonly tested on standardized tests. The grammar skill or skills covered in any given Review are linked to the Vocabulary for Comprehension passage that precedes it. A list of the skills covered in this Level, together with an introduction to the Grammar in Context feature, appears on page 16 of the Student Text.

TWO-WORD COMPLETIONS (PART 3)

This part of the Review has been designed to familiarize students with the type of word-omission (cloze) exercise that appears on typical standardized tests, including the SAT. Again the aim here is to refine students' critical-thinking skills. Context clues are embedded within the passages to guide students to the correct choice.

CHOOSING THE RIGHT MEANING (PART 4)

Focusing on usage-discrimination skills, this part of the Review challenges students to choose, from among two or more taught meanings of a word, the only one that the specific context will reasonably allow. This activity gives students useful practice in determining a word's meaning by careful attention to the context in which it appears, a skill assessed in the Critical Reading section of the SAT.

Note: Explanations for the correct answers to the Two-Word Completions and the Choosing the Right Meaning exercises can be found in the supplemental answer key on pages T38–T48.

ONLINE COMPONENTS
www.vocabularyworkshop.com

Practice Worksheets for the Passage-based Reading, Grammar, and Timed Essay sections of the new SAT and ACT are now available online. See page T21 for details.

OTHER SECTIONS OF THE REVIEW

ANTONYMS (PART 5)

As it requires of students that they recall the meaning of a key word in order to determine its opposite, this activity helps students "situate" a word within the cluster of words of related meanings.

WORD FAMILIES (PART 6)

This part extends the work of the Units by showing students that by learning one English word they often are acquiring a whole family of related words.

WORD ASSOCIATIONS (PART 7)

The purpose of this activity is to reinforce understanding of the meanings of key words with brief definitions or allusions that suggest key words.

BUILDING WITH CLASSICAL ROOTS (PART 8)

Building on the foundation laid down in the Vocabulary of Vocabulary section titled Vocabulary Strategy: Word Structure (Student Text pages 11–12), this part of the Review introduces students to English words derived from common Latin and Greek stems and gives practice in the strategy of finding meaning by analyzing the parts of a word.

The Cumulative Reviews

Once students have completed the Reviews (and any follow-up activities), they may turn to the Cumulative Reviews.

Of the four parts of the Cumulative Reviews, two mirror activities presented in the Reviews: Choosing the Right Meaning and Two-Word Completions. These are presented in the same format and serve the same purpose as their counterparts in the Reviews, primarily to give students practice in types of questions they will encounter on the SAT and other standardized tests.

Each of the Cumulative Reviews begins with a set of analogy exercises. Analogies are valuable and revealing, not merely as a kind of mental gymnastics, but also as a means of pinning down the exact meanings of words and of remedying misconceptions or uncertainties about how those words are used. They also provide an excellent means of testing and refining the critical-thinking skills used on the college level. Furthermore, words that receive the attention necessary to complete an analogy successfully are much more likely to become part of the student's active daily-use vocabulary.

An introduction to the structure of analogies and strategies with which to solve them is provided in "Working with Analogies" on page 17 of the Student Text. It is recommended that students read this introduction and discuss it with their teacher before they undertake the analogies exercises in the Cumulative Reviews.

The fourth part of the Cumulative Review, Enriching Your Vocabulary, is designed to broaden and enhance student knowledge of the interesting origins, history, and relationships of the words that make up the English language.

The Final Mastery Test

The Final Mastery Test in the Student Text of Levels A–H is designed as a practice test of 100 items that gives students and teachers reasonably good insight into how much progress has been made during the year and what kind of additional work is in order.

The purpose of the Final Mastery Test is fourfold.

- It can serve as a dry run in preparation for the more formal (and "secure") tests available as optional components of this program.
- It can serve as an informal evaluation of achievement to date.
- It can serve as a reinforcement activity.
- It can serve as a before-and-after comparison when used in conjunction with the Diagnostic Test.

For whichever purpose the test is used, it is both a testing and a teaching device, the culminating step in a process involving many class periods and, therefore, should be given careful attention.

Supplemental Assessment Components (Optional)

Test Generator with ExamView® Assessment Suite (Levels A–H)

The VOCABULARY WORKSHOP **Test Generator** allows teachers to quickly and easily create secure student tests that support the Student Texts for Levels A–H. With the Test Generator, countless unique vocabulary tests with a variety of question types and formats are available for use within minutes. With a database of nearly 4000 test items per Level, teachers never have to administer the same test twice.

Every CD of the Test Generator provides:

- a variety of user-friendly methods for selecting questions to include on customized tests

- the ability to scramble answer choices and/or questions so that multiple versions of the same test can be administered securely

- a wide assortment of question types to choose from: pronunciation, part of speech, spelling, definitions, synonyms and antonyms, sentence completions, sentence framing

- preformatted Unit tests, ready for immediate use

- the option to print tests, publish tests on a Local Area Network (LAN), or deliver tests or study guides on a Web site

- automatic scoring for LAN and Web-based tests

- a number of student and teacher reports designed to inform instruction and study needs

- an on-screen Help program

- an in-depth User Manual on every CD

The VOCABULARY WORKSHOP Test Generator is a convenient and secure source of assessment and/or extra practice that saves teachers precious time. Effortlessly creating customized tests tailored to suit the specific needs of either individual students or an entire class, receiving test results automatically, and generating informative reports in seconds allows more time for what students need most: instruction.

The flexibility of the Test Generator makes it easy to use either as needed or more systematically, as an integral part of the VOCABULARY WORKSHOP series. See pages T22–29 for recommendations on how it may be used in conjunction with the Student Text and other components of the program.

Test Booklets (Levels A–H)

Two Test Booklets (Form A and Form B) are available for each of Levels A–H. These Test Booklets have been designed to be used in alternating years, thereby reducing the risk of answers being passed on. Though the formats of the Test Booklets are the same, the items tested in any given section are completely different. The contents of the Test Booklets have been organized to reflect that of the Student Text and include the following:

- a Warm-Up Test (corresponding to the Diagnostic Test in the Student Text)

- 15 Unit Tests, each consisting of 25 items focusing on pronunciation, part of speech, spelling, definitions, synonyms, antonyms, and sentence completions

- 5 Cumulative Tests of 50 items each (plus 2 optional items)

Each Unit Test has been designed for use as soon as the students have completed work on the Unit to which it corresponds or at any point thereafter.

Each Cumulative Test, including the Final Cumulative Test, covers all the work of the Student Text to the point at which it occurs and is designed to be used after the corresponding Review in the Student Text.

For recommendations on how to employ the Test Booklets as part of the complete VOCABULARY WORKSHOP program, see pages T22–T29.

TEST PREP Blackline Masters (Levels A–H)

For further assessment options, a booklet of reproducible TEST PREP Blackline Masters is available for each Level A–H. The TEST PREP component is designed to provide both practice in working with SAT-type test questions and formats *and* review tests covering the entire content of the corresponding Student Text.

- Prep Tests approximate as closely as possible, given the vocabulary that is to be covered, the word-omission sections of the SAT and provide practice in the vocabulary-in-context strand with brief reading passages as well.

- Answer sheets provide an SAT-type test format to develop student ease and familiarity with standardized testing materials.

- Mastery Tests are meant to be used when students have completed the corresponding group of three Units in the Student Text. Each test covers basic meanings, synonyms, antonyms, sentence completions, and analogies.

- Answer keys, including selected answer rationales, are provided for all tests.

For recommendations on the implementation of the TEST PREP Blackline Masters as part of the complete VOCABULARY WORKSHOP program, see pages T22–T25.

The VOCABULARY WORKSHOP program now offers the following online components, as well as other valuable teacher resources, at **www.vocabularyworkshop.com**.

Audio Program (Levels A–F Only)

The VOCABULARY WORKSHOP **Online Audio Program** provides students with pronunciations, definitions, and examples of usage for all of the key words presented in each of Levels A–F. Students can listen to one word at a time or, if they wish, download to an MP3 player all of the words of any given Unit and then listen to the Audio Program for that Unit at their convenience.

- The audio program is ideal for English Language Learners of all cultures and backgrounds and for use in ESL classrooms.

- Students hear the recommended pronunciation of each word at least 6 times, both alone and in context, and are provided with two opportunities to pronounce each word themselves.

- Pronunciations are followed by brief definitions and examples in complete-sentence form.

- Teacher's notes for the program are provided in Spanish as well as English.

For recommendations on when to use the program, see pages T22–T27.

SAT and ACT Practice Worksheets (Levels A–H)

For teachers who wish to offer their students practice for the SAT or ACT in addition to that supplied in the Student Texts (see pages T16–17), 45 standardized-test worksheets are available online for each of Levels A–H. These practice worksheets are accessible *only to teachers*, who may print them and distribute them to their students as they see fit.

- For each Level, 15 worksheets in standardized-test format provide practice in the comprehension and vocabulary skills assessed on the new SAT and ACT.

- For each Level, 15 worksheets in standardized-test format provide practice in the types of multiple-choice grammar and usage items included in the new Writing section of the SAT and in the ACT.

- For each Level, 15 worksheets provide step-by-step guidance and practice in crafting a timed essay of the kind that now is required on the SAT (and is optional on the ACT).

Interactive Online Vocabulary Activities (Levels A–H)

For each Level, students are provided interactive word games using the vocabulary presented in the Units. These activities, which include crossword puzzles, word searches, "hangman," matching games, and others, are designed to reinforce and enrich student understanding of word meanings and usage.

IMPLEMENTING THE PROGRAM

The format of the VOCABULARY WORKSHOP program allows for great flexibility. The teacher can easily adjust the activity assignments to conform to the special needs of an entire class, of groups within the class, or of individual students.

Schedule for the Year (28 Weeks)

The chart on pages T23–T25 shows how the various components of the VOCABULARY WORKSHOP program for Levels A–H can be scheduled effectively over an academic year lasting 28 weeks. The following notes should prove helpful when adapting the chart to individual needs:

- Though the chart shows a disposition of material over 28 weeks, the time period can be extended to as many as 34 weeks simply by increasing to two weeks the time allotment for the items under weeks 6, 11, 16, 21, 26, and 28.

- It is not to be supposed that every item listed under Follow-Up Activities is meant to be covered during the week specified. The listings here are designed to offer the teacher options from which to choose in order to tailor the VOCABULARY WORKSHOP program to the specific needs of a particular class.

KEY

OAP = Online Audio Program
    (Levels A–F only)

BLM = TEST PREP Blackline
    Masters

TB A/B = Test Booklet
      Form A/Form B

TG = Test Generator

ONLINE COMPONENTS
www.vocabularyworkshop.com

Note that of the online components for VOCABULARY WORKSHOP only the **Audio Program** has been woven into the yearly and weekly schedules that appear on the following pages, chiefly because the Audio Program lends itself most naturally to a unit-by-unit integration with the Student Texts. The **Interactive Games and Puzzles** are linked to the reviews because they depend on a larger pool of words than is available in any one Unit, but they may be used at any point in the school year. Similarly, the **SAT and ACT Practice Worksheets**, which are accessible only to teachers, might be distributed on a regular basis over the course of the year or on an accelerated schedule if they are being used in the time leading up to a standardized-test date.

Using the Program Over the Year (28 Weeks)

Note: "Framing Sentences" and "Story/Essay Writing" are to be supplied by the teacher.

Week	Student Text	Follow-Up Activities
1	Vocabulary of Vocabulary	
2	Diagnostic Test	Warm-Up Test (TB A/B) Warm-Up Prep Test (BLM)
3	Unit 1 OAP	Framing Sentences Story/Essay Writing Unit Test 1 (TB A/B) Unit 1 Test (TG)
4	Unit 2 OAP	Framing Sentences Story/Essay Writing Unit Test 2 (TB A/B) Unit 2 Test (TG)
5	Unit 3 OAP	Framing Sentences Story/Essay Writing Unit Test 3 (TB A/B) Unit 3 Test (TG)
6	Review 1–3	Mastery Test 1–3 (BLM) Mastery Test (TG)*
7	—	Cumulative Test 1–3 (TB A/B) Prep Worksheet 1–3 (BLM)
8	Unit 4 OAP	Framing Sentences Story/Essay Writing Unit Test 4 (TB A/B) Unit 4 Test (TG)
9	Unit 5 OAP	Framing Sentences Story/Essay Writing Unit Test 5 (TB A/B) Unit 5 Test (TG)

* Customized by teacher   *(Continued on pg. T24)*

(Continued from pg. T23)

Week	Student Text	Follow-Up Activities
10	Unit 6 OAP	Framing Sentences Story/Essay Writing Unit Test 6 (TB A/B) Unit 6 Test (TG)
11	Review 4–6	Mastery Test 4–6 (BLM) Mastery Test (TG)*
12	Cumulative Review 1–6	Cumulative Test 1–6 (TB A/B) Prep Worksheet 4–6 (BLM)
13	Unit 7 OAP	Framing Sentences Story/Essay Writing Unit Test 7 (TB A/B) Unit 7 Test (TG)
14	Unit 8 OAP	Framing Sentences Story/Essay Writing Unit Test 8 (TB A/B) Unit 8 Test (TG)
15	Unit 9 OAP	Framing Sentences Story/Essay Writing Unit Test 9 (TB A/B) Unit 9 Test (TG)
16	Review 7–9	Mastery Test 7–9 (BLM) Mastery Test (TG)* Mid-Year Test (TG)*
17	Cumulative Review 1–9	Cumulative Test 1–9 (TB A/B) Prep Worksheet 7–9 (BLM) Cumulative Test (TG)*
18	Unit 10 OAP	Framing Sentences Story/Essay Writing Unit Test 10 (TB A/B) Unit 10 Test (TG)
19	Unit 11 OAP	Framing Sentences Story/Essay Writing Unit Test 11 (TB A/B) Unit 11 Test (TG)

* Customized by teacher

Week	Student Text	Follow-Up Activities
20	Unit 12 OAP	Framing Sentences Story/Essay Writing Unit Test 12 (TB A/B) Unit 12 Test (TG)
21	Review 10–12	Mastery Test 10–12 (BLM) Mastery Test (TG)*
22	Cumulative Review 1–12	Cumulative Test 1–12 (TB A/B) Prep Worksheet 10–12 (BLM) Cumulative Test (TG)*
23	Unit 13 OAP	Framing Sentences Story/Essay Writing Unit Test 13 (TB A/B) Unit 13 Test (TG)
24	Unit Test 14 OAP	Framing Sentences Story/Essay Writing Unit Test 14 (TB A/B) Unit 14 Test (TG)
25	Unit 15 OAP	Framing Sentences Story/Essay Writing Unit Test 15 (TB A/B) Unit 15 Test (TG)*
26	Review 13–15	Mastery Test 13–15 (BLM) Mastery Test (TG)*
27	Cumulative Review 1–15	Cumulative Test 1–15 (TB A/B) Prep Worksheet 13–15 (BLM) Cumulative Test (TG)*
28	Final Mastery Test	Cumulative Mastery Test (BLM) Cumulative Prep Test (BLM) Final Mastery Test (TG)*

* Customized by teacher

Using the Units

On the top of these 2 pages the teacher will find 2 models for using the Units effectively on a weekly basis. Though there is no single formula or plan that will be sure to yield optimum results all the time, the models presented here and on the next 2 pages are designed to get the teacher thinking about how best to adapt the program to the needs of individual classes.

KEY: OAP = Online Audio Program

TB = Test Booklet Form A or Form B

TG = Test Generator

** Item to be supplied by teacher/student

Assignment
Classwork
Homework

MODEL B: 5 Sessions/Periods (20 Minutes)		
Assignment	**Day 1**	**Day 2**
Classwork	**1.** Collect Framing Sentences** **2.** Review Unit Test **3.** Present Definitions	Review Completing the Sentences
Homework	**1.** Completing the Sentence **2.** OAP	Synonyms and Antonyms

Using the Reviews

On the bottom of these 2 pages the teacher will find 2 models for using the Reviews effectively on a weekly basis.

Assignment
Classwork
Homework

MODEL B: 5 Sessions/Periods (20 Minutes)		
Assignment	**Day 1**	**Day 2**
Classwork	Present Vocabulary for Comprehension	**1.** Review homework **2.** Grammar in Context
Homework	**1.** Word Associations **2.** Antonyms	Choosing the Right Meaning

Weekly Lesson Plans

MODEL A: 3 Sessions/Periods (35–40 Minutes)

Day 1	Day 2	Day 3
1. Collect Framing Sentences** **2.** Present Definitions	**1.** Review Completing the Sentence, Synonyms and Antonyms **2.** Present Choosing the Right Word and Vocabulary in Context	**1.** Unit Test (TB or TG) **2.** Review last week's Framing Sentences**
1. Completing the Sentence, Synonyms and Antonyms **2.** OAP	Test Study	Framing Sentences**

Day 3	Day 4	Day 5
Review Synonyms and Antonyms	**1.** Review Choosing the Right Word **2.** Present Vocabulary in Context	**1.** Unit Test (TB or TG) **2.** Review last week's Framing Sentences**
Choosing the Right Word	Test Study	Framing Sentences**

MODEL A: 3 Sessions/Periods (35–40 Minutes)

Day 1	Day 2	Day 3
Present Vocabulary for Comprehension, Antonyms Word Families	**1.** Review homework **2.** Present Grammar in Context Two-Word Completions Word Associations	**1.** Mastery Test (TB or TG) **2.** Review homework
Choosing the Right Meaning	**1.** Test Study **2.** Building with Classical Roots	Remedial work as required

Day 3	Day 4	Day 5
1. Review homework **2.** Present Two-Word Completions	Mastery Test (TB or TG)	**1.** Review Mastery Test **2.** Review homework
1. Test Study **2.** Word Families	Building with Classical Roots	Remedial work as required

Using the Cumulative Reviews

On the top of these 2 pages the teacher will find 2 models for using the Cumulative Reviews effectively on a weekly basis.

Assignment
Classwork
Homework

MODEL B: 5 Sessions/Periods (20 Minutes)		
Assignment	**Day 1**	**Day 2**
Classwork	Present Cumulative Review	Cumulative Test Parts 1–4 (TB)
Homework	Test Study	Test Study

Implementing the Weekly Schedules

The following may prove helpful when adapting the foregoing schedules to specific situations.

- The models shown are, as their designation suggests, purely models—that is, starting points. Accordingly, the teacher is expected to adapt them to the particular situation at hand.

- The models make only minimal use of the Follow-Up Activities suggested earlier and no use whatsoever of the Alternative Approaches to Using the Program suggested on the following pages. The teacher should in all cases feel free to introduce such alternative approaches as are convenient.

- Place assignments and timings are to some extent hypothetical. Teachers should switch items around and adjust timings as needed. Similarly, items may be modified or deleted and new items inserted as the teacher sees fit.

- Multiple listings in a Day's entry for either Classwork or Homework are to be seen as options from which the teacher should select appropriate material. It is unlikely that the teacher could cover all the suggested material in the indicated time allotment.

- With some adjustment, the allotments for each Day can accommodate a 2- or 4-day arrangement. There is usually too much material to cover in 1 day, and a 1-day approach is, therefore, not suggested.

MODEL A: 3 Sessions/Periods (35–40 Minutes)		
Day 1	**Day 2**	**Day 3**
Present Cumulative Review	Cumulative Test (TB or TG)	**1.** Review Cumulative Test **2.** Review Prep Worksheet
Test Study	Prep Worksheet	Remedial work as required

Day 3	**Day 4**	**Day 5**
Cumulative Test Parts 5–6 (TB)	Review Cumulative Test	Review Prep Worksheet
—	Prep Worksheet	Remedial work as required

Alternative Approaches to Using the Program

Writing Approach

Research has shown that vocabulary acquisition is maximized when learning is authentically contextualized—when learners have a "real-life" purpose for acquiring and using a new word. Activities such as the following can provide these authentic contexts.

- Students can create journals or logs in which they use the key words to express experiences, thoughts, or feelings that are personally meaningful. They are free to keep these entries for their eyes only or to share them with others.

- Students can use the key words in personal letters to friends and relatives or in letters to the editor of the school or local newspaper. Students should write about subjects of real interest and concern to them.

- Students can use the key words to write descriptions of people they know or characters they are interested in. These character sketches or personality profiles may be written for a class yearbook, for a book report, or as a reference for a friend.

Literature-Based Approach

The VOCABULARY WORKSHOP program can be combined with some of the items listed below to form a *literature-based* approach to vocabulary study. Each of the items listed has been surveyed for use of some of the key words presented in the specified level of VOCABULARY WORKSHOP. Seeing the words they are studying in classic world literature will reinforce student appreciation of the value of possessing a good active-use vocabulary.

Classic Literature To Use With The Program

Levels D and E

Louisa May Alcott *Little Women*

Maya Angelou *I Know Why the Caged Bird Sings*

Ray Bradbury *Fahrenheit 451*

Charlotte Brontë *Jane Eyre*

Emily Brontë *Wuthering Heights*

Pearl S. Buck *The Good Earth*

Lewis Carroll *Alice's Adventures in Wonderland*

Willa Cather *My Antonia*

Sandra Cisneros *The House on Mango Street*

Daniel Defoe *Robinson Crusoe*

Charles Dickens *A Tale of Two Cities*

Arthur Conan Doyle *The Hound of the Baskervilles*

George Eliot *Silas Marner*

William Golding *Lord of the Flies*

Frank Herbert *Dune*

Harper Lee *To Kill a Mockingbird*

Carson McCullers *Member of the Wedding*

Nicholasa Mohr *El Bronx Remembered*

Walter Dean Myers *Fallen Angels*

George Orwell *Animal Farm*

Alan Paton *Cry, the Beloved Country*

John Steinbeck *The Pearl*

Level F

Sherwood Anderson *Winesburg, Ohio*

James Baldwin *Go Tell It on the Mountain*

Stephen Crane *The Red Badge of Courage*

Kate Chopin *The Awakening*

Ralph Ellison *Invisible Man*

Louise Erdrich *Love Medicine*

Jack Finney *Time and Again*

F. Scott Fitzgerald *The Great Gatsby*

Joseph Heller *Catch-22*

Ernest Hemingway *A Farewell to Arms*

Zora Neale Hurston *Their Eyes Were Watching God*

Nathaniel Hawthorne *The Scarlet Letter*

Henry James *Washington Square*

Maxine Hong Kingston *Woman Warrior*

N. Scott Momaday *The Way to Rainy Mountain*

Toni Morrison *Beloved*

John Steinbeck *The Grapes of Wrath*

Amy Tan *The Joy Luck Club*

Mark Twain *The Adventures of Huckleberry Finn*

Kurt Vonnegut, Jr. *Slaughterhouse Five*

Alice Walker *The Color Purple*

Edith Wharton *The House of Mirth* and *The Age of Innocence*

Richard Wright *Black Boy*

Levels G and H

Margaret Atwood *The Handmaid's Tale*

Chinua Achebe *Things Fall Apart*

Jane Austen *Pride and Prejudice*

Joseph Conrad *Lord Jim* and *Heart of Darkness*

Charles Dickens *David Copperfield*

Isak Dinesen *Out of Africa*

George Eliot *The Mill on the Floss*

Thomas Hardy *The Return of the Native*

Aldous Huxley *Brave New World*

James Joyce *A Portrait of the Artist as a Young Man*

Gabriel Garcia Marquez *One Hundred Years of Solitude*

Mark Mathabane *Kaffir Boy*

V.S. Naipaul *A House for Mr. Biswas*

Mary Shelley *Frankenstein*

Muriel Spark *The Prime of Miss Jean Brodie*

Jonathan Swift *Gulliver's Travels*

Virginia Woolf *A Room of One's Own* and *To the Lighthouse*

To coordinate reading and vocabulary study, the following may prove helpful:

- Instruct students to devote a special notebook to vocabulary. As they come across key words in their reading, they should head a page of the notebook with the word; copy the title of the work; and then indicate (a) the definition of the word used in that sentence, (b) its part of speech, and (c) whether it is used in a literal or figurative sense.

- Students may then be instructed to check *Bartlett's Familiar Quotations* for other famous examples of the use of the key word in question. These may be copied into the notebook and shared with others in the class.

Content-Area Approach

VOCABULARY WORKSHOP can be used to enhance student understanding and use of vocabulary in subjects such as social studies and history, science and health, and other curriculum areas.

In the following list of nonfiction print and video titles you will find works that relate in content to Vocabulary in Context exercises appearing in specific Units and Reviews of the VOCABULARY WORKSHOP Student Texts for Levels D–H. Students may wish to read or view some of these works and report on the topics and issues that they treat. In their reports, whether oral or written, students should be encouraged to use words they have come to know through their Student Texts.

Other content-related activities to which students might apply vocabulary study are:

- Working in pairs or small groups, they can choose sentences from Completing the Sentence or Choosing the Right Word and discuss a larger context in which these sentences could have appeared, such as a history or mathematics textbook, a daily newspaper, a book review, a personal letter, or a scientific article.

- Students can work together to link individual vocabulary words to a particular content area. Then working in pairs, they can find "real-world" examples of the words used in context in that content area.

- Students can work cooperatively to create sentence and paragraph contexts that illustrate the meaning of the content-area words that they have identified.

Useful Classroom Techniques

Classroom experience and research have shown that some students learn more readily when they can exercise a great deal of personal choice and can interact with others. VOCABULARY WORKSHOP can be adapted in the following ways to accommodate such students.

Cooperative Activities

Working cooperatively does not just mean working in proximity to other students or dividing an assignment or project into discrete tasks. Rather it means that students take individual and collective responsibility for the learning of all members of the group and for the successful completion of the group goal. Students who cooperate to develop their vocabulary should maintain an ongoing dialogue to monitor the comprehension of all group members.

Oral and Kinesthetic

- One student can write the key words in a given unit on the chalkboard while the rest of the class is divided into pairs or small groups. A member of each group will read a numbered item from the Unit aloud. The rest of the group will confer and then supply the required vocabulary word. The student reader will evaluate each answer and give reasons why it is correct or incorrect based on the word's definition and any context clues.

- Students in groups can discuss the shades of meaning or connotations among selected synonyms and antonyms for a given Unit and among the alternative answers in Choosing the Right Meaning.

- Students can work together to create puns, riddles, Tom Swifties, and limericks to illustrate the multiple meanings of appropriate vocabulary words. They may want to collect and publish their creations in illustrated books or an audio-anthology.

- Members of a group can work together to improvise stories, skits, or pantomimes that illustrate the meaning of a key word in a given Unit, while other group members guess the word being illustrated.

Written

- Students can work cooperatively to brainstorm their own vocabulary word lists based on their current reading and writing in all areas of the curriculum and on their personal reading and writing experiences.

- The class can collaborate to create their own Unit, covering vocabulary words they have chosen. Different groups can be assigned to develop each of the unit activities.

- Students may want to create their own minidictionaries, based on the word lists in VOCABULARY WORKSHOP or on categories of words that are especially meaningful or useful to them, such as sports, fashion, music, and career terms.

- Students can make use of semantic mapping and other graphic devices, such as flowcharts, to generate new vocabulary or to demonstrate understanding of word relationships. Semantic mapping, or webbing, can be used to illustrate word families, synonyms, and antonyms. Flowcharts can illustrate etymological and grammatical relationships.

Alternative Types of Assessment

The following types of assessment may be used in addition to or in lieu of the objective-scoring materials provided in the VOCABULARY WORKSHOP, Levels A–H. The emphasis here is on monitoring understanding rather than on ranking students.

Self-Evaluation

Students can use their journals to reflect on their own process of learning and use of new words. They may consider, for example, which words from VOCABULARY WORKSHOP they understood quickly and used frequently and why. They may want to use these insights to design their own vocabulary-acquisition strategies.

Teacher-Student Conferencing

Meetings take place at every stage of the vocabulary-acquisition process. Meeting over time allows teachers to assess students' developing understanding of words as used in specific contexts.

Observation

Using a checklist of 2 or 3 important criteria, the teacher can observe and evaluate students while they are interacting in groups or engaging in other oral activities. Teachers can also probe for deeper levels of comprehension by asking students to clarify or give reasons for their choice of word or context.

Peer Evaluation

Students meet in pairs or small groups to develop standards or criteria to evaluate their vocabulary acquisition. They then apply their standards to their peers' oral or written expression, giving positive feedback and concrete suggestions for improvement.

Portfolio Assessment

By having students collect and save self-selected samples of their writing over a period of time, teachers have an ongoing record of students' vocabulary development and of their facility in using words in context.

Multimodal Assessment

Students with strong nonverbal competencies can be given the opportunity to demonstrate in nonverbal media their understanding of new vocabulary. For example, they can draw, paint, model, dance, compose music, or construct objects to communicate their comprehension of a word and its definition.

TEACHER RESOURCES

The following lists have been compiled to assist the teacher in the effective presentation of the VOCABULARY WORKSHOP program, Levels A–H.

I. DICTIONARIES

Recommended

Merriam-Webster *Collegiate Dictionary* [Eleventh Edition] (Springfield, MA: Merriam-Webster, 2003)

Webster's Third New International Dictionary (Springfield, MA: G. & C. Merriam, 1993)

American Heritage Dictionary (Boston: Houghton Mifflin, 2000)

Oxford English Dictionary [Compact Edition] (Oxford: Oxford University Press, 1971)

Skeat, W.W. *A Concise Etymological Dictionary of the English Language* (NY: G.P. Putnam, 1980)

Supplemental

12,000 Words [A Supplement to Webster's *Third International Dictionary*] (Springfield, MA: Merriam-Webster, 1993)

The Random House Dictionary of the English Language [Unabridged Edition] (NY: Random House, 1987)

II. THESAURI

Recommended

Roget's II The New Thesaurus (Boston: Houghton Mifflin, 1995)

Random House Roget's Thesaurus (NY: Random House, 2001)

Rodale, J. [Revised by Urdang, L. and La Roche, N.] *The Synonym Finder* (Emmaus, PA: Rodale Press, 1979)

Supplemental

Chapman, R.L. (Ed.). *Roget A to Z* (NY: Harper Perennial, 1994)

Laird, C. *Webster's New World Thesaurus* (NY: Warner Books, 1990)

Roget's International Thesaurus [Fifth Edition] (NY: HarperCollins, 1992)

Abate, F. *The Oxford Dictionary and Thesaurus: The Ultimate Language Reference for American Readers* (NY: Oxford University Press, 1996)

III. OTHER REFERENCE WORKS

Recommended

Carroll, J., Davies, P., and Richman, B. *Word Frequency Book* (Boston: Houghton Mifflin, 1971)

Dale, E. and O'Rourke, J. *The Living Word Vocabulary* (Chicago: Scott & Fetzer, 1981)

Supplemental

Harris, A. and Jackson, M. *Basic Reading Vocabularies* (NY: Macmillan, 1982)

Thorndike, E. and Lorge, I. *The Teacher's Book of 30,000 Words* (NY: Teachers College Press, Columbia University, 1968)

IV. HISTORY

General

Baugh, A.C. and Cable, T. *A History of the English Language* [Third Edition] (Englewood Cliffs, NJ: Prentice-Hall, 1992)

Carver, C. *A History of English in Its Own Words* (NY: HarperCollins, 1991)

Jespersen, O. *Growth and Structure of the English Language* (Chicago: University of Chicago Press, 1982)

McCrum, R., Cran, W., and MacNeil, R. *The Story of English* (NY: Penguin, 1993)

Myers, L.M. *The Roots of Modern English* (Boston: Little, Brown, 1961)

Pyles, T. *The Origins and Development of the English Language* [Fourth Edition] (NY: Harcourt, Brace, Jovanovich, 1993)

Robinson, O. *Old English and Its Closest Relatives* (Stanford, CA: Stanford University Press, 1993)

American English

Dillard, J.L. *All-American English* (NY: Random House, 1975)

Dillard, J.L. *American Talk* (NY: Random House, 1976)

Flexner, S.B. *I Hear America Talking* (NY: Simon & Schuster, 1976)

Mencken, H.L. *The American Language* (NY: Alfred A. Knopf, 1979)

V. OTHER USEFUL RESOURCES

A Dictionary of American Idioms (Woodbury, NY: Barron's Educational Series, Inc., 1995)

Bryson, B. *A Dictionary of Troublesome Words* (NY: Viking Penguin, 1988)

Carroll, D. *Dictionary of Foreign Terms in the English Language* (NY: Hawthorn Books, 1973)

Dixson, R. *Essential Idioms in English* (Englewood Cliffs, NJ: Pearson ESL, 1993)

Evans, I.H. (Ed.) *Brewer's Dictionary of Phrase & Fable* (NY: Harper & Row, 2000)

Harrison, G. *Vocabulary Dynamics* (NY: Warner Books, 1992)

Hendrickson, R. *The Dictionary of Eponyms* (NY: Stein and Day, 1985)

Morris, W. and M. *Morris Dictionary of Word & Phrase Origins* (NY: Harper & Row, 1988)

Orgel, J.R. *Building an Enriched Vocabulary* (NY: William H. Sadlier, Inc., 1999)

Paxson, W. *New American Dictionary of Confusing Words* (NY: NAL-Dutton, 1990)

Room, A. *Dictionary of Contrasting Pairs* (NY: Routledge Educational Series Inc., 1988)

Room, A. *The Penguin Dictionary of Confusibles* (NY: Penguin Books, 1989)

Shipley, J. *Dictionary of Word Origins* (Glenville, IL: Greenwood Press, 1988)

Smith, R. *Dictionary of English Word-Roots* (Totowa, NJ: Littlefield, Adams & Co., 1980)

Spears, R. *Slang and Euphemisms* (NY: NAL-Dutton, 1991)

Webster's Word Histories (Springfield, MA: Merriam-Webster, 1989)

ANSWERS TO EXERCISES IN REVIEWS AND CUMULATIVE REVIEWS

Two-Word Completions (page 45)

1. (d) cavorted (Inference clue: What do people do on a beach?) . . . halcyon (Inference clue: How would you describe the weather on a cloudless spring day?)

2. (b) temporize (Restatement clue: "or vacillate"; Inference clue: How might an overly cautious person act in a crisis?) . . . unwonted (Inference clue: How would you describe an action that a person has done for the first and only time in his or her life?)

3. (a) credence (Inference clue: What doesn't a skeptical person usually give to allegations of any kind?) . . . substantiated (Inference clue: What must be done to allegations in order for a skeptical person to accept them?)

4. (c) animadversions (Inference clue: With what might professional critics respond if they disliked a work?) . . . carping (Inference clue: What are pedants usually guilty of?)

5. (c) verdant (Inference clue: How would you describe the appearance of fields and pasturelands in the summer?) . . . undulated (Restatement clue: "slithering")

6. (b) devious (Inference clue: What kind of people are good at not telling the truth?) . . . dissembling (Restatement clue: "not telling the truth")

Choosing the Right Meaning (page 46)

1. (b) (Clue: What would a government do to its currency in order to "spur exports"?) (a), (c): wrong sense of word for context (ws); (d): irrelevant to meaning of word (ir).

2. (b) (Clue: Context indicates language understandable only to the initiated ["thoroughly versed in such matters"]) (a), (c): ws; (d): ir.

3. (d) (Clue: How would a boom be constructed so that it could "deploy and retrieve" objects?) (a), (c): ws; (b): ir.

4. (c) (Clue: How would one describe the effect of an "ultimatum" such that defiance is the reply?) (a), (d): ws; (b): ir.

5. (d) (Clue: Correct sense is restated in "vortex") (a), (b): ws; (c): ir.

6. (a) (Clue: What sort of person would fire marshals seek and "apprehend"?) (b), (c): ws; (d): ir.

Two-Word Completions (page 75)

1. (b) dereliction (Inference clue: With what would an officer who had failed to carry out orders be charged?) . . . incarcerated (Inference clue: What use do the military police make of the stockade?)

2. (d) frenetic (Inference clue: How might you describe a harried officer's attempts to do something?) . . . disarray (Inference clue: In what condition do troops usually flee from a field?)

3. (c) testy (Inference clue: How would you describe the personality of someone who was easily exasperated?) . . . nettle (Restatement clue: "or exasperate")

4. (c) consummate (Inference clue: How would you characterize the technical skill of an artist who could delineate every nuance of nature with a mere stroke of the brush?) . . . delineate (Inference clue: What does an artist do with his or her brush?)

5. (a) indictment (Inference clue: What legal instrument do you bring against someone accused of a crime?) . . . complicity (Inference clue: Of what may someone who is thought to have been involved in a crime be suspected?)

6. (d) incumbent (Restatement clue: "responsibility") . . . bastion (Inference clue: How would a journalist react against zealotry and indifference?)

Choosing the Right Meaning (page 76)

1. (d) (Clue: Restatement of "honored") (a), (c): ws; (b): ir.

2. (c) (Clue: Context indicates contrast with informal, special-interest meetings ["caucuses"]) (a), (b), (d): ws.

3. (c) (Clue: Context indicates story is not to be printed *despite* the "undeniable" trustworthiness of the source. What sort of source would be deemed trustworthy?) (a), (b): ws; (d): ir.

4. (d) (Clue: Context indicates sense related to money value) (a), (b): ws; (c): ir.

5. (a) (Clue: By what sort of "cost" would one judge a queen's "worth"?) (b), (c), (d): ws.

Analogies (page 81)

1. (b) Someone who is A would not be likely to B easily.
2. (a) Someone who is A would be able to B things easily.
3. (c) A indicates a state of B.
4. (d) A means the same as B.
5. (c) An A comment is completely lacking in B.
6. (b) One would A something with one's B.
7. (a) Something that is A has B.
8. (c) In an A, you would be likely to find many B.
9. (b) You would use an A for a job involving B.
10. (d) Someone who is A you can B easily.

Choosing the Right Meaning (pages 81–82)

1. (a) (Clue: Context indicates sense related to slavery; restatement in "slavish")
(b), (c), (d): ws.

2. (c) (Clue: Correct sense is given as restatement of "treaty") (a), (b): ws; (d): ir.

3. (d) (Clue: How might one term a "miserly" character who cares for nothing but money?) (a), (b), (c): ws.

4. (d) (Clue: Correct sense expounded in words of oath, which describe obligations of office) (a), (b): ws; (c): ir.

5. (b) (Clue: How might a character "appear" in a play that involves "mistaken identity"?) (a), (c), (d): ws.

Two-Word Completions (page 82)

1. (a) bastion (Inference clue: In what might you find enemy resistance?) . . . intermittent (Restatement clue: "occasionally")

2. (d) murky (Contrast clue: "once clear") . . . flotsam (Inference clue: What would you call industrial waste that is covering a lake?)

3. (b) avid (Inference clue: What are proponents of war?) . . . celerity (Inference clue: With what speed did Northerners join the war?)

4. (c) derelicts (Inference clue: What is a bag lady an example of?) . . . ubiquitous (Inference clue: How might you describe the occurrence of traffic lights in a modern city?)

5. (c) fiat (Inference clue: How do autocrats rule?) . . . atrophied (Restatement clue: died)

Two-Word Completions (page 108)

1. (b) misanthrope (Inference clue: What sort of person might enjoy castigating other people's behavior?) . . . vituperative (Restatement clue: "unremittingly harsh and")

2. (d) countermanded (Contrast clues: "issued," "reissued") . . . vacillating (Inference clue: What type of person would issue, countermand, and reissue the same order in quick succession?)

3. (c) unremitting (Inference clue: What type of rains would make the ground squish and gurgle?) . . . saturated (Inference clue: What would unremitting rains do to the ground?)

4. (a) counterpart (Inference clue: With which Soviet official did the President meet at "summit meetings") . . . allay (Restatement clue: "deal with sources of friction")

5. (c) alleged (Inference clue: How would you describe a charge that has not been proven?) . . . collusion (Inference from: "to have been in cahoots")

6. (c) echelons (Inference clue: What word defines various groups from a society?) . . . coterie (Inference clue: What would a close-knit group of travelers be called?)

Choosing the Right Meaning (page 109)

1. (d) (Clues: Of what is "Crime doesn't pay" an example? To what would facts "put the lie"?) (a), (b), (c): ws.

2. (b) (Clue: Context indicates the sense of excising, or "plucking") (a), (c), (d): ws.

3. (c) (Clue: How best describe progress "on foot" through mud?) (a), (b): ws; (d): ir.

4. (a) (Clue: Sentence structure indicates contrast with ability greater than human ["eclipsed"]) (b) (c): ws; (d): ir.

Analogies (page 114)

1. (a) A means the opposite of B.
2. (b) An A functions like a B.
3. (d) A means the same as B.
4. (b) A means the same as B.
5. (c) A is by definition something that is B.
6. (d) A means the opposite of B.
7. (a) A indicates that there is B of something.
8. (a) A means the same as B.
9. (c) A is by definition B.
10. (c) A means the same as B.

Choosing the Right Meaning (pages 114–115)

1. (c) (Clue: What would a politician who has given up a "hard-line stance" probably be prepared to do?) (a), (d): ws; (b): ir.

2. (b) (Clue: Context indicates the sense of elements uniting to some purpose.) (a), (c): ws; (d): ir.

3. (d) (Clue: What sort of goods would petty thieves likely bring to a fencing operation?) (a), (b), (c): ws.

4. (b) (Clue: Correct sense restated in "joy"); (d): ws (derived from adjectival form); (a), (c): ir.

Two-Word Completions (page 115)

1. (a) diatribe (Restatement clues: "address", "intemperate"; Inference clue: What kind of address would a heated speaker be likely to deliver?) . . . vituperative (Restatement clue: "scathing and")

2. (d) depraved (Inference clue: What kind of mind would Count Dracula or the Marquise de Sade have been likely to possess? . . . bestial (Inference clue: What kind of appetites would they have been likely to have?)

3. (a) equity (Restatement clue: "justice"; Inference clue: The people who are conducting a trial must have a sense of what?) . . . Travesty (Inference clue: What would people without a sense of equity do to the concept of justice?)

4. (b) tenable (Inference clue: What would a theory no longer be if evidence pointed to a different scenario?) . . . irrefutable (Inference clue: What kind of evidence would make a theory untenable?)

5. (c) peregrinations (Inference clue: What would a person be engaged in if he or she suddenly came upon various forest creatures?) . . . sylvan (Inference clue: What kind of animals inhabit a forest?)

REVIEW UNITS 10–12

Two-Word Completions (page 141)

1. (d) plaintive (Inference clue: What adjective would adequately describe a cry for help?) . . . hapless (Inference clue: How would you describe an animal that continually got its paw caught in the grillwork on the front porch?)

2. (c) espoused (Restatement clue: "embraced") . . . eclectic (Inference clue: How would you describe someone who picked and chose ideas from a wide variety of philosophies?)

3. (b) asperities (Inference clue: Of what would rough-and-tumble living be likely to possess a great deal?) . . . inured to (Restatement clue: "cope with"; Inference clue: What would a hardy group of people be likely to do in regard to the asperities of frontier life?)

4. (d) discomfited (Restatement clue: "external adversity . . . self-consciousness") . . . hapless (Inference clue: How would you characterize someone born with an unlucky affliction?)

5. (a) charlatans (Inference clue: What kind of people would "truth-in-advertising" laws be designed to discourage? Restatement clue: "crooks and") . . . mendacious (Inference clue: What kind of claims would crooks and charlatans be likely to make about their products?)

6. (b) impecunious (Inference clue: What would a pauper be by definition?) . . . sequestered (Inference clue: What would you use a hiding place for?)

Choosing the Right Meaning (page 142)

1. (a) (Clue: What might the slaying of a family member prompt that family to do?) (b), (c): ws; (d): ir.

2. (d) (Clue: What would a gust of wind likely do to the pages of an open book?) (a), (b): ws; (c): ir.

3. (d) (Clue: What is the most commanders could hope to do with respect to a "juggernaut" posed by an enemy?) (a), (c): ws; (b): ir.

4. (b) (Clue: Context indicates sense of solitude as a tonic, refreshing and restoring in nature.) (a), (c): ws; (d): ir.

5. (a) (Clue: How might one describe the "potions" concocted by a "mad scientist"?) (b): ws; (c), (d): ir.

CUMULATIVE REVIEW III

Analogies (page 147)

1. (d) The purpose of A is to B something.
2. (a) A means the same as B.
3. (a) A means the same as B.
4. (c) An A is something that would B when it moved.
5. (a) A person who is an A would by definition B.
6. (b) A means the same as B.
7. (c) A means the same as B.
8. (a) Someone who possesses A would not be B.
9. (d) A means the same as B.
10. (d) An A is a person who would be likely to B money.

Choosing the Right Meaning (pages 147–148)

1. (a) (Clue: What sort of manner would yield the impression of "humility" and "modesty"?) (b), (c), (d): ir.

2. (b) (Clue: Context compares "rogues" with rats and birds ["beaks"].) (a), (c), (d): ws.

3. (d) (Clue: Imitations, especially those produced by "hacks," are usually what in comparison with their originals?) (a), (b), (c): ws.

4. (b) (Clue: Context indicates that purpose of analysis is reductive, i.e., to probe the elementary makeup, rather than the provenance, of matter.) (a), (c), (d): ws.

5. (d) (Clue: Correct sense implied by contrast with "sting" and "scathing.")
(a), (b), (c): ws.

Two-Word Completions (page 148)

1. (b) incarcerated (Inference clue: What was the Bastille, a famous French prison, used for?) . . . languish (Inference clue: How would you describe what had happened to a person who had been left in a prison for over twenty years?)

2. (b) ludicrous (Inference clue: What adjective would best characterize the antics of a troupe of clowns?) . . . paroxysms (Inference clue: What reaction would a troupe of clowns' antics be likely to produce in an audience? Restatement clue: "salvos")

3. (c) razing (Inference clue: What are bulldozers and wrecking balls used for?) . . . detritus (Inference clue: What would dump trucks cart off from a construction site?)

4. (a) unremitting (Inference clue: How would you describe an artillery barrage that went on for two solid hours?) . . . decimated (Inference clue: What would have happened to the enemy's ranks if barely one in ten soldiers was left alive?)

5. (d) coterie (Inference clue: What would all your friends be members of?) . . . convivial (Inference clue: How would you describe a "get-together" at which everybody likes everybody else?)

REVIEW UNITS 13–15

Two-Word Completions (page 174)

1. (d) dissident (Restatement clue: "Disgruntled") . . . coup (Inference clues: What would you call the sudden development that toppled a duly elected government? To what do disgruntled army officers resort to topple a duly elected government?)

2. (b) facade (Inference clue: What noun might best describe a deceptive outward demeanor?) . . . febrile (Inference clue: What adjective might best characterize the brain activity of an inveterate opportunist? Contrast clue: "decorous sloth")

3. (a) rectitude (Inference clue: About what must a public official be concerned in regard to his or her behavior?) . . . chicanery (Restatement clue: "backroom shenanigans")

4. (c) opprobrium (Inference clue: What would the public be likely to have heaped on a hapless official?) . . . pariah (Inference clue: What does an official on whom the public has heaped opprobrium often become?)

5. (b) cynosure (Inference clue: What does a famous movie star often become when he or she suddenly appears in a crowd of ordinary people?) . . . mesmerized (Inference clues: What would a spell be likely to do to a person? How do people act when under a spell?)

6. (c) decorous (Inference clue: How would you characterize manners that obey social convention?) . . . minutae (Inference clue: How would you describe the conventions listed?)

Choosing the Right Meaning (page 175)

1. (c) (Clue: What might prompt a "tug-of-war" between committees?) (a), (b), (d): ws.

2. (d) (Clue: Context indicates figurative usage.) (b), (c): ws; (a): ir.

3. (b) (Clue: Who of his "contemporaries" would one expect to find in the presence of a "guiding light"?) (a), c), (d): ws.

4. (b) (Clue: Context indicates that the "fear" spoken of is groundless and imaginary.) (a), (c): ws; (d): ir.

5. (a) (Clue: Quoted passage speaks of "luxuries," not of taste.) (b): ws; (c), (d): ir.

CUMULATIVE REVIEW IV
Analogies (page 180)

1. (b) An A is a person who is usually the object of public B.
2. (c) A means the same as B.
3. (a) You would A something by the application of a great deal of B.
4. (a) Someone who is A would by definition B a lot.
5. (c) A indicates a feeling of B.
6. (d) An A is by definition something that is B.
7. (a) A means the same as B.
8. (b) A means the opposite of B.
9. (c) Someone who is A lacks B.
10. (d) An A would by definition not be B.

Choosing the Right Meaning (pages 180–181)

1. (c) (Clue: Quoted passage suggests that the very being of material things depends upon the "mind.") (a), (b), (d): ws (all derived from verb form).

2. (d) (Clue: What sort of objects would not be expected to survive "rude treatment"?) (a), (b), (c): ws.

3. (b) (Clue: What sort of body would a navigator look to for its "faithful and steadfast" qualities?) (a), (d): ws; (c): ir.

4. (a) (Clue: What sort of dish ["trencher"] would by definition be carved of oak, aspen, or pine?) (b), (c): ws; (d): ir.

Two-Word Completions (page 181)

1. (c) subsist (Restatement clue: "live") . . . pittance (Restatement clue: "pennies a day")

2. (c) propriety (Restatement clue: "straightlaced") . . . askance (Inference clue: How would straightlaced Victorians react to casual social conventions?)

3. (a) ephemeral (Restatement clue: "quick fixes") . . . exacerbating (Contrast clue: "rather than solving")

4. (b) neophyte (Contrast clue: "experts") . . . rudiments (Contrast clue: "finer points")

5. (d) ghoulish (Inference clue: What adjective would aptly describe the business of exhuming a body?) . . . exhuming (Inference clue: What might the court order cemetery workers to do to a body that is already buried?)

Notes

Vocabulary Workshop
New Edition

Level G

Jerome Shostak

Series Consultants

Sylvia A. Rendón, Ph.D.
Coord., Secondary Reading
Cypress-Fairbanks I.S.D.
Houston, Texas

John Heath, Ph.D.
Department of Classics
Santa Clara University
Santa Clara, California

Mel H. Farberman
Director of English
   Language Arts, K–12
Bay Shore U.F.S.D.
Bay Shore, New York

Sadlier-Oxford
A Division of William H. Sadlier, Inc.

Reviewers

The publisher wishes to thank for their comments and suggestions the following teachers and administrators, who read portions of the series prior to publication.

Anne S. Crane
Clinician, English Education
Georgia State University
Atlanta, GA

Susan W. Keogh
Curriculum Coordinator
Lake Highland Preparatory
Orlando, FL

Mary Louise Ellena-Wygonik
English Teacher
Hampton High School
Allison Park, PA

Lisa Anne Pomi
Language Arts Chairperson
Woodside High School
Woodside, CA

Arlene A. Oraby
Dept. Chair (Ret.), English 6–12
Briarcliff Public Schools
Briarcliff Manor, NY

Susan Cotter McDonough
English Department Chair
Wakefield High School
Wakefield, MA

Sr. M. Francis Regis Trojano
Sisters of St. Joseph (CSJ)
Educational Consultant
Boston, MA

Keith Yost
Director of Humanities
Tomball Ind. School District
Tomball, TX

Patricia M. Stack
English Teacher
South Park School District
South Park, PA

Joy Vander Vliet
English Teacher
Council Rock High School
Newtown, PA

Karen Christine Solheim
English Teacher
Jefferson High School
Jefferson, GA

Photo Credits

Corbis/Bettmann: 27, 90, 104, 163; Galen Rowell: 41; Robert Holmes: 57; George McCarthy: 97; Kelly-Mooney Photography: 116, 170; Joe McDonald: 123; Hulton-Deutsch Collection: 137; Free Agents Limited: 156. *Getty Images*/Stone/Kim Westerskov: 34; The Bridgeman Art Library: 83; Taxi/Chip Simons: 182. *Hans Namuth Ltd*: 64. *The Kobal Collection*: 130. *Lonely Planet Images*/Catherine Hanger: 149. *Picturequest*/Corbis: 71.

Printed in the United States of America.
ISBN: 0-8215-7112-5
14 15 16 RRDH 14 13 12 11

PREFACE

For more than five decades, VOCABULARY WORKSHOP has proven a highly successful tool for guiding systematic vocabulary growth and developing vocabulary skills. It has also been shown to be a valuable help to students preparing for standardized tests. This New Edition of VOCABULARY WORKSHOP has been prepared in recognition of important changes to these tests, with the introduction of two features designed to address the new emphasis on writing skills, including grammar, and reading skills on those tests.

A new **Vocabulary for Comprehension** section appears in each of the five Reviews. This two-page feature is modeled on the reading sections of standardized tests, and as in those tests, presents reading comprehension questions, including specific vocabulary-related ones, based on a reading passage. (For more on Vocabulary for Comprehension, see page 13.)

Following Vocabulary for Comprehension in each of the Reviews is another new feature called **Grammar in Context**. This one-page exercise is linked to the reading passage that precedes it, referring to a grammar or usage topic illustrated in the passage and then reviewing that topic with a brief explanation and practice questions. (For more on Grammar in Context, see page 16.)

The 15 Units that form the core of VOCABULARY WORKSHOP remain unchanged. Each of the Units comprises a five-part lesson consisting of **Definitions**, **Completing the Sentence**, **Synonyms and Antonyms**, **Choosing the Right Word**, and **Vocabulary in Context**. Together, these exercises provide multiple and varied exposures to the taught words, an approach that has been shown to be consistent with and supportive of research-based findings in vocabulary instruction.

Enrichment and vocabulary-building exercises also remain in the form of **Building with Classical Roots**, **Word Associations**, and **Word Families** in the Reviews, and **Analogies** and **Enriching Your Vocabulary** in the Cumulative Reviews.

In this Level of Vocabulary Workshop you will study 300 key words. The words in this Level, as well as all of the other Levels of this series, have been selected on the following bases: currency and general usefulness; frequency of appearance on recognized vocabulary lists; applicability to, and appearance on, standardized tests; and current grade-level research.

ONLINE COMPONENTS
www.vocabularyworkshop.com

At the **www.vocabularyworkshop.com** Web site you will also find **interactive vocabulary games and puzzles** that will help reinforce and enrich your understanding of the key words in this level of VOCABULARY WORKSHOP.

CONTENTS

PRONUNCIATION KEY

The pronunciation is indicated for every basic word introduced in this book. The symbols used for this purpose, as listed below, are similar to those appearing in most standard dictionaries of recent vintage. (Pronunciation keys and given pronunciations sometimes differ from dictionary to dictionary.) The author has consulted a large number of dictionaries for this purpose but has relied primarily on *Webster's Third New International Dictionary* and *The Random House Dictionary of the English Language (Unabridged)*.

There are, of course, many English words for which two (or more) pronunciations are commonly accepted. In virtually all cases where such words occur in this book, the author has sought to make things easier for the student by giving just one pronunciation. The only significant exception occurs when the pronunciation changes in accordance with a shift in the part of speech. Thus we would indicate that *project* in the verb form is pronounced prə jekt', and in the noun form, präj' ekt.

It is believed that these relatively simple pronunciation guides will be readily usable by the student. It should be emphasized, however, that the *best* way to learn the pronunciation of a word is to listen to and imitate an educated speaker.

Vowels	ā	lake	e	str*e*ss	ü	l*oo*t, n*ew*
	a	m*a*t	ī	kn*i*fe	u̇	f*oo*t, p*u*ll
	â	c*a*re	i	s*i*t	ə	j*u*mping, brok*e*n
	ä	b*a*rk, b*o*ttle	ō	fl*o*w	ər	b*ir*d, bett*er*
	au̇	d*ou*bt	ô	*a*ll, c*o*rd		
	ē	b*ea*t, word*y*	oi	*oi*l		

Consonants	ch	*ch*ild, lec*t*ure	s	*c*ellar	wh	*wh*at
	g	*g*ive	sh	*sh*un	y	*y*earn
	j	*g*entle, bri*dg*e	th	*th*ank	z	i*s*
	ŋ	si*ng*	t̶h̶	*th*ose	zh	mea*s*ure

All other consonants are sounded as in the alphabet.

Stress	The accent mark *follows* the syllable receiving the major stress: en rich'

Abbreviations	*adj.* adjective	*n.* noun	*prep.* preposition
	adv. adverb	*part.* participle	*v.* verb
	int. interjection	*pl.* plural	

See page T21 for information about the Interactive Audio Pronunciation Program.

THE VOCABULARY OF VOCABULARY

There are some interesting and useful words that we use to describe and identify words. The exercises that follow will help you to check and strengthen your knowledge of this "vocabulary of vocabulary."

Denotation and Connotation

The **denotation** of a word is its specific dictionary meaning. Here are a few examples:

Word	Denotation
bereft	deprived of
adroit	skillful
swerve	turn

The **connotation** of a word is its **tone**—that is, the emotions or associations it normally arouses in people using, hearing, or reading it. Depending on what these feelings are, the connotation of a word may be *favorable* (*positive*) or *unfavorable* (*negative, pejorative*). A word that does not normally arouse strong feelings of any kind has a *neutral* connotation. Here are some examples of words with different connotations:

Word	Connotation
bereft	unfavorable
adroit	favorable
swerve	neutral

Exercises *In the space provided, label the connotation of each of the following words* **F** *for "favorable,"* **U** *for "unfavorable," or* **N** *for "neutral."*

U	**1.** hackneyed	F	**3.** affable	N	**5.** motley
U	**2.** heinous	F	**4.** fortuitous	F	**6.** amenable

Literal and Figurative Usage

When a word is used in a **literal** sense, it is being employed in its strict (or primary) dictionary meaning in a situation (or context) that "makes sense" from a purely logical or realistic point of view. For example:

Yesterday I read an old tale about a knight who slew a *fire-breathing* dragon.

In this sentence, *fire-breathing* is employed literally. The dragon is pictured as breathing real fire.

Sometimes words are used in a symbolic or nonliteral way in situations that do not "make sense" from a purely logical or realistic point of view. We call this nonliteral application of a word a **figurative** or **metaphorical** usage. For example:

Suddenly my boss rushed into my office, *breathing fire*.

In this sentence *breathing fire* is not being used in a literal sense. That is, the boss was not actually breathing fire out of his nostrils. Rather, the expression is intended to convey graphically that the boss was very angry.

Exercises *In the space provided, write **L** for "literal" or **F** for "figurative" next to each of the following sentences to show how the italicized expression is being used.*

___F___ **1.** She was so forgetful that she sometimes said her mind was a *sieve*.

___L___ **2.** He strained his tea with a *sieve*.

___F___ **3.** That suitcase weighed a *ton*!

Synonyms

A **synonym** is a word that has *the same* or *almost the same* meaning as another word. Here are some examples:

silent—quiet
ephemeral—transitory
happy—jovial

bellow—yell
pensive—thoughtful
proficient—skillful

Exercises *In each of the following groups, circle the word that is most nearly the **synonym** of the word in **boldface** type.*

1. amnesty	2. curtail	3. debase	4. aura
a. equanimity	(a. diminish)	a. raise	a. hemisphere
b. culpability	b. aggrandize	(b. lower)	b. stratosphere
c. gratitude	c. acknowledge	c. deny	(c. atmosphere)
(d. forgiveness)	d. eschew	d. accept	d. color

Antonyms

An **antonym** is a word that means *the opposite* of or *almost the opposite* of another word. Here are some examples:

dark—light
prudent—foolish
lax—strict

lethargic—energetic
gigantic—tiny
trivial—significant

Exercises *In each of the following groups, circle the word that is most nearly the **antonym** of the word in **boldface** type.*

1. berate	2. erudite	3. galvanize	4. jejune
a. castigate	a. encumbering	a. embroil	(a. interesting)
(b. laud)	b. absorbing	(b. inhibit)	b. dry
c. equivocate	c. scholarly	c. elucidate	c. southern
d. extenuate	(d. ignorant)	d. gesticulate	d. ecumenical

VOCABULARY STRATEGY: USING CONTEXT

How do you go about finding the meaning of an unknown or unfamiliar word that you come across in your reading? You might look the word up in a dictionary, of course, provided one is at hand. But there are two other useful strategies that you might employ to find the meaning of a word that you do not know at all or that is used in a way that you do not recognize. One strategy is to analyze the **structure** or parts of the word. (See pages 11 and 12 for more on this strategy.) The other strategy is to try to figure out the meaning of the word by reference to context.

When we speak of the **context** of a word, we mean the printed text of which that word is part. By studying the context, we may find **clues** that lead us to its meaning. We might find a clue in the immediate sentence or phrase in which the word appears (and sometimes in adjoining sentences or phrases, too); or we might find a clue in the topic or subject matter of the passage in which the word appears; or we might even find a clue in the physical features of a page itself. (Photographs, illustrations, charts, graphs, captions, and headings are some examples of such features.)

One way to use context as a strategy is to ask yourself what you know already about the topic or subject matter in question. By applying what you have learned before about deserts, for example, you would probably be able to figure out that the word *arid* in the phrase "the arid climate of the desert" means "dry."

The **Vocabulary in Context** exercises that appear in the Units and the **Vocabulary for Comprehension** and the **Choosing the Right Meaning** exercises that appear in the Reviews and Cumulative Reviews both provide practice in using context to determine the meaning of given words.

When you do the various word-omission exercises in this book, look for **context clues** built into the sentence or passage to guide you to the correct answer. Three types of context clues appear in the exercises in this book.

A **restatement clue** consists of a *synonym* for, or a *definition* of, the missing word. For example:

The summer <u>humidity</u> seemed to make everything wilt, and I could feel the _____ in the air.
(a. wetness)   b. pollen   c. excitement   d. boredom

In this sentence, *humidity* is a synonym of the missing word, *wetness*, and acts as a restatement clue for it.

A **contrast clue** consists of an *antonym* for, or a phrase that means the *opposite* of, the missing word. For example:

Though she was <u>exhausted</u>, she worked on the production with admirable (**energy,** lethargy).

In this sentence, *exhausted* is in contrast with the missing word, *energy*. This is confirmed by the presence of the word *though*. *Exhausted* thus functions as a contrast clue for *energy*.

An **inference clue** implies but does not directly state the meaning of the missing word or words. For example:

It took a great deal of _____ to <u>keep up with the rest of the pack</u> as they sped across the broken and hilly _____ that separated them from the finish line in the cross country race.

a. dispatch . . . apparel
b. misgiving . . . repast

c. stamina . . . terrain
d. diversity . . . barrage

In this sentence, there are several inference clues: (a) *keep up with the rest of the pack* suggests the word *stamina* because people who keep up must by definition have stamina; the word *sped* suggests the same thing; (b) the words *broken* and *hilly* suggest *terrain* because they are both terms that describe terrain. Accordingly, all these words are inference clues because they suggest or imply, but do not directly state, the missing word or words.

Exercises   *Use context clues to choose the word or words that complete each of the following sentences or sets of sentences.*

1. It's better not to paraphrase lines from great works of literature if you can _____ them directly.
a. quote
b. copy
c. interpret
d. extrapolate

2. The town was the _____ it had been all year, and we trudged in thick boots through feet of white _____ every day on our way home from school.
a. wettest . . . rain
b. hottest . . . popcorn
c. quietest . . . air
d. coldest . . . snow

3. If you call my house before seven in the morning, it is (**unlikely,** **necessary**) that I will answer the phone.

VOCABULARY STRATEGY: WORD STRUCTURE

One important way to build your vocabulary is to learn the meaning of word parts that make up many English words. These word parts consist of **prefixes**, **suffixes**, and **roots**, or **bases**. A useful strategy for determining the meaning of an unknown word is to "take apart" the word and think about the parts. For example, when you look at the word parts in the word *invisible,* you find the prefix *in-* ("not") + the root *-vis-* ("see") + the suffix *-ible* ("capable of"). From knowing the meanings of the parts of this word, you can figure out that *invisible* means "not capable of being seen."

Following is a list of common prefixes. Knowing the meaning of a prefix can help you determine the meaning of a word in which the prefix appears.

Prefix	Meaning	Sample Words
bi-	two	bicycle
com-, con-	together, with	compatriot, contact
de-, dis-	lower, opposite	devalue, disloyal
fore-, pre-	before, ahead of time	forewarn, preplan
il-, im-, in-, ir, non-, un-	not	illegal, impossible, inactive, irregular, nonsense, unable
in-, im-	in, into	inhale, import
mid-	middle	midway
mis-	wrongly, badly	mistake, misbehave
re-	again, back	redo, repay
sub-	under, less than	submarine, subzero
super-	above, greater than	superimpose, superstar
tri-	three	triangle

Following is a list of common suffixes. Knowing the meaning and grammatical function of a suffix can help you determine the meaning of a word.

Noun Suffix	Meaning	Sample Nouns
-acy, -ance, -ence, -hood, -ity, -ment, -ness, -ship	state, quality, or condition of, act or process of	adequacy, attendance, persistence, neighborhood, activity, judgment, brightness, friendship
-ant, -eer, -ent, -er, -ian, -ier, -ist, -or	one who does or makes something	contestant, auctioneer, resident, banker, comedian, financier, dentist, doctor
-ation, -ition, -ion	act or result of	organization, imposition, election

Verb Suffix	Meaning	Sample Verbs
-ate	to become, produce, or treat	validate, salivate, chlorinate
-en	to make, cause to be	weaken
-fy, -ify, -ize	to cause, make	liquefy, glorify, legalize

Adjective Suffix	Meaning	Sample Adjectives
-able, -ible	able, capable of	believable, incredible
-al, -ic	relating to, characteristic of	natural, romantic
-ful, -ive, -ous	full of, given to, marked by	beautiful, protective, poisonous
-ish, -like	like, resembling	foolish, childlike
-less	lacking, without	careless

A **base** or **root** is the main part of a word to which prefixes and suffixes may be added. Many roots come to English from Latin, such as *-socio-,* meaning "society," or from Greek, such as *-logy-,* meaning "the study of." Knowing Greek and Latin roots can help you determine the meaning of a word such as *sociology,* which means "the study of society."

In the **Building with Classical Roots** sections of this book you will learn more about some of these Latin and Greek roots and about English words that derive from them. The lists that follow may help you figure out the meaning of new or unfamiliar words that you encounter in your reading.

Greek Root	Meaning	Sample Word
-astr-, -aster-, -astro-	star	astral, asteroid, astronaut
-auto-	self	autograph
-bio-	life	biography
-chron-, chrono-	time	chronic, chronological
-cosm-, -cosmo-	universe, order	microcosm, cosmopolitan
-cryph-, -crypt-	hidden, secret	apocryphal, cryptographer
-dem-, -demo-	people	epidemic, democracy
-dia-	through, across, between	diameter
-dog-, -dox-	opinion, teaching	dogmatic, orthodox
-gen-	race, kind, origin, birth	generation
-gnos-	know	diagnostic
-graph-, -graphy-, -gram-	write	graphite, autobiography, telegram
-log-, -logue-	speech, word, reasoning	logic, dialogue
-lys-	break down	analysis
-metr-, -meter-	measure	metric, kilometer
-micro-	small	microchip
-morph-	form, shape	amorphous
-naut-	sailor	cosmonaut
-phon-, -phone-, -phono-	sound, voice	phonics, telephone, phonograph
-pol-, -polis-	city, state	police, metropolis
-scop-, -scope-	watch, look at	microscope, telescope
-tele-	far off, distant	television
-the-	put or place	parentheses

Latin Root	Meaning	Sample Word
-cap-, -capt-, -cept-, -cip-	take	capitulate, captive, concept, recipient
-cede-, -ceed-, -ceas-, -cess-	happen, yield, go	precede, proceed, decease, cessation
-cred-	believe	incredible
-dic-, -dict-	speak, say, tell	indicate, diction
-duc-, -duct-, -duit-	lead, conduct, draw	educate, conduct, conduit
-fac-, -fact-, -fect-, -fic-, -fy-	make	faculty, artifact, defect, beneficial, clarify
-ject-	throw	eject
-mis-, -miss-, -mit-, -mitt-	send	promise, missile, transmit, intermittent
-note-, -not-	know, recognize	denote, notion
-pel-, -puls-	drive	expel, compulsive
-pend-, -pens-	hang, weight, set aside	pendulum, pension
-pon-, -pos-	put, place	component, position
-port-	carry	portable
-rupt-	break	bankrupt
-scrib-, -scribe-, -script-	write	scribble, describe, inscription
-spec-, -spic-	look, see	spectator, conspicuous
-tac-, -tag-, -tang-, -teg-	touch	contact, contagious, tangible, integral
-tain-, -ten-, -tin-	hold, keep	contain, tenure, retinue
-temp-	time	tempo
-ven-, -vent-	come	intervene, convention
-vers-, -vert-	turn	reverse, invert
-voc-, -vok-	call	vocal, invoke

VOCABULARY AND READING

Word knowledge is essential to reading comprehension. Quite simply, the more words you know, the easier it is to make sense of what you read. Your growing knowledge of word meanings combined with an ability to read carefully and think about what you read will help you succeed in school and do well on standardized tests, including the new SAT, the ACT, and the PSAT.

The **Vocabulary for Comprehension** exercises in this book will give you the opportunity to put your vocabulary knowledge and critical reading skills to use. Each exercise consists of a nonfiction reading passage followed by comprehension questions. The passages and questions are similar to those that you are likely to find on standardized tests.

Kinds of Questions

The questions on the reading sections of standardized tests are formulated in many different ways, but they are usually only of a small number of kinds, or types— the same ones that appear most frequently in the Vocabulary for Comprehension exercises in this book.

Main Idea Questions generally ask what the passage as a whole is about. Questions about the main idea may begin like this:

- The primary or main purpose of the passage is

- The primary focus of the passage is on

- The passage is best described as

- The passage is primarily concerned with

- The title that best describes the content of the passage is

Often the main idea is stated in the first paragraph of the passage. Sometimes, however, the first paragraph serves as an introduction and the main idea is included later on. When you answer questions about the main idea, you should make sure that the answers you choose reflect the focus of the entire passage and not just part of it. You may also be asked the main idea of a specific paragraph.

Detail Questions focus on important information that is explicitly stated in the passage. Often, however, the correct answer choices do not use the exact language of the passage. They are instead restatements, or paraphrases, of the text. So, for example, the answer to a question about "trash production and disposal" might use the term "waste management."

Vocabulary-in-Context Questions check your ability to use context to identify a word's meaning. All vocabulary-in-context questions include line references so that you can refer back to the passage to see how and in what context the word is used.

Here are some examples:

- **Condone** (line 6) most nearly means
- **Eminent** (line 8) is best defined as
- The meaning of **diffuse** (line 30) is

It is important to use context to check your answer choices, particularly when the vocabulary word has more than one meaning. Among the choices may be two (or more) correct meanings of the word in question. Your task is to choose the meaning that best fits the context.

Inference Questions ask you to make inferences or draw conclusions from the passage. These questions often begin like this:

- It can be inferred from the passage that
- The author implies that
- The passage suggests that
- Evidently the author feels that

The inferences you make and the conclusions you draw must be based on the information in the passage. Your own knowledge and reasoning come into play in understanding what is implied and in reaching conclusions that are logical.

Questions about Tone show your understanding of the author's attitude toward the subject of the passage. Words that describe tone, or attitude, are "feeling" words, for example, *indifferent, ambivalent, scornful, astonished, respectful*. These are typical questions:

- The author's attitude toward . . . is best described as
- The author's perspective is that of . . .
- Which word best describes the author's tone . . .

To determine the tone, it's important to pay attention to the author's choice of words and note your personal reaction. The author's attitude may be positive *(respectful, astonished)*, negative *(scornful)*, or neutral *(indifferent, ambivalent)*.

Questions about Author's Technique focus on the way a text is organized and the language the author uses. These questions ask you to think about structure and function. For example:

- The final paragraph serves to
- What is the function of the phrase . . . ?
- What does the author mean by . . . ?
- The author cites . . . in order to . . . .

To answer the questions, you must demonstrate an understanding of the way the author presents information and develops ideas.

Strategies

Here are some general strategies to help you in reading each passage and answering the questions.

- Read the introduction first. The introduction will provide a focus for the selection.

- Be an active reader. As you read, ask yourself questions about the passage, for example: What is this paragraph about? What does the writer mean here? Why does the writer include this information?

- Refer back to the passage when you answer the questions. In general, the order of the questions mirrors the organization of the passage, and many of the questions include paragraph or line references. It is often helpful to go back and reread before choosing an answer.

- Read carefully, and be sure to base your answer choices on the passage. There are answer choices that make sense, but are not based on the information in the passage. These are true statements, but incorrect answers. The correct answers are either restatements of ideas in the text or inferences that can be made from the text.

- Consider each exercise a learning experience. Keep in mind that your ability to answer the questions correctly shows as much about your understanding of the questions as about your understanding of the passage.

GRAMMAR AND WRITING

In order to write well, so that your meaning and your purpose are clearly understood, you must use words correctly; but, more than that, you must also make sure that what you write is grammatically correct. Knowing the rules of grammar, usage, and mechanics—the conventions of standard English—make your writing not just correct but more powerful and persuasive, too.

As a student you are regularly challenged to write effectively and correctly not only in your English classes but in your social studies, science, and history classes, too. Furthermore, high schools and colleges have raised their expectations for graduates. If you have taken a standardized test recently or are preparing to take one, you know this only too well. The writing and grammar sections of these tests have grown more demanding than ever.

On these grammar sections, questions usually appear in one or two multiple-choice formats. In one, you must decide if a mistake has been made in a sentence and, if one has been made, identify it. In another format, you must decide if an identified word or phrase is incorrect and, if it is incorrect, choose from several options the best way to correct it.

The **Grammar in Context** exercise that appears in each of the five Reviews in this book will provide you with opportunity to review and apply grammar and usage rules that are critical to good writing and that are frequently tested on the multiple-choice parts of standardized tests. In Level G, these topics are:

- Adjectives and adverbs
- Pronoun-antecedent agreement
- Pronoun reference and shift
- Dangling participles
- Faulty subordination

(For the sake of convenience, we sometimes use the term *grammar* to embrace all of the "rules" of English; but it's important to note that grammar, usage, and mechanics each represents a different aspect of writing. Grammar deals mostly with parts of speech and with parts of sentences and their relations. Usage, as the name suggests, concerns the way that words and phrases are used; usage topics would include, for example, irregular verbs, active and passive voice, subject-verb agreement, and double negatives. Mechanics deals with punctuation, capitalization, and spelling.)

There are many reasons to write and speak correctly other than to score well on standardized tests. You are judged by the way you write and speak. Your use of English is evaluated in the writing you do in school, on college applications, and in many different kinds of careers. You should be able to write and speak correctly when the situation calls for it—in a formal writing assignment, on a test, or in an interview. The more you practice standard English, the more comfortable and confident you will become when you write and speak.

WORKING WITH ANALOGIES

A verbal analogy expresses a relationship or comparison between sets of words. Normally, an analogy contains two pairs of words linked by a word or symbol that stands for an equals (=) sign. A complete analogy compares the two pairs of words and makes a statement about them. It asserts that the relationship between the first pair of words is the same as the relationship between the second pair.

In the **Analogies** exercises that appear in the Cumulative Reviews, you will be asked to complete analogies, that is, to choose the pair of words that best matches or parallels the relationship of the key, or given, pair of words. Here are two examples:

1. maple is to **tree** as	**2. joyful** is to **gloomy** as
a. acorn is to oak	a. cheerful is to happy
b. hen is to rooster	b. strong is to weak
c. rose is to flower	c. quick is to famous
d. shrub is to lilac	d. hungry is to starving

In order to find the correct answer to exercise 1, you must first determine the relationship between the two key words, **maple** and **tree**. In this case, that relationship might be expressed as "a maple is a kind (or type) of tree." The next step is to select from choices a, b, c, and d the pair of words that best reflects the same relationship. Clearly, the correct answer is (c); it is the only choice that parallels the relationship of the key words: a rose is a kind (or type) of flower, just as a maple is a kind (or type) of tree. The other choices do not express the same relationship.

In exercise 2, the relationship between the key words can be expressed as "joyful means the opposite of gloomy." Which of the choices best represents the same relationship? The answer, of course, is (b): "strong" means the opposite of "weak."

Here are examples of some other common analogy relationships:

Analogy	Key Relationship
big is to **large** as **little** is to **small**	**Big** means the same thing as **large**, just as **little** means the same thing as **small**.
brave is to **favorable** as **cowardly** is to **unfavorable**	The tone of **brave** is **favorable**, just as the tone of **cowardly** is **unfavorable**.
busybody is to **nosy** as **klutz** is to **clumsy**	A **busybody** is by definition someone who is **nosy**, just as a **klutz** is by definition someone who is **clumsy**.
cowardly is to **courage** as **awkward** is to **grace**	Someone who is **cowardly** lacks **courage**, just as someone who is **awkward** lacks **grace**.
visible is to **see** as **audible** is to **hear**	If something is **visible**, you can by definition **see** it, just as if something is **audible**, you can by definition **hear** it.
liar is to **truthful** as **bigot** is to **fair-minded**	A **liar** is by definition not likely to be **truthful**, just as a **bigot** is by definition not likely to be **fair-minded**.
eyes are to **see** as **ears** are to **hear**	You use your **eyes** to **see** with, just as you use your **ears** to **hear** with.

There are many different kinds of relationships represented in the analogy questions you will find in this book, but the key to solving any analogy is to find and express the relationship between the two key words.

This test contains a sampling of the words that are to be found in the exercises in this Level of VOCABULARY WORKSHOP. It will give you an idea of the types of words to be studied and their level of difficulty. When you have completed all the units, the Final Mastery Test at the end of this book will assess what you have learned. By comparing your results on the Final Mastery Test with your results on the Diagnostic Test below, you will be able to judge your progress.

Synonyms

*In each of the following groups, circle the word or phrase that **most** **nearly** expresses the meaning of the word in **boldface** type in the given phrase.*

1. improvident behavior
a. conservative   b. funny   c. mysterious   (d. rash)

2. tended to **decry** our efforts
(a. condemn)   b. assist   c. hinder   d. finance

3. embellish a story
a. confirm   (b. adorn)   c. ridicule   d. translate

4. carping supervisors
a. cooperative   (b. critical)   c. efficient   d. clumsy

5. jettison the ballast
a. analyze   (b. cast off)   c. describe   d. conceal

6. an **overt** act
a. rebellious   (b. obvious)   c. nearly fatal   d. habitual

7. a **febrile** imagination
a. inhibited   (b. feverish)   c. disciplined   d. sentimental

8. an **insatiable** appetite
a. temporary   b. shallow   (c. limitless)   d. informed

9. germane to the problem
(a. relevant)   b. inappropriate   c. indispensable   d. foreign

10. spoke with the **distraught** parents
a. strict   b. permissive   (c. agitated)   d. indifferent

11. respond with **celerity**
a. intelligence   b. satisfaction   c. distrust   (d. promptness)

12. the **acclamation** of the crowd
(a. applause)   b. derision   c. indifference   d. criticism

13. a **utopian** community
a. restricted   b. backward   (c. idealistic)   d. successful

14. a **prepossessing** smile
(a. engaging)   b. sarcastic   c. tentative   d. timid

15. nothing but a **dilettante**
(a. dabbler)   b. skeptic   c. thief   d. lout

16. hallow the ground on which they fought
- a. observe
- b. consecrate
- c. tread
- d. profane

17. a minor **idiosyncrasy**
- a. inclination
- b. setback
- c. error
- d. peculiarity

18. received **intermittent** signals
- a. interrupted
- b. weak
- c. clear
- d. coded

19. accuse of **collusion**
- a. theft
- b. slander
- c. conspiracy
- d. negligence

20. tantamount to a victory
- a. equivalent
- b. opposed
- c. favorable
- d. unrelated

21. a **paucity** of resources
- a. dearth
- b. variety
- c. oversupply
- d. sample

22. used the Faust **motif**
- a. theme
- b. copyright
- c. costume
- d. scenery

23. dressed with **impeccable** taste
- a. vulgar
- b. modern
- c. faultless
- d. strange

24. a **sylvan** scene
- a. marine
- b. horrifying
- c. wooded
- d. urban

25. a **luminous** moon
- a. sizeable
- b. ostentatious
- c. glowing
- d. forbidding

26. allay our fears
- a. analyze
- b. intensify
- c. lessen
- d. ridicule

27. delineate the character
- a. guess
- b. portray
- c. obscure
- d. replace

28. a **delectable** dish
- a. delightful
- b. foreign
- c. crude
- d. expensive

29. belabor the point
- a. ignore
- b. sharpen
- c. overwork
- d. accept

30. attenuated the effect of the measure
- a. questioned
- b. diluted
- c. enhanced
- d. reassessed

Antonyms

*In each of the following groups, circle the word that is **most nearly opposite** in meaning to the word in **boldface** type in the given phrase.*

31. a **perfunctory** explanation
- a. new
- b. long
- c. incisive
- d. shallow

32. a **testy** reply
- a. even-tempered
- b. evasive
- c. brilliant
- d. impatient

33. exhumed the corpse
- a. examined
- b. unearthed
- c. buried
- d. revived

34. illusory gains
- a. imaginary
- b. actual
- c. spectacular
- d. supplemental

35. an **abstruse** theory
a. difficult   b. psychological   c. boring   (d. straightforward)

36. compose a **panegyric**
(a. philippic)   b. recipe   c. tribute   d. reply

37. sporadic precipitation
a. intermittent   (b. steady)   c. record   d. unseasonable

38. a **moot** point
(a. indisputable)   b. pertinent   c. new   d. debatable

39. an **obsequious** manner
a. fawning   b. courtly   (c. overbearing)   d. clumsy

40. the **acuity** of her mind
(a. dullness)   b. flexibility   c. tidiness   d. keenness

41. a **hapless** contestant
(a. lucky)   b. nervous   c. professional   d. brilliant

42. plenary powers
a. absolute   (b. limited)   c. acute   d. superhuman

43. manifest an interest in tennis
a. reveal   b. create   c. claim   (d. conceal)

44. a **pejorative** connotation
a. bad   b. colloquial   (c. favorable)   d. illegal

45. the **ephemeral** joys of summer
(a. long-lasting)   b. transitory   c. masculine   d. profound

46. a **defunct** organization
a. profitable   (b. ongoing)   c. charitable   d. dead

47. the man's **foibles**
a. wealth   b. background   c. children   (d. strong suits)

48. a **reputed** mobster
a. fearsome   b. celebrated   c. deceased   (d. proven)

49. lend **credence** to a statement
a. support   b. credibility   (c. disbelief)   d. eloquence

50. ubiquitous ants
(a. scarce)   b. omnipresent   c. aggressive   d. bestial

Definitions

Note carefully the spelling, pronunciation, part(s) of speech, and definition(s) of each of the following words. Then write the word in the blank space(s) in the illustrative sentence(s) following. Finally, study the lists of synonyms and antonyms given at the end of each entry.

1. acquisitive
(ə kwiz′ ə tiv)

(*adj.*) able to get and retain ideas or information; concerned with acquiring wealth or property

In an _____**acquisitive**_____ society, there is a great deal of emphasis on buying and selling.
SYNONYMS: greedy, grasping, avaricious, retentive
ANTONYMS: altruistic, unretentive

2. arrogate
(a′ rə gāt)

(*v.*) to claim or take without right

The ambitious noblemen will put the young king under house arrest and _____**arrogate**_____ royal privileges to themselves.
SYNONYMS: expropriate, usurp, commandeer
ANTONYMS: relinquish, renounce, abdicate, abandon

3. banal
(bə nal′)

(*adj.*) hackneyed, trite, commonplace

The new play's _____**banal**_____ dialogue made it seem more like a soap opera than a serious drama.
SYNONYMS: stale, insipid
ANTONYMS: fresh, novel, original, new

4. belabor
(bi lā′ bər)

(*v.*) to work on excessively; to thrash soundly

His tendency to _____**belabor**_____ the small points often made him miss the big picture.
SYNONYM: overwork

5. carping
(kär′ piŋ)

(*adj.*) tending to find fault, especially in a petty, nasty, or hairsplitting way; (*n.*) petty, nagging criticism

The trainee resigned after a week rather than put up with the _____**carping**_____ complaints of the sales manager.

Most artists choose to ignore the _____**carping**_____ of critics and simply go on with their work.
SYNONYMS: (*adj.*) nit-picking, caviling
ANTONYMS: (*adj.*) approving, uncritical

6. coherent
(kō hēr′ ənt)

(*adj.*) holding or sticking together; making a logical whole; comprehensible, meaningful

The physics teacher gave a surprisingly _____**coherent**_____ description of quantum mechanics.
SYNONYMS: connected, unified, consistent, cohesive
ANTONYMS: muddled, chaotic, disjointed

7. congeal
(kən jēl′)

(v.) to change from liquid to solid, thicken; to make inflexible or rigid

If you do not wash your dishes right away, the food on them will _____ congeal _____.

SYNONYMS: harden, jell, coagulate, solidify
ANTONYMS: melt, liquefy

8. emulate
(em′ yə lāt)

(v.) to imitate with the intent of equaling or surpassing the model

Most beginning writers try to _____ emulate _____ a great writer and later develop their own individual styles.

SYNONYMS: copy, mimic, rival, match, measure up to

9. encomium
(en kō′ mē əm)

(n.) a formal expression of praise, a lavish tribute

On Veterans Day, the President delivered a heartfelt _____ encomium _____ to those who died for their country.

SYNONYMS: panegyric, eulogy, commendation
ANTONYMS: condemnation, castigation, criticism

10. eschew
(es chü′)

(v.) to avoid, shun, keep away from

The young athletes promised the coach that they would train vigorously and _____ eschew _____ bad habits.

SYNONYMS: abstain from, steer clear of, forgo
ANTONYMS: embrace, adopt

11. germane
(jər mān′)

(adj.) relevant, appropriate, apropos, fitting

Bringing up examples from the past is not _____ germane _____ to the present discussion.

SYNONYM: pertinent
ANTONYMS: irrelevant, extraneous, inappropriate

12. insatiable
(in sā′ shə bəl)

(adj.) so great or demanding as not to be satisfied

People with an _____ insatiable _____ appetite for gossip often do not have compelling stories of their own.

SYNONYMS: unquenchable, ravenous, voracious

13. intransigent
(in tran′ sə jənt)

(adj.) refusing to compromise, irreconcilable

Little will get accomplished if the legislators of both parties maintain their _____ intransigent _____ attitudes.

SYNONYMS: uncompromising, unyielding, obdurate
ANTONYMS: lukewarm, halfhearted, yielding

14. invidious
(in vid′ ē əs)

(*adj.*) offensive, hateful; tending to cause bitterness and resentment

Teachers should avoid making _____ **invidious** _____ comparisons between their students.

SYNONYMS: malicious, spiteful, prejudicial, pejorative
ANTONYMS: complimentary, flattering, ameliorative

15. largesse
(lär jes′)

(*n.*) generosity in giving; lavish or bountiful contributions

The university was the fortunate beneficiary of the _____ **largesse** _____ of many of its graduates.

SYNONYMS: liberality, munificence, bounty
ANTONYMS: stinginess, miserliness, niggardliness

16. reconnaissance
(ri kän′ ə səns)

(*n.*) a survey made for military purposes; any kind of preliminary inspection or examination

The field officer required a thorough _____ **reconnaissance** _____ before ordering any troop movements.

SYNONYM: scouting expedition

17. substantiate
(səb stan′ shē āt)

(*v.*) to establish by evidence, prove; to give concrete or substantial form to

The prospector was unable to _____ **substantiate** _____ his claim to the land where the gold was found.

SYNONYMS: verify, confirm, validate, authenticate
ANTONYMS: refute, disprove, invalidate

18. taciturn
(tas′ ə tərn)

(*adj.*) habitually silent or quiet, inclined to talk very little

Abraham Lincoln has the reputation of having a dour and _____ **taciturn** _____ personality.

SYNONYMS: tight-lipped, uncommunicative, laconic
ANTONYMS: garrulous, loquacious, prolix, verbose

19. temporize
(tem′ pə rīz)

(*v.*) to stall or act evasively in order to gain time, avoid a confrontation, or postpone a decision; to compromise

For most of Shakespeare's greatest tragedy, the protagonist Hamlet chooses to _____ **temporize** _____ rather than act.

SYNONYMS: hedge, dillydally, procrastinate

20. tenable
(ten′ ə bəl)

(*adj.*) capable of being held or defended

The researchers put forth a _____ **tenable** _____ theory, but their conclusions would be reviewed carefully by others.

SYNONYMS: defensible, justifiable, maintainable
ANTONYMS: indefensible, unjustifiable

Completing the Sentence

From the words for this unit, choose the one that best completes each of the following sentences. Write the word in the space provided.

1. The novel contains an interesting study of a miser's _____ **insatiable** _____ lust for gold and its evil effects on those around him.

2. Some of the episodes in the series were wonderfully fresh and original; others were just plain _____ **banal** _____.

3. I don't object to the inclusion of anecdotes in a serious lecture, but they should at the very least be _____ **germane** _____ to the subject.

4. "There is no need for you to _____ **belabor** _____ the point," I replied, "when I already understand clearly what your criticism is."

5. There is nothing wrong with _____ **emulating** _____ the great singers of the past as long as you eventually develop a style that is all your own.

6. When the temperature outside dropped suddenly, the water in the ditch _____ **congealed** _____ into a mass of icy sludge.

7. Your essay would be a great deal tighter and more _____ **coherent** _____ if you removed all the extraneous information it now contains.

8. I would rather work at the most menial, ill-paying job than be the recipient of the government's _____ **largesse** _____.

9. The purpose of military _____ **reconnaissance** _____ remains the same whether cavalry or helicopters are used: to learn as much as possible about the enemy.

10. I doubt very much that he can _____ **substantiate** _____ his assertion that he won two gold medals in the 1956 Olympics.

11. Despite the _____ **carping** _____ and nit-picking of a few petty minds, I feel we have substantially improved our local school system of late.

12. In any crisis, the longer a person _____ **temporizes** _____, the greater the danger is likely to become.

13. In my humble opinion, there is absolutely no justification for making such _____ **invidious** _____ distinctions between the two types of product.

14. Never having any money in one's pockets can be a real trial for someone born with the _____ **acquisitive** _____ instincts of a pack rat.

15. Students who seek high grades must learn to _____ **eschew** _____ the joys of the one-eyed monster, the TV set.

16. As a result of recent research, earlier theories about the origin of the universe are no longer _____ **tenable** _____.

17. In spite of his size, he was so _____ **taciturn** _____ that we tended to forget that he was even in the room.

18. By whose authority did you _____ arrogate _____ to yourself the right to decide how the club's money would be spent?

19. Even the most severe critics showered _____ encomiums _____ on the young writer for the remarkable narrative power of her first novel.

20. How can we "meet them halfway" when they are so _____ intransigent _____ in their opposition to what we propose to do?

Synonyms

Choose the word from this unit that is **the same** or **most nearly the same** in meaning as the **boldface** word or expression in the given phrase. Write the word on the line provided.

1. harp on the same point again and again — belabor

2. the **grasping** real estate developer — acquisitive

3. tries to **copy** her social graces — emulate

4. tends to **hedge** when confronted by direct questions — temporize

5. the **nit-picking** comments of a perfectionist — carping

6. the **voracious** hunger — insatiable

7. led the **scouting expedition** into the jungle — reconnaissance

8. was thanked for her **munificence** — largesse

9. could not **verify** the alibi — substantiate

10. received a well-deserved **commendation** — encomium

11. blood that does not **coagulate** — congeal

12. was **pertinent** to the investigation — germane

13. obdurate on certain points — intransigent

14. a **justifiable** reason for disagreeing — tenable

15. tried to **usurp** control of the finances — arrogate

Antonyms

Choose the word from this unit that is **most nearly opposite** in meaning to the **boldface** word or expression in the given phrase. Write the word on the line provided.

16. made a very **complimentary** remark — invidious

17. questioned the **garrulous** witness — taciturn

18. the **novel** lyrics to that song — banal

19. a **disjointed** essay on foreign policy — coherent

20. adopted the use of technology — eschewed

Choosing the Right Word

Circle the **boldface** word that more satisfactorily completes each of the following sentences.

1. Aristotle had such a(n) (**tenable,** **acquisitive**) mind that his writings are a veritable gold mine of odd and interesting information.

2. The mood of easy cordiality with which we began the meeting soon (**congealed,** **temporized**) into icy politeness.

3. "That word has such (**invidious,** germane) connotations in modern American parlance," I said, "that I would hesitate to use it, even in jest."

4. In that moment of grief, the conventional expressions of sympathy I had always considered (**tenable,** **banal**) were surprisingly comforting.

5. The speech was so filled with (**encomiums,** reconnaissance) that I found it hard to believe that the subject of all this acclaim was plain old me.

6. When the evidence of his misconduct became irrefutable, he saw that his position was not (**banal,** **tenable**) and resigned.

7. I am proud to have it said of me that I am stubborn and (**invidious,** **intransigent**) when genuine moral issues are involved.

8. His figure bears witness to his (**acquisitive,** **insatiable**) appetite for the pleasures of the table.

9. Ethelred the Unready was so reluctant to face the Vikings who invaded his kingdom that in effect he (**arrogated,** **temporized**) himself off the throne.

10. After I mowed the lawn for an hour, he gave me a whole dollar with the air of a feudal lord bestowing (**largesse,** intransigence) on a grateful serf.

11. The poor woman was in such a state of shock after the accident that she couldn't give a (**coherent,** taciturn) account of what had happened.

12. Your critical comments about my "lack of social background" may be true, but they are not (**coherent,** **germane**) to my qualifications for office.

13. Aerial (**reconnaissance,** encomium) of the enemy's positions provided the general with the information he needed to plan his attack.

14. What evidence can you offer to (**substantiate,** eschew) the assertion that capital punishment does not deter potential murderers?

15. In our attempt to improve the quality of life in America, we should not be too quick to (**eschew,** cohere) old ideas simply because they are old.

16. The new batting champion in our softball league is a(n) (**insatiable,** **taciturn**) young man who prefers to let his bat to do his talking for him.

17. Suddenly a band of ruffians set upon us and began to (**congeal,** **belabor**) us with blows and curses.

18. After the editor read the story, he returned it to the author with only a few (**carping,** coherent) criticisms of minor faults penciled in the margin.

19. Even a very imperfect human being may sometimes have virtues of mind or character that are worthy of (**carping,** **emulation**).

20. The Constitution is uniquely designed to provide protection against those who might seek to (**substantiate,** **arrogate**) undue power to themselves.

Read the following passage, in which some of the words you have studied in this unit appear in **boldface** type. Then complete each statement given below the passage by circling the letter of the item that is **the same** or **almost the same** in meaning as the highlighted word.

All That Glitters

(Line)

While the decades following the American Civil War were troubled by two serious economic depressions and rampant political corruption epitomized by the machinations of Boss Tweed at Tammany Hall in New York City, they were also a period of unprecedented economic growth and opportunity. "Robber Barons" with an

(5) apparently **insatiable** hunger for success amassed huge empires unregulated by anti-monopoly laws or income taxes. Mark Twain dubbed this era of growth, industry, and contrasting poverty "The

(10) Gilded Age" in a novel of the same name. The title sums up the **acquisitive** energy and desire to display wealth that seemed to possess every level of American society in that freewheeling era. The

(15) former distaste for the energetic pursuit of money was **eschewed** and replaced by an uncritical admiration for those who acquired great wealth. Getting rich quick was now the dream of millions, and it was

(20) upstart entrepreneurs like Cornelius Vanderbilt and Andrew Carnegie whom the masses wished to **emulate**.

Lampoon of Tammany Hall corruption published in *Harper's Magazine*

When French Premier Georges Clemenceau visited the U.S. during the

(25) Gilded Age, he intimated that the effects of capitalism on American society were **invidious**, and that the nation had gone from a stage of barbarism to one of decadence—without achieving anything in between. But Clemenceau's observation does not tell the whole story. While there was an increasing disparity between the working and leisure classes during this time, a new economy increased the overall

(30) standard of living so that laborers were less dependent on the **largesse** of their employers, and more able to care for themselves.

---

1. The meaning of **insatiable** (line 5) is
  a. admirable
  (c.) unquenchable
  b. lifelong
  d. humble

2. The meaning of **acquisitive** (line 11) is
  a. enthusiastic
  c. unflagging
  b. remarkable
  (d.) grasping

3. Eschewed (line 16) most nearly means
  a. embraced
  c. digested
  (b.) shunned
  d. blamed

4. Emulate (line 22) is best defined as
  (a.) copy
  c. condemn
  b. discuss
  d. escape

5. Invidious (line 26) most nearly means
  (a.) malicious
  c. original
  b. clever
  d. controversial

6. Largesse (line 30) most nearly means
  a. display
  (c.) munificence
  b. decency
  d. modesty

Definitions

Note carefully the spelling, pronunciation, part(s) of speech, and definition(s) of each of the following words. Then write the word in the blank space(s) in the illustrative sentence(s) following. Finally, study the lists of synonyms and antonyms given at the end of each entry.

1. accost
(ə käst′)

(*v.*) to approach and speak to first; to confront in a challenging or aggressive way

The nobleman was _____ accosted _____ by beggars on his way to the castle.

SYNONYMS: buttonhole, approach, confront
ANTONYMS: evade, avoid, shun

2. animadversion
(an ə mad vər′ zhən)

(*n.*) a comment indicating strong criticism or disapproval

The inexperienced filmmaker was disheartened by the _____ animadversion _____ of the film critic.

SYNONYMS: rebuke, reproof
ANTONYMS: praise, compliment

3. avid
(av′ id)

(*adj.*) desirous of something to the point of greed; intensely eager

Most writers are also _____ avid _____ readers who have loved books since childhood.

SYNONYMS: keen, enthusiastic, grasping
ANTONYMS: reluctant, indifferent, unenthusiastic

4. brackish
(brak′ ish)

(*adj.*) having a salty taste and unpleasant to drink

The shipwrecked passengers adrift on the lifeboat became ill after drinking _____ brackish _____ water.

SYNONYMS: briny, saline
ANTONYMS: fresh, clear, sweet

5. celerity
(sə ler′ ə tē)

(*n.*) swiftness, rapidity of motion or action

Although the heavy snowfall was not expected, the highway department responded with surprising _____ celerity _____.

SYNONYMS: promptness, alacrity, speed
ANTONYMS: slowness, sluggishness, dilatoriness

6. devious
(dē′ vē əs)

(*adj.*) straying or wandering from a straight or direct course; done or acting in a shifty or underhanded way

The interrogator used _____ devious _____ methods to try to get the suspect to incriminate himself.

SYNONYMS: roundabout, indirect, tricky, sly, artful
ANTONYMS: direct, straightforward, open, aboveboard

7. gambit
(gam' bit)

(*n.*) in chess, an opening move that involves risk or sacrifice of a minor piece in order to gain a later advantage; any opening move of this type

Asking an interesting stranger about his or her job is a popular party _____gambit_____.

SYNONYMS: ploy, stratagem, ruse, maneuver

8. halcyon
(hal' sē ən)

(*n.*) a legendary bird identified with the kingfisher; (*adj.*) of or relating to the halcyon; calm, peaceful; happy, golden; prosperous, affluent

The teacher read the legend of the _____halcyon_____, a mythic bird that nested in a calm sea.

The woman often spoke of the _____halcyon_____ days of her childhood.

SYNONYMS: (*adj.*) tranquil, serene, placid, palmy
ANTONYMS: (*adj.*) turbulent, chaotic, tumultuous

9. histrionic
(his trē än' ik)

(*adj.*) pertaining to actors and their techniques; theatrical, artificial; melodramatic

Upon receiving his award, the young actor gave a _____histrionic_____ speech.

SYNONYMS: affected, stagy
ANTONYMS: low-keyed, muted, untheatrical, subdued

10. incendiary
(in sen' dē er ē)

(*adj.*) deliberately setting or causing fires; designed to start fires; tending to stir up strife or rebellion; (*n.*) one who deliberately sets fires, arsonist; one who causes strife

The arsonist planted an _____incendiary_____ device in the basement of the store.

The radical _____incendiary_____ was sentenced to life imprisonment.

SYNONYMS: (*adj.*) inflammatory, provocative, (*n.*) firebrand
ANTONYMS: (*adj.*) soothing, quieting, (*n.*) peacemaker

11. maelstrom
(māl' strəm)

(*n.*) a whirlpool of great size and violence; a situation resembling a whirlpool in violence and destruction

Many innocent people caught in the _____maelstrom_____ of the revolution lost their lives and property.

SYNONYMS: vortex, chaos, turbulence, tumult

12. myopic
(mī äp' ik)

(*adj.*) nearsighted; lacking a broad, realistic view of a situation; lacking foresight or discernment

The _____myopic_____ foreign policy of the last administration has led to serious problems with our allies.

SYNONYM: shortsighted
ANTONYM: farsighted

13. overt
(ō vert')

(*adj.*) open, not hidden, expressed or revealed in a way that is easily recognized

In order for Congress to declare war, the President must demonstrate an _____ overt _____ threat.

SYNONYMS: clear, obvious, manifest, patent
ANTONYMS: secret, clandestine, covert, concealed

14. pejorative
(pə jôr' ə tiv)

(*adj.*) tending to make worse; expressing disapproval or disparagement, derogatory, deprecatory, belittling

The lawyer was accused of making a _____ pejorative _____ remark when referring to the defendant's background.

ANTONYMS: complimentary, ameliorative

15. propriety
(prə prī' ə tē)

(*n.*) the state of being proper, appropriateness; (*pl.*) standards of what is proper or socially acceptable

The social worker questioned the _____ propriety _____ of the police's request to see confidential records.

SYNONYMS: fitness, correctness, decorum
ANTONYMS: unseemliness, inappropriateness

16. sacrilege
(sak' rə lij)

(*n.*) improper or disrespectful treatment of something held sacred

The anthropologist was accused of committing a _____ sacrilege _____ when she disturbed an ancient burial ground.

SYNONYMS: desecration, profanation, defilement

17. summarily
(sə mer' ə lē)

(*adv.*) without delay or formality; briefly, concisely

As soon as there was evidence of criminal wrongdoing, the official was _____ summarily _____ ousted from his post.

SYNONYMS: promptly, peremptorily, abruptly

18. suppliant
(səp' lē ənt)

(*adj.*) asking humbly and earnestly; (*n.*) one who makes a request humbly and earnestly, a petitioner, suitor

He made a _____ suppliant _____ address to the parole board.

Stranded in the deserted city of Moscow, Napoleon had to turn to the Czar not as a conqueror but as a _____ suppliant _____.

19. talisman
(tal' iz mən)

(*n.*) an object that serves as a charm or is believed to confer magical powers, an amulet, fetish

Most people do not believe that rabbit's feet and other _____ talismans _____ actually bring good luck.

20. undulate
(ən' dyə lāt)

(*v.*) to move in waves or with a wavelike motion; to have a wavelike appearance or form

The baseball fans began to _____ undulate _____ as they cheered, so that they appeared to move in a wave.

SYNONYMS: ripple, fluctuate, rise and fall

Completing the Sentence

From the words for this unit, choose the one that best completes each of the following sentences. Write the word in the space provided.

1. To our dismay, we discovered that the water we had worked so hard to bring to the surface was too _____**brackish**_____ for human consumption.

2. As an employee of the local polling service last summer, it was my job to _____**accost**_____ people on the street and ask their opinions.

3. Many a rich southern planter saw all his or her financial resources swallowed up in the _____**maelstrom**_____ of the Civil War.

4. After the prisoner had been found guilty of treason, he was led before a firing squad and _____**summarily**_____ executed.

5. Saying that "people who live in glass houses shouldn't throw stones" is not an effective response to their _____**animadversions**_____ on your conduct.

6. During the rainy season, the highway sank at so many points that its surface began to _____**undulate**_____ like the track for a roller coaster.

7. I stand before you an abject _____**suppliant**_____, hoping against hope for a sign of your forgiveness.

8. My brother is such a(n) _____**avid**_____ collector of toy soldiers that I sometimes think our house has been invaded by a pint-sized army.

9. The suffix *-ling* often has a(n) _____**pejorative**_____ connotation, as in the word *princeling*, derived from *prince*.

10. On the return trip, we cut straight across the meadows rather than take the more _____**devious**_____ path along the river.

11. In Grandmother's day, standards of _____**propriety**_____ required that a young lady wear a hat and gloves when she went out in public.

12. The _____**celerity**_____ with which he accepted our invitation to dinner suggested that he was badly in need of a good meal.

13. The tons of _____**incendiary**_____ material ignited and turned the waste disposal plant into a roaring inferno.

14. In the eyes of most Americans, people who burn or spit on our flag are guilty of an intolerable _____**sacrilege**_____.

15. We looked back on those _____**halcyon**_____ years before the war broke out as a kind of "golden age" in our history.

16. Any book on chess strategy usually discusses the standard opening moves, such as the "knight's _____**gambit**_____."

17. The Japanese attack on Pearl Harbor was a(n) _____**overt**_____ act of war.

18. Down in the main square, a wrinkled old peasant was selling charms and _____ talismans _____ to ward off the evil eye.

19. To be really convincing on stage, an opera singer must possess both vocal and _____ histrionic _____ abilities.

20. His pale face, hunched shoulders, and _____ myopic _____ stare showed that he had spent his life poring over old books and documents.

Synonyms

*Choose the word from this unit that is **the same** or **most nearly the same** in meaning as the **boldface** word or expression in the given phrase. Write the word on the line provided.*

1. a tireless **petitioner** _____ suppliant _____

2. a lucky **amulet** _____ talisman _____

3. the **vortex** of public opinion _____ maelstrom _____

4. **ripple** in the current _____ undulate _____

5. was taken in by her **stratagem** _____ gambit _____

6. outraged by the **desecration** _____ sacrilege _____

7. apologized for his unnecessary **rebuke** _____ animadversion _____

8. swam in the **briny** water _____ brackish _____

9. **abruptly** resigned from the Cabinet _____ summarily _____

10. behaved with her usual **decorum** _____ propriety _____

11. memories of our **serene** beginnings _____ halcyon _____

12. **confronted** the thief at the door _____ accosted _____

13. completed the job with **alacrity** _____ celerity _____

14. their **derogatory** references to his past _____ pejorative _____

15. took an **indirect** route _____ devious _____

Antonyms

*Choose the word from this unit that is **most nearly opposite** in meaning to the **boldface** word or expression in the given phrase. Write the word on the line provided.*

16. identified the **peacemaker** _____ incendiary _____

17. made a very **low-keyed** plea for mercy _____ histrionic _____

18. one of the most **reluctant** participants _____ avid _____

19. known for **farsighted** thinking _____ myopic _____

20. took **secret** action to avoid a crisis _____ overt _____

Choosing the Right Word

Circle the **boldface** word that more satisfactorily completes each of the following sentences.

1. His reckless words had an (**incendiary,** overt) effect on the already excited crowd, and large-scale rioting resulted.

2. He is the kind of person who is concerned not with real moral values but simply with appearances and (**propriety,** celerity).

3. He regarded his Phi Beta Kappa key as a(n) (**talisman,** animadversion) that would open all doors and win him universal acceptance.

4. After years of failure to sell a single story, the young writer described himself bitterly as "a(n) (pejorative, **avid**) collector of rejection slips."

5. She was buffeted about in a veritable (gambit, **maelstrom**) of emotions, caused mainly by her own dissatisfaction with herself.

6. His methods were so complicated and his purposes so (avid, **devious**) that we were not sure if he was spying on the enemy or on us.

7. Without even considering the new evidence that I was prepared to present, they (deviously, **summarily**) denied my appeal to reopen the case.

8. In an age when the United States has truly global responsibilities, we can ill afford leaders with (**myopic,** pejorative) points of view.

9. The adoring fan regarded my negative comments about his favorite singer as tantamount to (maelstrom, **sacrilege**).

10. I certainly do not claim that my performance in office was beyond criticism, but I deeply resent (**animadversions,** maelstroms) on my honesty.

11. Although all politicians must have some ability to dramatize themselves, it is very easy to overdo the (proprieties, **histrionics**).

12. As the defendant left the courtroom, he was (gambited, **accosted**) by a group of reporters seeking his reaction to the verdict.

13. Walt tends to react slowly, but when he feels that his own interests are at stake he can move with striking (**celerity,** myopia).

14. Since the word appeasement is associated with disastrous concessions to Adolf Hitler, it has acquired a(n) (**pejorative,** overt) connotation.

15. John Masefield's poem "Sea Fever" has an (avid, **undulating**) rhythm that actually gives one the feeling of being on a rolling ship.

16. "His acts of defiance have been so (myopic, **overt**) and premeditated that I have no choice but to fire him," she said sadly.

17. Instead of imbibing the (**brackish,** suppliant) waters of superstition, let us refresh ourselves with long drafts of pure, clean common sense.

18. "I realize that this kind of financial (**gambit,** sacrilege) has its risks," she said, "but I expect it to pay off handsomely in the end."

19. Nary a ripple disturbed the (**halcyon,** brackish) calm of the sea on that glorious summer's afternoon.

20. The infatuated schoolboy, in one of his more restrained expressions, described himself as "a (sacrilege, **suppliant**) at the altar of love."

*Read the following passage, in which some of the words you have studied in this unit appear in **boldface** type. Then complete each statement given below the passage by circling the letter of the item that is **the same** or **almost the same** in meaning as the highlighted word.*

The Wonder Around Us

(Line)

Most people today have a far greater appreciation of the preciousness of the land and sea than the general public living just a half century ago. In the 1940s and 1950s, many held the **myopic** view that natural resources were limitless and impervious to pollution. The marine biologist Rachel Carson (1907–1964) was one of the first scientists to challenge these widely held assumptions. She did so by (5) writing a series of evocative books about the sea, culminating in the 1951 bestseller, *The Sea Around Us.* To the surprise of many, Carson found an **avid** audience for her

unique blend of science and lyricism and became one of the pioneers of the growing ecological movement. (10)

Through her imaginative prose, Carson made the **brackish** waters of the world's oceans come alive for her readers. She helped them see that the ocean was not a deep, dark, empty (15) abyss, but a living home to a fascinating array of plants and animals.

Carson also dramatized the intricate relationship between wind and water. The rotation of the earth, water (20) temperature, and wind combine to produce the great ocean currents— giant global **maelstroms** that carry the sea's waters in roughly circular

The endangered blue whale is indigenous to oceans all over the world.

patterns. The wind also whips up the ocean waters into waves that **undulate** across (25) the sea's surface. Carson explained that these waves vary from the smallest ripples to giant mountains of water, called *tsunamis*, that travel up to 600 miles per hour—with a sometimes startling **celerity**—and cause great damage when they come ashore. No matter what force of nature Carson evoked, she never failed to make her reader feel a part of the process she was describing, and to respect the earth and seas. (30)

---

1. The meaning of **myopic** (line 3) is
a. imaginative   c. democratic
b. enlightened   d. shortsighted ✓

2. Avid (line 7) most nearly means
a. enthusiastic ✓   c. critical
b. grateful   d. varied

3. Brackish (line 12) is best defined as
a. frigid   c. deep
b. briny ✓   d. mysterious

4. The meaning of **maelstroms** (line 23) is
a. whirlpools ✓   c. motors
b. explosions   d. earthquakes

5. Undulate (line 25) most nearly means
a. creep   c. ripple ✓
b. sing   d. reflect

6. Celerity (line 28) most nearly means
a. quantity   c. speed ✓
b. cost   d. time

Definitions

Note carefully the spelling, pronunciation, part(s) of speech, and definition(s) of each of the following words. Then write the word in the blank space(s) in the illustrative sentence(s) following. Finally, study the lists of synonyms and antonyms given at the end of each entry.

1. articulate
(*v.*, är tik' yə lāt;
adj., är tik' yə lit)

(*v.*) to pronounce distinctly; to express well in words; to connect by a joint or joints; (*adj.*) expressed clearly and forcefully; able to employ language clearly and forcefully; jointed

Few people can _____**articulate**_____ their emotions during times of stress.

The most _____**articulate**_____ student in the class was chosen to mediate the debate.

SYNONYMS: (*v.*) pronounce, elucidate; (*adj.*) eloquent
ANTONYMS: (*v.*) mumble, slur; (*adj.*) tongue-tied, halting

2. cavort
(kə vôrt')

(*v.*) to romp or prance around exuberantly; to make merry

The actors in the musical _____**cavort(ed)**_____ on stage.

SYNONYM: gambol

3. credence
(krēd' əns)

(*n.*) belief, mental acceptance

The government and the public failed to give __**credence**__ to the reports of an impending water shortage.

SYNONYMS: credit, trust, confidence
ANTONYMS: disbelief, skepticism, incredulity

4. decry
(di krī')

(*v.*) to condemn, express strong disapproval; to officially depreciate

Every arm of government and every educational institution should _____**decry**_____ bigotry in all its forms.

SYNONYMS: denounce, censure, devalue
ANTONYMS: tout, commend, extol, laud, praise

5. dissemble
(di sem' bəl)

(*v.*) to disguise or conceal, deliberately give a false impression

The young man was unable to _____**dissemble**_____ his feelings and admitted to having committed the crime.

SYNONYMS: dissimulate, mask, feign

6. distraught
(dis trôt')

(*adj.*) very much agitated or upset as a result of emotion or mental conflict

The workforce became _____**distraught**_____ in the wake of the 1929 stock market crash.

SYNONYMS: frantic, distracted
ANTONYMS: calm, composed, collected

7. eulogy
(yü′ lə jē)

(*n.*) a formal statement of commendation; high praise

The best friend and longtime law partner of the deceased delivered the _____**eulogy**_____ at the funeral.

SYNONYMS: panegyric, encomium, tribute, testimonial
ANTONYMS: philippic, diatribe, invective

8. evince
(i vins′)

(*v.*) to display clearly, to make evident, to provoke

The crowd did not _____**evince**_____ any signs of panic but moved in an orderly fashion to the nearest exits.

SYNONYMS: exhibit, manifest, occasion

9. exhume
(eks hyüm′)

(*v.*) to remove from a grave; to bring to light

Suspecting foul play, the coroner issued an order to
_____**exhume**_____ the body immediately.

SYNONYMS: disinter, unearth, uncover
ANTONYMS: bury, inter

10. feckless
(fek′ ləs)

(*adj.*) lacking in spirit and strength; ineffective, weak; irresponsible, unreliable

Although a _____**feckless**_____ youth, he eventually matured into a hard-working and responsible citizen.

SYNONYMS: feeble, helpless, incompetent, ineffectual
ANTONYMS: competent, capable, effective

11. murky
(mər′ kē)

(*adj.*) dark and gloomy, obscure; lacking in clarity and precision

Many visitors have claimed to see a mysterious creature in the _____**murky**_____ waters of Loch Ness in Scotland.

SYNONYMS: dim, cloudy, unclear
ANTONYMS: clear, transparent, lucid, limpid

12. nefarious
(nə fâr′ ē əs)

(*adj.*) wicked, depraved, devoid of moral standards

Brutus and Cassius hatched a _____**nefarious**_____ plot to assassinate Julius Caesar on the steps of the Roman Senate.

SYNONYMS: iniquitous, reprehensible
ANTONYMS: virtuous, honorable, praiseworthy, meritorious

13. piquant
(pē′ kənt)

(*adj.*) stimulating to the taste or mind; spicy, pungent; appealingly provocative

The chef was an expert in making those _____**piquant**_____ dishes that are characteristic of South Indian cooking.

SYNONYMS: tangy, zestful
ANTONYMS: bland, insipid, tasteless, mild

14. primordial
(prī môr′ dē əl)

(*adj.*) developed or created at the very beginning; going back to the most ancient times or earliest stage; fundamental, basic

The _____ **primordial** _____ stages of most civilizations are founded on common needs met by common goals.

SYNONYMS: original, primeval, primal

15. propinquity
(prō piŋ′ kwə tē)

(*n.*) nearness in place or time; kinship

The _____ **propinquity** _____ of the two cities has created a greater metropolitan area that in effect is one city.

SYNONYMS: proximity, similarity
ANTONYMS: remoteness, distance

16. unwonted
(un wōn′ tid)

(*adj.*) not usual or expected; not in character

The listless student answered with _____ **unwonted** _____ spirit when the subject of military tactics was raised.

SYNONYMS: unusual, uncommon, unexpected, atypical
ANTONYMS: usual, customary, typical

17. utopian
(yü tō′ pē ən)

(*adj.*) founded upon or involving a visionary view of an ideal world; impractical

A number of American religious groups like the Shakers have built separate communities based on _____ **utopian** _____ schemes.

SYNONYM: idealistic
ANTONYMS: realistic, pragmatic

18. verbiage
(vər′ bē ij)

(*n.*) language that is too wordy or inflated in proportion to the sense or content, wordiness; a manner of expression

The contract was full of meaningless _____ **verbiage** _____ that seemed designed to confuse the lay person.

SYNONYMS: verbosity, prolixity, diction, jargon

19. verdant
(vər′ dənt)

(*adj.*) green in tint or color; immature in experience or judgment

The tourists on safari traveled over the _____ **verdant** _____ grasslands of Kenya in search of native wildlife.

SYNONYMS: artless, naíve
ANTONYMS: scorched, sere, barren, arid

20. viscous
(vis′ kəs)

(*adj.*) having a gelatinous or gluey quality, lacking in easy movement or fluidity

The varnish left a _____ **viscous** _____ residue on the wood that was hard to remove.

SYNONYMS: gummy, sticky, thick
ANTONYMS: runny, watery, aqueous

Completing the Sentence

From the words for this unit, choose the one that best completes each of the following sentences. Write the word in the space provided.

1. The assembly speaker couldn't be understood because he mumbled his words instead of _____**articulating**_____ them clearly.

2. For as far as the eye could see, _____**verdant**_____ fields of unripe corn swayed gently in the morning breeze.

3. An educated citizenry will not give _____**credence**_____ to wild charges of extremists seeking to undermine our political and economic system.

4. How could we draw any clear ideas from a talk that was so disorganized, confused in language, and generally _____**murky**_____?

5. Sadly, the _____**utopian**_____ schemes of high-minded idealists usually founder on the rocks of practical realities.

6. Such spices as red pepper make many of the sauces used in Cajun cooking delightfully _____**piquant**_____.

7. I believe there is an overall design to the universe that has been visible ever since the first thing crawled out of the _____**primordial**_____ ooze.

8. In the hands of our hopelessly _____**feckless**_____ producer, what should have been a surefire hit turned into a resounding fiasco.

9. When new evidence turned up in the case, the court ordered the coroner to _____**exhume**_____ the victim's body and reexamine it.

10. Though diesel fuels are not as thick as motor oil, they are a good deal more _____**viscous**_____ than regular gasoline.

11. Though I prefer to be as open and aboveboard as possible, I have learned that it is sometimes wiser or more tactful to _____**dissemble**_____.

12. When Bill was told that he had made the varsity wrestling team, he began to _____**cavort**_____ around the gym like a young colt.

13. The NCAA has in recent years cracked down hard on such _____**nefarious**_____ practices as "shaving points."

14. He clothes his puny ideas in such highfalutin _____**verbiage**_____ that they resemble gnats in top hats and tails.

15. The new chairman _____**decried**_____ what she called the "deplorable tendency of so many Americans to try to get something for nothing."

16. Even at an early age, my sister _____**evinced**_____ a strong interest in studying medicine.

17. When news of the school fire ran through town, _____**distraught**_____ parents rushed to the scene of the blaze.

18. Every Memorial Day, the Mayor delivers a(n) _____ eulogy _____ extolling the selfless devotion of those who have died in defense of this country.

19. Since my apartment is in such close _____ propinquity _____ to my office, I usually walk to work.

20. I have always regarded the man as something of a daredevil, but on this occasion he approached the problem with _____ unwonted _____ caution.

Synonyms

Choose the word from this unit that is **the same** or **most nearly the same** in meaning as the **boldface** word or expression in the given phrase. Write the word on the line provided.

1. did **exhibit** true remorse — evince

2. **primeval** history — primordial

3. burdened by unnecessary **verbosity** — verbiage

4. a very **tangy** salad dressing — piquant

5. distinguished by **uncommon** courtesy — unwonted

6. full of **idealistic** plans — utopian

7. the **iniquitous** traitor and spy — nefarious

8. a slightly **gummy** coating of wax — viscous

9. **gamboled** in the wading pool — cavorted

10. tried to **dissimulate** when confronted — dissemble

11. **uncovered** the buried treasure — exhumed

12. feared for the **helpless** child — feckless

13. an unwelcome **proximity** — propinquity

14. tried to calm the **frantic** parents — distraught

15. could not make out the **unclear** image — murky

Antonyms

Choose the word from this unit that is **most nearly opposite** in meaning to the **boldface** word or expression in the given phrase. Write the word on the line provided.

16. watered the **arid** lawn — verdant

17. managed to **mumble** a quick response — articulate

18. rose to **commend** the new regime — decry

19. published her lengthy **diatribe** — eulogy

20. treated the idea with **skepticism** — credence

Choosing the Right Word

*Circle the **boldface** word that more satisfactorily completes each of the following sentences.*

1. Far from being unpleasant, her slight foreign accent added an extra dash of spice to her already (**primordial, piquant**) personality.

2. Trying to read your (**viscous, utopian**) prose is just like trying to swim upstream through custard.

3. An accomplished hypocrite usually finds it very easy to (**dissemble, decry**) his or her true feelings as circumstances dictate.

4. The new mayor is a curious mixture of the hardheaded pragmatist and the (**utopian, murky**) reformer.

5. The book has an interesting plot, but the author has practically smothered it in endless (**verbiage, eulogy**).

6. Though the work hadn't seen the light of day for over a century, a daring impresario (**cavorted, exhumed**) and staged it to great public acclaim.

7. Not surprisingly, the address was a notably evenhanded affair in which the speaker cleverly mixed (**eulogy, verbiage**) with admonition.

8. The investigating committee (**decried, dissembled**) the use of substandard materials and slovenly workmanship in the housing project.

9. One of the duties of a President is to (**cavort, articulate**) the policies and programs of his administration in a forceful and convincing way.

10. The United States is cooperating with the other nations of the world in an effort to check the (**feckless, nefarious**) trade in narcotics.

11. (**Exhumed, Distraught**) with grief, they sat motionless for hours, staring blankly into space.

12. The extraordinary musical talents of Wolfgang Amadeus Mozart (**evinced, dissembled**) themselves at an amazingly early age.

13. Despite all the reports of "miraculous" cures, you would be well advised to withhold (**verbiage, credence**) until the drug has been fully tested.

14. The behavior of armies in wartime often evinces the (**murky, primordial**) blood lust that civilized people have not yet fully overcome.

15. When life was easy he was all dash and confidence, but in times of trouble his essentially (**piquant, feckless**) character came to the fore.

16. The (**credence, propinquity**) of our ideas on handling the problem made it very easy for my colleague and me to produce the report in record time.

17. From the bridge, the rescue team could just make out the blurred image of a car beneath the (**murky, unwonted**) waters of the river.

18. Unfortunately, the (**nefarious, verdant**) hopes and aspirations of my youth have been somewhat blighted by the icy blasts of reality.

19. From the deck of our luxury liner, we occasionally caught sight of schools of porpoises (**cavorting, evincing**) playfully in the waves.

20. His (**viscous, unwonted**) interest in the state of my finances strengthened my suspicions that he was about to ask for a loan.

3

Read the following passage, in which some of the words you have studied in this unit appear in **boldface** type. Then complete each statement given below the passage by circling the letter of the item that is **the same** or **almost the same** in meaning as the highlighted word.

The Great Green World

(Line)

Forests developed in marshlands about 365 million years ago. These **primordial** tracts covered the earth for eons, providing food and shelter first for animals and later for human beings. In fact, sixty percent of the earth's landmass was covered with forest until humans began clearing great

(5) swaths of timber for farmland and town-building. Although many **decry** the loss of so much forest habitat, few realize that today forests still occupy thirty percent of the planet.

The forest ecosystem is a very complex,

(10) interdependent environment that **evinces** a great variety of plants and animals that range from huge, towering trees to low shrubs and mosses to invisible, microscopic bacteria that break down larger organisms. This natural recycling process returns

(15) minerals to the soil where they can again be used by plants to make food. There are also different types of forests, depending on climate, soil, water, and geography. These include the **verdant** rain forests of the tropics, the mixed deciduous forests of the

(20) temperate zones, the cold boreal or northern forests with their short growing season, the grassy tree-pocked savannas of Africa, and the **murky** evergreen forests of the wet Pacific Northwest.

Actual life for forest creatures may contradict our

(25) **utopian** visions of a wild paradise. In reality, every animal, bird, and plant in the forest must compete with others of its kind and with similar species for food, breeding space, and water. Many plants and animals live by feeding on others, creating and sustaining a complex food chain. The

(30) truth of forest life is that, although individuals die, species survive and so does the forest, unless human beings disturb its delicate balance.

Hikers dwarfed by a California redwood tree

---

1. The meaning of **primordial** (line 1) is
  a. agricultural   c. expansive
  b. mysterious   d. original ✓

2. **Decry** (line 6) most nearly means
  a. extol   c. bemoan
  b. denounce ✓   d. publicize

3. **Evinces** (line 10) is best defined as
  a. destroys   c. hides
  b. boasts   d. exhibits ✓

4. The meaning of **verdant** (line 18) is
  a. barren   c. green ✓
  b. noisy   d. frightening

5. **Murky** (line 22) most nearly means
  a. wet   c. dim ✓
  b. merry   d. wild

6. **Utopian** (line 25) most nearly means
  a. idealistic ✓   c. charitable
  b. futuristic   d. primitive

Vocabulary for Comprehension

*Read the following passage, in which some of the words you have studied in Units 1–3 appear in **boldface** type. Then answer questions 1–12 on page 43 on the basis of what is <u>stated</u> or <u>implied</u> in the passage and in the introductory statement.*

Although the Chicago fire caused enormous destruction, the city recovered quickly, as this passage shows.

(Line)

On the evening of October 8, 1871, at around 9 o'clock, the city of Chicago went up in flames. The exact **incendiary** agent remains unknown,
(5) but historians have **substantiated** the Chicago Fire Department's discovery that the blaze began in or near the barn of Mr. and Mrs. Patrick O'Leary, on the southwest side of the city.
(10) Official **credence**, however, has not been extended to the popular belief that it all started when the O'Leary's cow knocked over a lighted lantern.
Whatever the initial spark, the city
(15) was a tinderbox. That summer had been unusually dry, and almost all the buildings, bridges, and even the sidewalks were made of wood. Construction over the previous years
(20) had proceeded rapidly and with little attention to fire safety. The **feckless** city council ignored all pleas to improve the level of fire protection, either by bolstering the fire
(25) department or by passing zoning laws. As a result, the city of Chicago averaged about two fires a day.
Driven by a strong wind out of the southwest, the October 8 fire was
(30) already out of control by the time the exhausted Chicago firefighters (who had been working the day before on another large fire) arrived. The wind

carried the flames to the center of
(35) the city, where they consumed nearly every structure in their path. In a panic, the **distraught** population fled northward toward Lincoln Park and Lake Michigan.
(40) The fire raged for more than twenty-four hours until it rained on the morning of October 10.
In the days that followed, **reconnaissance** missions were
(45) conducted over the rubble that remained of homes, businesses, and tunnels. Three hundred were dead, nearly 100,000 were homeless, and property damage
(50) amounted to $200 million. Yet, four years later, Chicago was almost completely rebuilt. And today, the Chicago Fire Academy stands on the site of the O'Leary cowshed.

1. The primary purpose of the passage is to
   a. expose the incompetence of the city council
   b. focus on the heroism of the firefighters
   c. tell the story of the Chicago fire of 1871
   d. highlight the geography of Chicago
   e. compare the Chicago fire with the San Francisco earthquake of 1906

2. The meaning of **incendiary** (line 3) is
   a. causative
   b. criminal
   c. foreign
   d. subversive
   e. inflammatory

3. **Substantiated** (line 5) most nearly means
   a. ignored
   b. verified
   c. dismissed
   d. disputed
   e. analyzed

4. From the passage, it is clear that
   a. Mr. and Mrs. O'Leary were responsible for setting the fire
   b. the fire started when the O'Learys' cow knocked over a lighted lantern
   c. no one really knows how or where the fire started
   d. the fire started in or near the O'Learys' barn
   e. the fire spread slowly but steadily

5. **Credence** (line 10) is best defined as
   a. acceptance
   b. pardon
   c. enthusiasm
   d. mourning
   e. condemnation

6. Which of the following best describes the organizational structure of paragraph 2 (lines 14–27)?
   a. order of importance
   b. chronological order
   c. spatial order
   d. comparison and contrast
   e. cause and effect

7. The meaning of **feckless** (line 21) is
   a. popular
   b. corrupt
   c. incompetent
   d. conservative
   e. effective

8. From the passage, you can reasonably infer that all of the following played a role in the spread of the fire EXCEPT
   a. the unusually dry summer
   b. a strong wind
   c. the minimal attention to safety in construction
   d. the fleeing population
   e. the exhaustion of the firefighters

9. **Distraught** (line 37) is best defined as
   a. frightened
   b. frantic
   c. disheveled
   d. angry
   e. bemused

10. **Reconnaissance** (line 44) is best defined as
   a. calm evacuation
   b. court decision
   c. slow deliberation
   d. scouting expedition
   e. detailed analysis

11. The effect of the last sentence in the passage (lines 52–54) might best be described as
   a. ironic
   b. tragic
   c. farcical
   d. melancholy
   e. fanciful

12. Which of the following best describes the author's attitude toward the subject of the passage?
   a. disillusioned
   b. satiric
   c. enthusiastic
   d. factual
   e. skeptical

Grammar in Context

In the sentence "Construction over the previous years had proceeded rapidly and with little attention to fire safety" (lines 19–21 on page 42), the word *little* is an **adjective**. Adjectives tell *what kind, which one, how many,* or *how much.* Adjectives always modify a noun or pronoun. The word *rapidly* in the sentence is an **adverb**. Adverbs tell *where, when, in what way,* or *to what extent.* An adverb modifies a verb, an adjective, or another adverb. Sometimes the same word can be either an adjective or an adverb, depending on how it is used in the sentence. For example in the sentence "Determining the cause of the fire posed a hard challenge for investigators," *hard* is an adjective. But in the sentence "Firefighters worked hard to extinguish the blaze," *hard* is an adverb.

Many adverbs are formed by adding the suffix *–ly* to an adjective: for example, *rapid* and *rapidly.* Keep in mind, though, that not all words ending in *–ly* are adverbs. A few of these words are adjectives: for example, *gingerly, leisurely,* and *ungainly.* A few others may be either adjectives or adverbs: for example, *early* and *daily.*

On the lines provided, identify each underlined word as an adjective or an adverb.

1. The <u>specific</u> cause of the Chicago fire was never determined <u>exactly</u>.
   specific: **adjective**; *exactly*: **adverb**

2. The <u>most</u> <u>likely</u> location for the origin of the blaze was the O'Learys' barn.
   most: **adverb**; *likely*: **adjective**

3. It was <u>widely</u> rumored that the O'Learys' cow knocked over a lighted lantern.
   widely: **adverb**

4. In Chicago, the summer of 1871 had been <u>unusually</u> dry.
   unusually: **adverb**

5. Ignoring <u>urgent</u> pleas to improve fire protection, the city council proved to be <u>incompetent</u>.
   urgent: **adjective**; *incompetent*: **adjective**

6. As a result, <u>several</u> fires broke out in the city on a <u>daily</u> basis.
   several: **adjective**; *daily*: **adjective**

7. <u>Distraught</u> citizens fled <u>northward</u> toward Lincoln Park and Lake Michigan.
   distraught: **adjective**; *northward*: **adverb**

8. The buildings destroyed by the fire included dozens of <u>stately</u> homes.
   stately: **adjective**

Two-Word Completions

Circle the pair of words that best complete the meaning of each of the following passages.

See pages T38–T48 for explanations of answers.

1. Little did we realize, as we _____ blithely on the beach during those _____ and cloudless days of spring 1914, that the world was moving inexorably into the maelstrom of total war.

a. evinced . . . piquant
b. belabored . . . utopian
c. emulated . . . insatiable
d. cavorted . . . halcyon

2. For what must have been the first and only time in his life, the overly cautious general did not _____ or vacillate but committed his troops to battle with _____ celerity.

a. arrogate . . . overt
b. temporize . . . unwonted
c. carp . . . myopic
d. dissemble . . . feckless

3. Someone who is by nature as skeptical as I am usually refuses to give any _____ to the kinds of wild allegations thrown about in an election until they have been _____ by solid evidence.

a. credence . . . substantiated
b. celerity . . . decried
c. largesse . . . exhumed
d. propriety . . . eschewed

4. Despite the somewhat strident _____ of some professional critics and the inane _____ of a few literary pedants, the work enjoyed a notable popular success.

a. encomiums . . . largesse
b. verbiage . . . eulogies
c. animadversions . . . carping
d. gambits . . . sacrilege

5. From the top of the mountain that summer afternoon, I looked out on a(n) _____ panorama of fields and pasturelands through which countless streams and rivulets _____ like so many serpents slithering lazily across a carpet.

a. murky . . . articulated
b. avid . . . congealed
c. verdant . . . undulated
d. primordial . . . cavorted

6. Someone with a _____ nature is generally very good at _____, while more honest people give off unconscious cues that they are not telling the truth.

a. distraught . . . emulating
b. devious . . . dissembling
c. ubiquitous . . . strategizing
d. acquisitive . . . decrying

Read each sentence carefully. Then circle the item that best completes the statement below the sentence.

See pages T38–T48 for explanations of answers.

By decrying the nation's currency, the government hoped to both spur exports and curb inflation. (2)

1. The word **decrying** in line 1 is used to mean

   a. denouncing   (b. devaluating)   c. condemning   d. supporting

Unfortunately, the procurement specifications were framed in technical verbiage that only those thoroughly versed in such matters could understand. (2)

2. In line 1 the word **verbiage** most nearly means

   a. prolixity   (b. jargon)   c. verbosity   d. code

The space vehicle was equipped with an articulated boom designed to deploy and retrieve small satellites and scientific devices. (2)

3. The best definition for the word **articulated** in line 1 is

   a. elucidated   b. state-of-the-art   c. well-spoken   (d. jointed)

The ultimatum delivered to the besieged American forces at Bastogne in December 1944 is reputed to have evinced the succinct response "Nuts!" (2)

4. The best definition for the **evinced** in line 2 is

   a. displayed   b. demanded   (c. provoked)   d. exhibited

The narrator of Edgar Allan Poe's tale "Descent Into the Maelstrom" tells the harrowing story of his deliverance from a gigantic vortex. (2)

5. In line 1 the word **maelstrom** most nearly means

   a. chaos   b. turbulence   c. mine   (d. whirlpool)

Fire marshals soon apprehended the incendiary responsible for the conflagration that reduced to smoking embers the historic waterfront hotel. (2)

6. The word **incendiary** in line 1 is used to mean

   (a. arsonist)   b. rabble-rouser   c. agitator   d. criminal

Antonyms

*In each of the following groups, circle the word or expression that is most nearly the **opposite** of the word in **boldface** type.*

1. propriety
a. tactfulness
b. correctness
c. morality
(d. unseemliness)

2. avid
a. enthusiastic
(b. indifferent)
c. quick
d. intelligent

3. myopic
a. sincere
b. scholarly
(c. farsighted)
d. foolish

4. coherent
a. recent
(b. disjointed)
c. strange
d. workable

5. nefarious
a. intelligent
b. feasible
c. new
(d. meritorious)

6. propinquity
(a. remoteness)
b. importance
c. size
d. splendor

7. largesse
a. haste
b. rudeness
(c. stinginess)
d. skill

8. overt
(a. concealed)
b. obvious
c. humorous
d. unnecessary

9. animadversions
(a. compliments)
b. salaries
c. backgrounds
d. quirks

10. germane
(a. irrelevant)
b. worthy
c. unprotected
d. disloyal

11. acquisitive
a. fault-finding
b. deliberate
(c. altruistic)
d. retentive

12. substantiate
(a. refute)
b. introduce
c. report
d. confirm

13. tenable
a. scientific
(b. indefensible)
c. interesting
d. complicated

14. piquant
(a. bland)
b. foreign
c. expensive
d. spicy

15. murky
a. salty
b. turbulent
(c. clear)
d. polluted

16. taciturn
a. arrogant
b. mean
c. stupid
(d. garrulous)

Word Families

A. *On the line provided, write the word you have learned in Units 1–3 that is related to each of the following nouns.*
EXAMPLE: acquisitiveness—**acquisitive**

1. utopia, utopianism — utopian

2. viscosity — viscous

3. murkiness, murk — murky

4. myopia — myopic

5. coherence — coherent

6. banality — banal

7. undulation — undulate

8. piquancy — piquant

9. intransigence — intransigent

10. emulation — emulate

11. deviousness — devious

12. substantiation — substantiate

13. exhumation, exhumer — exhume

14. articulation, articulator, articulateness — articulate

15. arrogation — arrogate

B. *On the line provided, write the word you have learned in Units 1–3 that is related to each of the following verbs.*
EXAMPLE: acquire—**acquisitive**

16. eulogize — eulogy

17. cohere — coherent

18. supplicate — suppliant

19. satiate — insatiable

20. reconnoiter — reconnaissance

In each of the following groups, circle the word that is best defined or suggested by the given phrase.

1. what a person who vacillates would probably do in a crisis
a. cavort   **b. temporize**   c. propound   d. articulate

2. going back to the time of the first appearance of life on this planet
a. primordial   b. feckless   c. viscous   d. taciturn

3. what a nitpicker seems always to be doing
a. cavorting   b. decrying   c. articulating   **d. carping**

4. one who is unwilling to compromise
a. tenable   b. invidious   **c. intransigent**   d. pejorative

5. hiding one's disappointment behind a brave smile
a. arrogate   b. congeal   **c. dissemble**   d. evince

6. the rate at which gossip travels
a. celerity   b. encomium   c. maelstrom   d. credence

7. lavish tips given to waiters, parking lot attendants, etc.
a. eulogy   b. gambit   c. credence   **d. largesse**

8. too agitated to continue
a. articulate   **b. distraught**   c. utopian   d. primordial

9. so nearsighted that one can't see the woods for the trees
a. avid   b. unwonted   **c. myopic**   d. devious

10. rolling hills and lush meadows in springtime
a. verdant   b. brackish   c. intractable   d. germane

11. how you might properly characterize a cliché
a. piquant   b. insatiable   **c. banal**   d. halcyon

12. "So he came up to me and asked me for a quarter."
a. accost   b. eschew   c. emulate   d. exhume

13. improper use of a house of worship
a. suppliant   **b. sacrilege**   c. animadversion   d. verbiage

14. will consider only matters directly related to the question under discussion
a. incendiary   **b. germane**   c. pejorative   d. suppliant

15. a grasping society
a. feckless   **b. acquisitive**   c. overt   d. primordial

16. avoid bad habits
a. eschew   b. evince   c. belabor   d. articulate

17. disparaging remark
a. verdant   b. coherent   c. halcyon   **d. pejorative**

18. a rabbit's foot
a. talisman   b. gambit   c. suppliant   d. animadversion

19. condemn publicly
a. temporize   **b. decry**   c. exhume   d. substantiate

20. appropriateness
a. eulogy   b. credence   **c. propriety**   d. verbiage

Building with Classical Roots

cred—to believe

This root appears in **credence** (page 35). Some other words based on the same root are listed below.

accreditation	credibility	creditor	credulity
credentials	creditable	credo	credulous

From the list of words above, choose the one that corresponds to each of the brief definitions below. Write the word in the blank space in the illustrative sentence below the definition.

1. references, testimonials, or other (usually written) evidence of identity or status (*"that which provides a basis for belief"*)

The security guard demanded to see their _____credentials_____ before they could enter the building.

2. inclined to believe very readily, gullible

The naïve young man seemed as _____credulous_____ as a child.

3. worthiness of belief

At the hearing, a panel of experts questioned the _____credibility_____ of the advertisement.

4. a statement or summary of faith or fundamental belief; an authoritative statement of religious belief (*"I believe"*)

The _____credo_____ of our hiking club is "Take only pictures; leave only footprints."

5. bringing or deserving credit or honor

Despite limited rehearsal time, the cast did a(n) _____creditable_____ job on that play.

6. an undue readiness to believe; a lack of critical judgment

The wily con artists exploited their victim's _____credulity_____.

7. official authorization or approval (often used in regard to academic affairs)

The college received _____accreditation_____ as an institution of higher learning.

8. a person or an organization to which money is owed

The bank denied her request for a loan when they saw that she had made late payments to past _____creditors_____.

From the list of words above, choose the one that best completes each of the following sentences. Write the word in the space provided.

1. In view of the number of weeks he'd been absent from class with the chicken pox, he gave a very _____creditable_____ performance on the math final.

2. The salesperson making those absurd claims about the used car was clearly trying to take advantage of our _____credulity_____.

3. The new medical school will convene classes as soon as it receives its official
_____accreditation_____ from the state.

4. A physician's _____credo_____ is aptly summarized in the noble ideas and
attitudes set forth in the Hippocratic Oath.

5. The applicant submitted her résumé, along with several _____credentials_____ such
as a diploma and written references from former employers, in order to get the job.

6. After a series of financial setbacks, the entrepreneur was forced to dodge a
relentless wave of _____creditors_____.

7. The plot involved a series of coincidences so farfetched as to tax the patience of
even the most _____credulous_____ of readers.

8. The attorney attacked the _____credibility_____ of the star witness by demonstrating
that he had a poor reputation for honesty and reliability.

---

*Circle the **boldface** word that more satisfactorily completes each of the following
sentences.*

1. In researching day-care centers for her son, Ms. Lopez always asked to see the most
recent documents of (**accreditation,** **credo**).

2. We could tell by the (**creditable,** **credulous**) looks on their faces that the children
completely believed our story about flying carpets.

3. The first thing she did with her prize money was to pay off all her (**credentials,**
creditors).

4. My doctor's office is decorated with framed diplomas, certificates, awards, and other
(**credentials,** **credulities**) that attest to her excellent training.

5. Each week that they met, the boy scouts recited their (**accreditation,** **credo**).

6. During the 1960s, widespread distrust of government led to the "(**credibility,**
creditor) gap"—a general lack of confidence in statements made by public officials.

7. The children tried to take advantage of their babysitter's (**credulity,** **credibility**) when
they told him they were allowed eight cookies apiece.

8. In the American film classic *Gone with the Wind*, the ever-resourceful Scarlett O'Hara
creates a (**credulous,** **creditable**) ball gown out of green velvet drapes.

Definitions

Note carefully the spelling, pronunciation, part(s) of speech, and definition(s) of each of the following words. Then write the word in the blank space(s) in the illustrative sentence(s) following. Finally, study the lists of synonyms and antonyms given at the end of each entry.

1. atrophy
(aʹ trə fē)

(*n.*) the wasting away of a body organ or tissue; any progressive decline or failure; (*v.*) to waste away

The _____**atrophy**_____ of the downtown business district began when two huge malls opened.

The patient's muscles have _____**atrophied**_____.

SYNONYMS: (*n.*) degeneration, deterioration; (*v.*) wither
ANTONYMS: (*n.*) growth, development; (*v.*) mature, develop

2. bastion
(basʹ chən)

(*n.*) a fortified place, stronghold

Contrary to popular belief, the military is not always a _____**bastion**_____ of political conservatism.

SYNONYMS: citadel, rampart, bulwark, parapet

3. concord
(känʹ kôrd)

(*n.*) a state of agreement, harmony, unanimity; a treaty, pact, covenant

A spirit of _____**concord**_____ was restored when the company compensated its employees.

ANTONYMS: disagreement, strife, discord

4. consummate
(*v.*, känʹ sə māt;
adj., kənʹ sə mət)

(*adj.*) complete or perfect in the highest degree; (*v.*) to bring to a state of completion or perfection

Michelangelo's paintings on the ceiling of the Sistine Chapel in the Vatican are works of _____**consummate**_____ artistry.

The lawyers could not _____**consummate**_____ the settlement until the two parties met face to face.

SYNONYMS: (*adj.*) masterful; (*v.*) clinch, conclude
ANTONYMS: (*v.*) launch, initiate, begin, kick off

5. disarray
(dis ə rāʹ)

(*n.*) disorder, confusion; (*v.*) to throw into disorder

The burgled apartment was in a state of _____**disarray**_____.

If you leave the window open, a breeze may _____**disarray**_____ the papers on the desktop.

SYNONYMS: (*n.*) disorganization; (*v.*) dishevel, mess up
ANTONYMS: (*n.*) organization, order, tidiness

6. exigency
(ekʹ sə jən sē)

(*n.*, *often pl.*) urgency, pressure; urgent demand, pressing need; an emergency

The governor emphasized the _____**exigency**_____ of the situation by requesting the immediate dispatch of rescue teams.

SYNONYM: requirement, crisis

7. flotsam
(flät' səm)

(n.) floating debris; homeless, impoverished people

After the two ships collided, the survivors clung to various pieces of _____flotsam_____ and hoped for rescue.

SYNONYM: floating wreckage

8. frenetic
(frə net' ik)

(adj.) frenzied, highly agitated

When a court order was issued, the social services department made a _____frenetic_____ search for the missing report.

SYNONYMS: frantic, overwrought
ANTONYMS: calm, controlled, relaxed, leisurely

9. glean
(glēn)

(v.) to gather bit by bit; to gather small quantities of grain left in a field by the reapers

By means of painstaking investigation, the detectives will eventually _____glean_____ the truth.

SYNONYMS: collect, cull, pick up

10. grouse
(graůs)

(n.) a type of game bird; a complaint; (v.) to complain, grumble

The patient's latest _____grouse_____ was that he did not get any dessert with his dinner the night before.

Those who just stand around and _____grouse_____ about their low salaries are not likely to get raises.

SYNONYMS: (v.) gripe, kvetch, bellyache

11. incarcerate
(in kär' sə rāt)

(v.) to imprison, confine, jail

They will _____incarcerate_____ the convicted felon at the state penitentiary.

SYNONYMS: intern, immure
ANTONYMS: liberate, release, free

12. incumbent
(in kəm' bənt)

(adj.) obligatory, required; (n.) one who holds a specific office at the time spoken of

Voting on election day is a duty _____incumbent_____ on all Americans who value a democratic government.

The _____incumbent_____ has the advantage when standing for reelection but does not have a guarantee of victory.

SYNONYMS: (adj.) mandatory, necessary
ANTONYMS: (adj.) optional, unnecessary

13. jocular
(jäk' yə lər)

(adj.) humorous, jesting, jolly, joking

After receiving the news that she was ahead in the polls, the candidate was in a delightfully _____jocular_____ mood.

SYNONYMS: waggish, facetious, droll, witty
ANTONYMS: humorless, solemn, grave, earnest, grim

14. ludicrous
(lüd′ ə krəs)

(*adj.*) ridiculous, laughable, absurd

Her comment was so _____ludicrous_____ that we finally understood that she was joking.

SYNONYMS: risible, preposterous
ANTONYMS: heartrending, poignant, pathetic

15. mordant
(môr′ dənt)

(*adj.*) biting or caustic in thought, manner, or style; sharply or bitterly harsh

The actor was upset by the _____mordant_____ criticism of the gossip columnist who seemed out to ruin his reputation.

SYNONYMS: acrimonious, acidulous, sardonic, scathing
ANTONYMS: bland, mild, gentle, soothing

16. nettle
(net′ əl)

(*n.*) a prickly or stinging plant; (*v.*) to arouse displeasure, impatience, or anger; to vex or irritate severely

If you are pricked by a _____nettle_____, aloe cream will soothe and reduce the sting.

The principal was _____nettled_____ by the student's disrespectful behavior.

SYNONYMS: (*v.*) peeve, annoy, incense, gall, irk
ANTONYMS: (*v.*) please, delight, soothe, pacify

17. pecuniary
(pi kyü′ nē er ē)

(*adj.*) consisting of or measured in money; of or related to money

The couple was forced by _____pecuniary_____ considerations to sell their large home and buy a smaller one.

SYNONYMS: monetary, financial

18. pusillanimous
(pyü sə lan′ ə məs)

(*adj.*) contemptibly cowardly or mean-spirited

It is often said that bullies, when tested, are the most _____pusillanimous_____ people of all.

SYNONYMS: craven, lily-livered
ANTONYMS: stouthearted, courageous, daring

19. recumbent
(ri kəm′ bənt)

(*adj.*) in a reclining position, lying down, in the posture of one sleeping or resting

The tired toddlers were _____recumbent_____ on the couch after playing all afternoon in the yard.

SYNONYMS: prone, prostrate, supine, inactive
ANTONYMS: erect, upright, energetic, dynamic

20. stratagem
(strat′ ə jəm)

(*n.*) a scheme to outwit or deceive an opponent or to gain an end

The defense attorney used a clever _____stratagem_____ to curry sympathy for her client.

SYNONYMS: ruse, trick, ploy, subterfuge

Completing the Sentence

From the words for this unit, choose the one that best completes each of the following sentences. Write the word in the space provided.

1. I get my best ideas while lying down; the _____**recumbent**_____ position seems to stimulate my brain.

2. It was pleasant to see the usually quiet and restrained Mr. Baxter in such a(n) _____**jocular**_____ and expansive mood.

3. The _____**flotsam**_____ that we observed here and there in the harbor bore mute testimony to the destructive power of the storm.

4. Since I had had only one year of high-school French, my attempts to speak that language on my trip to Paris were pretty _____**ludicrous**_____.

5. The high ground east of the river formed a natural _____**bastion**_____, which we decided to defend with all the forces at our disposal.

6. I regret that Nancy was _____**nettled**_____ by my unfavorable review of her short story, but I had to express my opinion honestly.

7. Almost every case of muscle or tissue _____**atrophy**_____ is the result of disease, prolonged disuse, or changes in cell nutrition.

8. The _____**exigencies**_____ of my present financial situation demand that I curtail all unnecessary expenses for at least a month.

9. It is _____**incumbent**_____ on all of us to do whatever we can to help our community overcome this crisis.

10. Even critics of our penal system admit that so long as hardened criminals are _____**incarcerated**_____, they can't commit further crimes.

11. Despite all their highfalutin malarky about helping the poor, I suspect that their interest in the project is purely _____**pecuniary**_____.

12. The purpose of our _____**stratagem**_____ was to draw in the safety so that Tom could get behind him to receive a long pass.

13. The defeated army fled in such _____**disarray**_____ that before long it had become little more than a uniformed mob.

14. As soon as he struck the opening chords of the selection, we realized that we were listening to a(n) _____**consummate**_____ master of the piano.

15. Though next to nothing is known about Homer, historians have been able to _____**glean**_____ a few odd facts about him from studying his works.

16. Shakespeare's Timon of Athens is a disillusioned misanthrope who spends his time hurling _____**mordant**_____ barbs at the rest of mankind.

17. Peace is not just the absence of war but a positive state of _____**concord**_____ among the nations of the world.

18. I have yet to meet an adult who did not _____grouse_____ about the taxes he or she had to pay.

19. Most people regarded the government's attempt to avert a war by buying off the aggressor as not only shameful but ____pusillanimous____.

20. People who are used to the unhurried atmosphere of a country town often find it hard to cope with the _____frenetic_____ pace of big-city life.

Synonyms

*Choose the word from this unit that is **the same** or **most nearly the same** in meaning as the **boldface** word or expression in the given phrase. Write the word on the line provided.*

1. floating wreckage in the harbor — flotsam

2. gripes about every change in the routine — grouses

3. received **financial** compensation — pecuniary

4. the ill-conceived **ruse** — stratagem

5. collected tidbits of information — gleaned

6. a longtime **bulwark** of resistance — bastion

7. prostrate on a hospital bed — recumbent

8. craven behavior — pusillanimous

9. enthusiasm that **withered** — atrophied

10. left the room in a state of **disorganization** — disarray

11. a handshake that **clinched** the deal — consummated

12. immured for years in a dank dungeon — incarcerated

13. irks her coworkers with senseless chatter — nettles

14. the **obligatory** responsibilities of the new administrator — incumbent

15. the **requirements** of a wartime economy — exigencies

Antonyms

*Choose the word from this unit that is **most nearly opposite** in meaning to the **boldface** word or expression in the given phrase. Write the word on the line provided.*

16. maintained a **leisurely** pace — frenetic

17. disagreement among the family members — concord

18. the **poignant** story — ludicrous

19. a **gentle** reproof — mordant

20. a **humorless** manner — jocular

Choosing the Right Word

*Circle the **boldface** word that more satisfactorily completes each of the following sentences.*

1. We were fascinated by the (**mordant, frenetic**) scene on the floor of the stock exchange as brokers struggled to keep up with sudden price changes.

2. Before the ceremony began, we all bowed our heads and prayed for unity, peace, and (**concord, atrophy**) among all nations.

3. It has been said that the only way to handle a (**nettle, stratagem**), or any difficult problem, without being stung is to grasp it firmly and decisively.

4. There are few things in life as (**frenetic, ludicrous**) as an unqualified person trying to assume the trappings of authority.

5. In the shelter, I saw for the first time people who'd been beaten and discouraged by life—the so-called derelicts and (**flotsam, incumbents**) of the great city.

6. Do you really think that those (**jocular, recumbent**) remarks are appropriate on such a solemn occasion?

7. The affairs of our city are in such (**disarray, flotsam**) that the state may have to intervene to restore some semblance of order.

8. I have always regarded our schools and colleges as citadels of learning and (**bastions, stratagems**) against ignorance and superstition.

9. The huge influx of wealth that resulted from foreign conquests led in part to the physical and moral (**atrophy, flotsam**) of the Roman ruling class.

10. A born leader is someone who can rise to the (**incumbents, exigencies**) of any crisis that he or she may be confronted with.

11. Comfortably (**recumbent, frenetic**) in the shade of the elm tree, I watched the members of the football team go through a long, hard workout.

12. In Victorian times, fashionable ladies (**disarrayed, incarcerated**) their waists in tight corsets to achieve a chic "hourglass" figure.

13. I noticed with approval that his (**pecuniary, mordant**) remarks were intended to deflate the pompous and unmask the hypocritical.

14. All that I needed to (**consummate, nettle**) the most important deal of my career was her signature on the dotted line.

15. During the 19th century, it was fashionable to spend a few weeks in the fall hunting (**grouse, nettles**), pheasants, and other game birds.

16. Of the ten Congressional seats in our state, only one was won by a new member; all the other winners were (**incumbents, bastions**).

17. To feel fear in difficult situations is natural, but to allow one's conduct to be governed by fear is (**jocular, pusillanimous**).

18. We were able to (**consummate, glean**) only a few shreds of useful information from his long, pretentious speech.

19. What we need to cope with this crisis is not cute (**grouping, stratagems**) but a bold, realistic plan and the courage to carry it out.

20. The only way we'll really be able to increase productivity is to offer our employees a few solid (**frenetic, pecuniary**) incentives to work harder.

Vocabulary in Context

*Read the following passage, in which some of the words you have studied in this unit appear in **boldface** type. Then complete each statement given below the passage by circling the letter of the item that is **the same** or **almost the same** in meaning as the highlighted word.*

Tea Time

(Line)

Although people today tend to think of colonial Boston as a **bastion** of revolutionary fervor, anti-British sentiment there grew slowly in the 1760s and 1770s. Not surprisingly, the provocation that eventually turned many loyal colonists against their mother country was **pecuniary**. In 1767 a financially strapped British

(5) Parliament placed duties, or taxes, on several items imported into the American colonies. This **nettled** the colonists because they had no representatives in the British Parliament to speak against the taxes on their behalf.

The British government, on the other hand, saw the taxes as fair since it had

(10) incurred huge debts in the French and Indian War—a war the British believed benefited their American subjects. In the end, the British government repealed all of the taxes except the

(15) one on tea. In 1773 the British provoked the colonists once again when they decreed that the British East India Company would be the exclusive seller of tea to the American

(20) colonies. Such a monopoly was a clear threat to the businesses of local tea merchants.

When three shiploads of tea arrived in Boston Harbor in December 1773,

Boston Tea Party reenactment

(25) the colonists developed a **stratagem** to foil the British. Before the tea could be sold, colonists disguised as Indians boarded the ships and emptied 342 chests of tea into the harbor. The next morning the empty chests were mere **flotsam**, and the British had not earned a penny on tea. This incident has since been given the **jocular** title the Boston Tea Party, but unlike most tea parties, it did nothing to bring

(30) the colonists and the British together.

---

1. The meaning of **bastion** (line 1) is
a. broadcaster
c. citadel
b. cesspool
d. fountainhead

2. Pecuniary (line 4) most nearly means
a. superficial
c. premeditated
b. financial
d. unnecessary

3. Nettled (line 6) is best defined as
a. incensed
c. confused
b. amused
d. delighted

4. The meaning of **stratagem** (line 25) is
a. ruse
c. code
b. costume
d. company

5. Flotsam (line 27) most nearly means
a. paper
c. trinkets
b. symbols
d. wreckage

6. Jocular (line 29) most nearly means
a. appropriate
c. facetious
b. primitive
d. famous

Definitions

Note carefully the spelling, pronunciation, part(s) of speech, and definition(s) of each of the following words. Then write the word in the blank space(s) in the illustrative sentence(s) following. Finally, study the lists of synonyms and antonyms given at the end of each entry.

1. acuity
(ə kyü′ ə tē)

(*n.*) sharpness (particularly of the mind or senses)

The _____ **acuity** _____ of most people's hearing diminishes as they grow older.

SYNONYMS: keenness, acuteness
ANTONYMS: dullness, obtuseness

2. delineate
(di lin′ ē āt)

(*v.*) to portray, sketch, or describe in accurate and vivid detail; to represent pictorially

The architects will _____ **delineate** _____ the main features of their plan at the next client meeting.

SYNONYMS: depict, picture, render

3. depraved
(di prāvd′)

(*adj.*) marked by evil and corruption, devoid of moral principles

Oscar Wilde's novel *The Picture of Dorian Gray* is about a _____ **depraved** _____ man whose portrait reveals his wickedness.

SYNONYMS: perverted, degenerate, vicious, corrupt
ANTONYMS: moral, virtuous, upright, uncorrupted

4. enervate
(en′ ər vāt)

(*v.*) to weaken or lessen the mental, moral, or physical vigor of; enfeeble, hamstring

Unfortunately, the great musician's mind was _____ **enervated** _____ by disease in the last decade of her life.

SYNONYMS: impair, cripple, paralyze
ANTONYMS: invigorate, strengthen, buttress

5. esoteric
(es ə ter′ ik)

(*adj.*) intended for or understood by only a select few, private, secret

The fraternity developed a set of _____ **esoteric** _____ rites that had to be performed by anyone seeking membership.

SYNONYMS: occult, cryptic, arcane, recondite
ANTONYMS: accessible, comprehensible, intelligible

6. fecund
(fek′ und)

(*adj.*) fruitful in offspring or vegetation; intellectually productive

The remarkably _____ **fecund** _____ mind of Albert Einstein produced theories that revolutionized the science of physics.

SYNONYMS: fertile, teeming, prolific
ANTONYMS: infertile, barren, unproductive

7. fiat
(fē ət)

(*n.*) an arbitrary order or decree; a command or act of will or consciousness

The ruler instituted several new _____fiats_____.

SYNONYMS: edict, dictum, ukase

8. figment
(fig′ mənt)

(*n.*) a fabrication of the mind; an arbitrary notion

The silhouette of a man on the porch was a mere _____figment_____ of your overheated imagination.

SYNONYMS: creation, invention, fancy

9. garner
(gär′ nər)

(*v.*) to acquire as the result of effort; to gather and store away, as for future use

Over the years, the writer was able to _____garner_____ some wisdom that she passed on to others in her books.

SYNONYMS: collect, accumulate, accrue
ANTONYMS: scatter, squander, waste, dissipate

10. hallow
(hal′ ō)

(*v.*) to set apart as holy or sacred, sanctify, consecrate; to honor greatly, revere

In the Gettysburg Address, Lincoln _____hallowed_____ the battlefield on which the Union soldiers fought and died.

SYNONYMS: venerate, bless
ANTONYMS: desecrate, defile, profane

11. idiosyncrasy
(id ē ə siŋ′ krə sē)

(*n.*) a peculiarity that serves to distinguish or identify

The fact that the plurals of some nouns are formed irregularly is an _____idiosyncrasy_____ of English grammar.

SYNONYMS: eccentricity, quirk, mannerism

12. ignominy
(ig′ nə min ē)

(*n.*) shame and disgrace

He went from glory to _____ignominy_____.

SYNONYMS: dishonor, humiliation, disrepute, odium
ANTONYMS: honor, glory, acclaim

13. mundane
(mən dān′)

(*adj.*) earthly, worldly, relating to practical and material affairs; concerned with what is ordinary

The painter left all _____mundane_____ concerns to her sister while she single-mindedly pursued her artistic goals.

SYNONYMS: prosaic, humdrum, routine, sublunary
ANTONYMS: heavenly, unworldly, spiritual, transcendental

14. nuance
(nü' äns)

(*n.*) a subtle or slight variation (as in color, meaning, quality), delicate gradation or shade of difference

In his writing, the poet paid close attention to every _____ **nuance** _____ of meaning in the words he chose.

SYNONYMS: shade, nicety, refinement

15. overweening
(ō vər wē 'niŋ)

(*adj.*) conceited, presumptuous; excessive, immoderate

It was the _____ **overweening** _____ confidence of the candidate that prevented her from acknowledging her weaknesses.

SYNONYMS: arrogant, unbridled, inflated
ANTONYMS: restrained, understated, modest, meek

16. penchant
(pen' chənt)

(*n.*) a strong attraction or inclination

A teacher with a _____ **penchant** _____ for belaboring the obvious is bound to be boring.

SYNONYMS: proclivity, propensity, predilection
ANTONYMS: disinclination, aversion

17. reputed
(ri pyüt' id)

(*adj.*) according to reputation or general belief; having widespread acceptance and good reputation; (*part.*) alleged

Although he is the _____ **reputed** _____ head of a crime syndicate, he has never spent time in jail.

SYNONYMS: putative, reputable, supposed
ANTONYMS: proven, corroborated, authenticated

18. sophistry
(säf' ə strē)

(*n.*) reasoning that seems plausible but is actually unsound; a fallacy

The couple was beguiled into buying a bigger house than they needed by the clever _____ **sophistry** _____ of the broker.

SYNONYMS: specious reasoning

19. sumptuous
(səmp' chü əs)

(*adj.*) costly, rich, magnificent

The _____ **sumptuous** _____ feast honoring the king's birthday was followed by musical entertainment.

SYNONYMS: lavish, munificent, opulent, splendid
ANTONYMS: skimpy, meager, stingy, niggardly, spartan

20. ubiquitous
(yü bik' wə təs)

(*adj.*) present or existing everywhere

The _____ **ubiquitous** _____ eye of the TV camera threatens to rob citizens of any sense of privacy.

SYNONYMS: omnipresent, pervasive, universal
ANTONYMS: restricted, limited, rare, scarce

Completing the Sentence

From the words for this unit, choose the one that best completes each of the following sentences. Write the word in the space provided.

1. The man is _____**reputed**_____ to have mob connections, but so far no one has actually substantiated the allegation.

2. During the eleven years of his "personal rule," King Charles I bypassed Parliament and ruled England by royal _____**fiat**_____.

3. The phonograph is but one of the wonderful new devices that sprang from the _____**fecund**_____ mind of Thomas Edison, our most prolific inventor.

4. American-style fast-food shops have gained such popularity all over the world that they are now truly _____**ubiquitous**_____.

5. His constant use of the word *fabulous,* even for quite ordinary subjects, is a(n) _____**idiosyncrasy**_____ that I could do without.

6. The passing years lessened her physical vigor but in no way diminished the _____**acuity**_____ of her judgment.

7. I was so _____**enervated**_____ by the oppressive heat and humidity of that awful afternoon that I could barely move.

8. Music can often express a(n) _____**nuance**_____ of mood or feeling that would be difficult to put into words.

9. The ground in which those soldiers are buried was _____**hallowed**_____ by the blood they shed on it.

10. Analysis will show that his "brilliant exposition" of how we can handle the pollution problem without cost to anyone is the merest _____**sophistry**_____.

11. His _____**overweening**_____ sense of superiority dominates his personality in much the same way as his beetling brow dominates his face.

12. The marathon not only brought in huge sums of money for Africa's starving masses but also _____**garnered**_____ much sympathy for their plight.

13. May I interrupt this abstruse discussion and turn your attention to more _____**mundane**_____ matters—like what's for dinner?

14. You may have many good traits, but I do not admire your _____**penchant**_____ for borrowing things and failing to return them.

15. The artist's sketch not only _____**delineated**_____ the model's appearance accurately, but also captured something of her personality.

16. "Your suspicion that I am constantly making fun of you behind your back is a mere _____**figment**_____ of your overheated brain," I replied.

17. There is quite a difference between the austere furnishings of my little apartment and the _____**sumptuous**_____ accommodations of a luxury hotel.

18. He was a changed young man after he suffered the _____ignominy_____ of expulsion from West Point for conduct unbecoming a gentleman.

19. Most people I know are so busy dealing with the ordinary problems of life that they have no time for _____esoteric_____ philosophical speculation.

20. Beneath the man's cultivated manner and impeccable grooming there lurked the _____depraved_____ mind of a brutal sadist.

Synonyms

*Choose the word from this unit that is **the same** or **most nearly the same** in meaning as the **boldface** word or expression in the given phrase. Write the word on the line provided.*

1. known for his **propensity** for exaggeration _____penchant_____

2. a distinct **shade** of meaning _____nuance_____

3. as a result of a general **edict** _____fiat_____

4. a **supposed** heir to a huge fortune _____reputed_____

5. an **eccentricity** of speech _____idiosyncrasy_____

6. **depicted** the view from the balcony _____delineated_____

7. sought **occult** knowledge in ancient books _____esoteric_____

8. the latest **fabrication** of his imagination _____figment_____

9. their **omnipresent** sense of dread _____ubiquitous_____

10. known for the **keenness** of her wit _____acuity_____

11. a truly **vicious** attack on an innocent person _____depraved_____

12. the **fertile** products of a lively intelligence _____fecund_____

13. **weakened** by the relentless repetition _____enervated_____

14. **collects** data from many sources _____garners_____

15. deceived by the **specious reasoning** of a lawyer _____sophistry_____

Antonyms

*Choose the word from this unit that is **most nearly opposite** in meaning to the **boldface** word or expression in the given phrase. Write the word on the line provided.*

16. **desecrated** the tombs of their ancestors _____hallowed_____

17. a man of **modest** aspirations _____overweening_____

18. the **unworldly** side of life _____mundane_____

19. made a **meager** meal _____sumptuous_____

20. the **glory** of her situation _____ignominy_____

Choosing the Right Word

*Circle the **boldface** word that more satisfactorily completes each of the following sentences.*

1. It is only in superior mental powers, not in physical strength or (ignominy, **acuity**) of the senses, that human beings surpass other living things.

2. Cleopatra took her own life rather than suffer the (figment, **ignominy**) of being led through the streets of Rome in chains.

3. Like a true fanatic, he considers anyone who disagrees with him on any issue to be either feebleminded or (**depraved**, mundane).

4. Your language is indeed clever and amusing, but your argument is nothing but a piece of outright (**sophistry**, idiosyncrasy).

5. In a democracy, the government must rule by persuasion and consent—not by mere (**fiat**, sophistry).

6. The conversation between the computer programmers was so (**esoteric**, ubiquitous) that I wasn't sure whether they were speaking English.

7. Her imagination is like a (**fecund**, depraved) field in which new ideas spring up like so many ripe ears of corn.

8. In that rarefied atmosphere, I was afraid to ask about anything quite so (sumptuous, **mundane**) as the location of the john.

9. We will never abandon a cause that has been (garnered, **hallowed**) by the achievements and sacrifices of so many noble people.

10. Someone with a pronounced (**penchant**, figment) for saying the wrong thing might justly be described as a victim of "foot-in-mouth" disease.

11. I appreciate all those kind expressions of gratitude for my services, but I had hoped also to (**garner**, nuance) some greenbacks.

12. Probably no complaint of young people is more (**ubiquitous**, depraved) than "My parents don't understand me!"

13. Scandal and corruption may so (**enervate**, delineate) an administration that it can no longer function effectively.

14. He means well, but we cannot tolerate his highly (**idiosyncratic**, fecund) behavior in an organization that depends on discipline and teamwork.

15. How I'd love to knock the wind out of the sails of that lout's (fecund, **overweening**) conceit!

16. Two synonyms are rarely exactly the same because (fiats, **nuances**) of tone or applicability make each of the words unique.

17. The alert defense put up by our team completely neutralized our opponents' (**reputedly**, sumptuously) unstoppable passing attack.

18. A true sign of intellectual maturity is the ability to distinguish the (**figments**, penchants) of wishful thinking from reality.

19. The (**sumptuous**, ubiquitous) banquet was a pleasant change of pace from the spartan fare to which I had become accustomed.

20. Few writers have J. D. Salinger's remarkable ability to (**delineate**, garner) the emotions and aspirations of the average teenager.

Vocabulary in Context

*Read the following passage, in which some of the words you have studied in this unit appear in **boldface** type. Then complete each statement given below the passage by circling the letter of the item that is **the same** or **almost the same** in meaning as the highlighted word.*

Lights! Action! Paint!

(Line)

The age-old aspiration of painters to **delineate** reality in recognizable forms was consciously abandoned in the United States in the 1940s and 1950s by a group of artists working mostly in New York. The most prominent member of the group was Wyoming-born Jackson Pollock. Other major figures included Willem de Kooning, Mark Rothko, and Barnett Newman. Although critics were quick to lump these (5) painters together under the rather **esoteric** label Abstract Expressionist, each one had an individual style, ranging from the explosive energy of Pollock's action paintings to the serene comtemplativeness of Rothko's color (10) field canvasses.

Pollock at work on one of his famous action paintings

Despite each artist's **idiosyncratic** technique, the critics continued to point to a set of common practices that marked these painters as members of a distinct movement in (15) modern art. These commonalties included a **penchant** for working on a huge scale, an interest in the surface qualities and flat plane of the canvas, and a preference for an all-over aesthetic in which no one area of the painting (20) is emphasized over any other. One product of Pollock's **fecund** mind, his series of "action paintings" of the 1940s, is a well-known example of these Abstract Expressionist traits. Instead of using the traditional easel and brush, Pollock laid a canvas on the floor (25) and moved around it rhythmically, pouring and dripping paint on it from a can.

The utter abstraction and seeming randomness of these revolutionary paintings initially baffled the public, but Pollock did succeed in **garnering** widespread critical acclaim, public recognition, and considerable financial rewards before his untimely death in a car accident in 1956 at the age of forty-four. (30)

---

1. The meaning of **delineate** (line 1) is
a. heighten
b. deny
c. escape
d. depict

2. Esoteric (line 6) most nearly means
a. cryptic
b. kind
c. critical
d. catchy

3. Idiosyncratic (line 12) is best defined as
a. excellent
b. similar
c. eccentric
d. delightful

4. Penchant (line 17) most nearly means
a. propensity
b. reputation
c. weakness
d. dislike

5. The meaning of **fecund** (line 22) is
a. fertile
b. insightful
c. brilliant
d. expository

6. Garnering (line 28) most nearly means
a. belittling
b. acquiring
c. ignoring
d. demanding

Definitions

Note carefully the spelling, pronunciation, part(s) of speech, and definition(s) of each of the following words. Then write the word in the blank space(s) in the illustrative sentence(s) following. Finally, study the lists of synonyms and antonyms given at the end of each entry.

1. abject
(ab' jekt)

(*adj.*) degraded; base, contemptible; cringing, servile; complete and unrelieved

In the American dream, those who work hard can escape lives of _____ **abject** _____ poverty.

SYNONYMS: wretched, miserable, ignoble, sheer, utter
ANTONYMS: lofty, noble, exalted

2. agnostic
(ag näs' tik)

(*n.*) one who believes that nothing can be known about God; a skeptic; (*adj.*) without faith, skeptical

Although he was a confirmed _____ **agnostic** _____, he supported the rights of others to practice their religion.

Her _____ **agnostic** _____ tendencies made it difficult for her to subscribe to any set of religious beliefs.

SYNONYM: (*n.*) doubter
ANTONYM: (*n.*) believer

3. complicity
(kəm plis' ə tē)

(*n.*) involvement in wrongdoing; the state of being an accomplice

If you know a crime is going to be committed but do nothing to prevent it, you may be accused of _____ **complicity** _____.

SYNONYMS: connivance, collusion
ANTONYMS: noninvolvement, innocence

4. derelict
(der' ə likt)

(*n.*) someone or something that is abandoned or neglected; (*adj.*) left abandoned; neglectful of duty

The family complained about the unsightly collection of _____ **derelict** _____ cars in their neighbor's driveway.

SYNONYMS: (*n.*) vagrant; (*adj.*) remiss, delinquent
ANTONYMS: (*adj.*) punctilious, conscientious, scrupulous

5. diatribe
(dī' ə trīb)

(*n.*) a bitter and prolonged verbal attack

The senator's speech was more of a _____ **diatribe** _____ than a reasoned address.

SYNONYMS: harangue, tirade
ANTONYMS: panegyric, encomium, eulogy

6. effigy
(ef' ə jē)

(*n.*) a crude image of a despised person

The night before the battle, the troops burned the despised enemy leader in _____ **effigy** _____.

SYNONYMS: figure, figurine, likeness

7. equity
(ek′ wət ē)

(*n.*) the state or quality of being just, fair, or impartial; fair and equal treatment; something that is fair; the money value of a property above and beyond any mortgage or other claim

Prompted by considerations of _____equity_____, the father decided to divide his estate equally among his children.

SYNONYMS: justice, fairness, impartiality
ANTONYMS: injustice, unfairness, bias, prejudice

8. inane
(in ān′)

(*adj.*) silly, empty of meaning or value

The politician made an _____inane_____ reply to the interviewer's probing question.

SYNONYMS: vapid, idiotic, moronic, fatuous
ANTONYMS: sensible, meaningful, profound

9. indictment
(in dīt′ mənt)

(*n.*) the act of accusing; a formal accusation

The Grand Jury delivered the _____indictment_____ for murder after deliberating in secret for two weeks.

SYNONYMS: charge, accusation

10. indubitable
(in dü′ bə tə bəl)

(*adj.*) certain, not to be doubted or denied

You cannot argue with _____indubitable_____ truths.

SYNONYMS: unquestionable, indisputable
ANTONYMS: questionable, debatable, dubious

11. intermittent
(in tər mit′ ənt)

(*adj.*) stopping and beginning again, sporadic

The pulled muscle in her back gave her _____intermittent_____ pains for about a week.

SYNONYMS: fitful, spasmodic, random
ANTONYMS: continuous, uninterrupted

12. moot
(müt)

(*adj.*) open to discussion and debate, unresolved; (*v.*) to bring up for discussion; (*n.*) a hypothetical law case argued by students

The class agreed that the question of whether Jefferson should have retaliated sooner against the Barbary Pirates was a _____moot_____ point.

The committee members decided to _____moot_____ the issue to the full Congress at the earliest opportunity.

The law student prepared for the _____moot_____ court.

SYNONYMS: (*adj.*) debatable, questionable; (*v.*) broach
ANTONYMS: (*adj.*) undebatable, indisputable, self-evident

13. motif
(mō tēf′)

(*n.*) a principal idea, feature, theme, or element; a repeated or dominant figure in a design

The collector admired the unusual Asian _____motif_____ that was woven into the fabric of the tapestry.

14. neophyte
(nē′ ə fīt)

(*n.*) a new convert, beginner, novice

In comparison to an experienced wilderness hiker, he is a mere _____ neophyte _____ in the woods.

SYNONYMS: tenderfoot, tyro, rookie
ANTONYMS: veteran, past master, expert, pro

15. perspicacity
(pər spə kas′ ət ē)

(*n.*) keenness in observing and understanding

The birdwatcher scans the surrounding trees and fields with the same _____ perspicacity _____ as a hawk looking for prey.

SYNONYMS: acuity, acumen, discernment
ANTONYMS: dullness, obtuseness

16. plenary
(plēn′ ə rē)

(*adj.*) complete in all aspects or essentials; absolute; attended by all qualified members

Because of its importance, the case was presented at a _____ plenary _____ session of the Superior Court.

SYNONYMS: unlimited, unrestricted
ANTONYMS: limited, restricted, incomplete

17. surveillance
(sər vā′ ləns)

(*n.*) a watch kept over a person; careful, close, and disciplined observation

The police kept the suspect under strict _____ surveillance _____ after she was released due to lack of evidence.

SYNONYMS: observation, scrutiny, monitoring

18. sylvan
(sil′ vən)

(*adj.*) pertaining to or characteristic of forests; living or located in a forest; wooded, woody

Once upon a time, Hansel and Gretel walked down a _____ sylvan _____ path, leaving only bread-crumbs in their wake.

SYNONYMS: forested, arcadian

19. testy
(tes′ te)

(*adj.*) easily irritated; characterized by impatience and exasperation

The lawyer's _____ testy _____ remarks during cross-examination probably affected her credibility with the jury.

SYNONYMS: irritable, peevish, waspish, petulant
ANTONYMS: even-tempered, imperturbable, unexcitable

20. travesty
(trav′ ə stē)

(*n.*) a grotesque or grossly inferior imitation; a disguise, especially the clothing of the opposite sex; (*v.*) to ridicule by imitating in a broad or burlesque fashion

Instead of modernizing Shakespeare's "Twelfth Night," they made a _____ travesty _____ of it.

The Restoration dramatists _____ travesty _____ the snobbery of the upper classes in their satirical comedies.

SYNONYMS: (*n.*) burlesque, parody, caricature, farce

From the words for this unit, choose the one that best completes each of the following sentences. Write the word in the space provided.

1. Though some writers have emphasized Jefferson's human weaknesses, his greatness is also a(n) _____**indubitable**_____ part of the historic record.

2. Since he neither affirms nor denies the existence of God, I'd classify him as a(n) _____**agnostic**_____ rather than an atheist.

3. During the emergency, the mayor assumed _____**plenary**_____ authority and did whatever was needed to provide essential services.

4. It was such a(n) _____**inane**_____ remark that I couldn't keep myself from laughing derisively when I heard it.

5. "Simple _____**equity**_____ demands that we distribute the tax burden as fairly as possible among the populace," the Senator remarked.

6. How can you call that a(n) _____**moot**_____ question when it is quite clearly a simple matter of right and wrong?

7. I would be _____**derelict**_____ in my duty to you if I did not warn you against the bad effects of smoking cigarettes.

8. Since the accused was never really given a chance to defend himself, his so-called "trial" was nothing but a(n) _____**travesty**_____ of justice.

9. The overthrown dictator was hanged in _____**effigy**_____ before a vast throng in the town square.

10. Those who saw the young woman being assaulted and did nothing to help her were guilty of _____**complicity**_____ in the crime.

11. At the slightest sound of thunder, my dog Rover dives under the bed in a state of _____**abject**_____ terror.

12. In her garland of leaves and acorns, the child looked very much like some _____**sylvan**_____ spirit from an Arthurian myth.

13. Throughout the period that the spy thought he had gone undetected, he was actually under close _____**surveillance**_____ by the CIA.

14. For years, we carried on a(n) _____**intermittent**_____ correspondence, sometimes allowing months to pass before a letter was answered.

15. Every time we did something to anger him, he delivered an intemperate _____**diatribe**_____ lambasting our "hopeless irresponsibility."

16. In Wagner's operas, brief musical _____**motifs**_____ associated with the characters or their actions recur again and again.

17. The fact that so many released prisoners return to a life of crime is in itself a terrifying _____**indictment**_____ of our penal system.

18. How could a mere _____ neophyte _____ in the teaching profession question the judgment of so experienced an educator?

19. I'd say that the phrase "having a short fuse" aptly describes my boss's decidedly _____ testy _____ disposition.

20. The _____ perspicacity _____ of her analysis not only clarified the nature of the problem but also suggested its most promising solution.

Synonyms *Choose the word from this unit that is **the same** or **most nearly the same** in meaning as the **boldface** word or expression in the given phrase. Write the word on the line provided.*

1. a crude **likeness** — effigy

2. a familiar **theme** in her poetry — motif

3. put under **scrutiny** — surveillance

4. a mere **parody** of fair play — travesty

5. the **forested** slopes of the Rockies — sylvan

6. announced the formal **charge** to the press — indictment

7. admired for his uncommon **acuity** — perspicacity

8. was given **unlimited** power to govern — plenary

9. indoctrinated the **rookie** — neophyte

10. a **doubter** in every aspect — agnostic

11. **remiss** in discharging her responsibilities — derelict

12. guilty of **collusion** — complicity

13. could not contain her own **tirade** — diatribe

14. the **vapid** chatter of thoughtless critics — inane

15. a **debatable** issue — moot

Antonyms *Choose the word from this unit that is **most nearly opposite** in meaning to the **boldface** word or expression in the given phrase. Write the word on the line provided.*

16. the **continuous** flow of water — intermittent

17. a history of **injustice** — equity

18. the **dubious** strength of the foundation — indubitable

19. calmed the **even-tempered** child — testy

20. her **lofty** plea for understanding — abject

Choosing the Right Word

Circle the **boldface** word that more satisfactorily completes each of the following sentences.

1. Today's forecast calls for variable cloudiness with (**abject,** **intermittent**) periods of rain.

2. Only an (**intermittent,** **abject**) coward would stand idly by while a defenseless old woman was mugged in the street.

3. All of a sudden, a strange young man rushed onto the speaker's platform and launched into a (**travesty,** **diatribe**) against "big government."

4. After over 30 years in Congress, he retains the idealism of the (**agnostic,** **neophyte**) but has gained the practical wisdom of the veteran.

5. As he sat before the fire absentmindedly puffing on his pipe, Grandfather seemed the very epitome of (**plenary,** **sylvan**) contentment.

6. According to voodoo belief, one can get rid of an enemy by making a tiny (**effigy,** **motif**) of him and sticking it full of pins.

7. My studies have convinced me that the one dominant (**motif,** **diatribe**) in American history has been the expansion of democracy.

8. The picture shows the three Graces dancing in a forest clearing, while nymphs, satyrs, and other (**sylvan,** **indubitable**) creatures cavort among the trees.

9. "I vetoed that idea when it was first (**mooted,** **indicted**) years ago," the Governor said, "and I have never regretted my decision."

10. The awkward pause in the conversation became even more painful when he interjected his (**plenary,** **inane**) attempts at humor.

11. His extraordinary ability to (**moot,** **travesty**) the works of popular writers is largely due to his keen eye for the ridiculous.

12. What qualities will he have to fall back on when his (**indubitable,** **testy**) charm and good looks begin to wear thin?

13. Though the book was written by an avowed (**agnostic,** **derelict**), it enjoyed a certain popularity with the faithful.

14. How can I be accused of (**indictment,** **complicity**) in that plot when I did not even know the conspirators?

15. Bag ladies and other homeless (**neophytes,** **derelicts**) roam our streets in increasing numbers.

16. Observers on the ground keep close (**surveillance,** **equity**) on air traffic at a busy airport by means of various electronic devices, such as radar.

17. Though I can sometimes be as (**testy,** **derelict**) as an irate wasp, I normally do not lose my temper very easily.

18. The historian had long been noted for the soundness of his scholarship and the (**complicity,** **perspicacity**) of his judgment.

19. His disgraceful behavior since he left college is in itself a(n) (**indictment,** **surveillance**) of the lax, overindulgent upbringing he received.

20. Since she is a fair-minded woman, I'm sure she will present both sides of the controversy with admirable (**equity,** **effigy**).

Read the following passage, in which some of the words you have studied in this unit appear in **boldface** type. Then complete each statement given below the passage by circling the letter of the item that is **the same** or **almost the same** in meaning as the highlighted word.

Judicial Heights

(Line)

The Supreme Court is the most powerful judicial body in the United States and, possibly, the world. But this esteemed branch of the American government has not always commanded quite so much respect. In its early days the court had to fight off **intermittent** infringements on its authority by the executive and legislative
(5) branches of the American government. Most challenging, it also had to assert its authority over fractious state and local courts in order to bolster the power of the federal government.

(10) The first justices were appointed to the Supreme Court by George Washington. They were all members of Washington's Federalist party and thus intensely sympathetic to his policies. These
(15) **neophytes** could not see any role for themselves beyond personal and party loyalty, and, as a result, the young court quickly became a hotbed of partisan controversy. Two of the first three justices,
(20) John Jay and Oliver Ellsworth, resigned after a few years, and the third, John Rutledge, was refused confirmation by a

Located in the nation's capital, the U.S. Supreme Court is open to the public year-round.

testy Senate after he had already served four months on the bench. The Court's most **abject** hour occurred, however, when Justice Samuel Chase, an outspoken
(25) Federalist, was impeached (but not convicted) by anti-Federalist forces in Congress following the election of Republican Thomas Jefferson.

The judicial tide turned in 1800 with the appointment of John Marshall by President John Adams. For 35 years the distinguished Judge Marshall steadily moved the Court toward what he saw as its rightful role: supreme arbiter of the
(30) Constitution. His **indubitable** integrity, personal courage, and judicial **perspicacity** permanently advanced the power and prestige of the Court.

---

1. The meaning of **intermittent** (line 4) is
a. rightful
b. malicious
c. sporadic
d. clever

2. Neophytes (line 15) most nearly means
a. novices
b. patriots
c. criminals
d. fools

3. Testy (line 23) is best defined as
a. indecisive
b. irritable
c. powerful
d. divided

4. The meaning of **abject** (line 24) is
a. triumphant
b. memorable
c. moving
d. ignoble

5. Indubitable (line 30) most nearly means
a. remarkable
b. indisputable
c. political
d. questionable

6. Perspicacity (line 30) most nearly means
a. manipulation
b. training
c. discernment
d. reputation

ONLINE COMPONENTS
www.vocabularyworkshop.com

Vocabulary for Comprehension

Read the following passage, in which some of the words you have studied in Units 4–6 appear in **boldface** *type. Then answer questions 1–12 on page 73 on the basis of what is* <u>stated</u> *or* <u>implied</u> *in the passage and in the introductory statement.*

As this passage shows, zoos have served a wide range of purposes during their long history.

(Line)

Zoos, or at least collections of **incarcerated** animals, have existed for millennia. The purpose of capturing and caging animals, however, has

(5) changed over time. In ancient Egypt, certain animals were deified or else considered very closely connected to gods. These animals were held in cages in temple complexes and

(10) treated as objects of worship. In a sense, these ancient zoos were **hallowed** grounds, but it is difficult not to see them as existing more for the benefit of humans than for animals.

(15) In the classical world, private menageries, or collections of exotic animals, were **ubiquitous** among **overweening** rulers who wished to advertise their power and wealth.

(20) The modern conception of a zoo emerged in Victorian England. In fact, the word *zoo* derives from the London zoological garden, which was established in the late nineteenth

(25) century. The purpose of this zoo, according to its founder Sir Stamford Raffles, was scientific study, not the "vulgar admiration" of animals. Despite Raffles's **fiat**, however, zoos

(30) on both sides of the Atlantic soon focused on entertaining the large crowds that paid money to view the animals. While exposure to both rare and commonplace creatures

(35) benefited many zoo patrons, the animals often suffered. The creatures, which had been either taken captive in the wild or bred in captivity, were usually housed singly

(40) in tiny metal cages or other bare enclosures, where they paced nervously or lay **recumbent** in a bored stupor.

Finally, with the rise of ecological

(45) consciousness in the 1970s, the bars began to come down in zoos all over the world. Increasingly, captive animals were placed in roomier, more natural environments not only for their

(50) own well-being but also as a way of educating the public about the need to preserve wild habitats.

1. The meaning of **incarcerated** (line 2) is
a. immense
b. exotic
c. imaginary
d. confined
e. dangerous

2. The primary purpose of the passage is
a. to compare modern zoos with ancient ones
b. to argue that zoos unjustifiably deprive wild animals of their freedom
c. to expose the shocking conditions in modern zoos
d. to present some aspects of the historical development of zoos
e. to offer insights into the religion of ancient Egypt

3. Hallowed (line 12) most nearly means
a. fertile
b. sacred
c. neutral
d. breeding
e. forbidden

4. Ubiquitous (line 17) is best defined as
a. pervasive
b. prohibited
c. unusual
d. traditional
e. coveted

5. The meaning of **overweening** (line 18) is
a. feuding
b. brutal
c. arrogant
d. benevolent
e. weak

6. According to the author, in the classical world private menageries of exotic animals served to
a. insure the progress of science
b. entertain large crowds of visitors
c. strengthen traditional religious attitudes
d. advertise the power and wealth of rulers
e. celebrate foreign conquests

7. The author states that the modern conception of a zoo emerged
a. in Victorian England
b. during the late Middle Ages in France
c. in China around 1900
d. during the Italian Renaissance
e. in the United States during the late nineteenth century

8. From paragraph 2 (lines 20–43), one can reasonably infer that the author
a. believes that zoo admission should be free
b. sympathizes with the animals' suffering
c. thinks that zoos are vital for scientific progress
d. rejects the techniques of captive breeding
e. thinks that zoos should be abolished

9. Fiat (line 29) most nearly means
a. title
b. request
c. decree
d. wealth
e. opinion

10. The organization of the passage as a whole is best defined as
a. chronological order
b. cause and effect
c. comparison and contrast
d. order of importance
e. spatial order

11. Recumbent (line 42) most nearly means
a. prostrate
b. contented
c. injured
d. relaxed
e. ignored

12. The tone of the final paragraph (lines 44–52) is best described as
a. satirical
b. positive
c. skeptical
d. humorous
e. philosophical

Grammar in Context

In the sentence "In a sense, these ancient zoos were hallowed grounds, but it is difficult not to see them as existing more for the benefit of humans than for animals" (lines 10–14 on page 72), the pronoun *them* refers to the noun *zoos*. A pronoun usually refers to a noun or another pronoun. This word is called the pronoun's **antecedent**. Proper **pronoun-antecedent agreement** requires that a pronoun agree with its antecedent in number and gender.

Singular pronouns are used to refer to antecedents such as *anyone, each, either, everyone, neither, no one, nothing,* and *someone.* A plural pronoun is used to refer to two or more singular antecedents connected by *and.* A singular pronoun is used to refer to two or more singular antecedents joined by *or* or *nor.* When a singular and a plural antecedent are joined by *or* or *nor,* the pronoun usually agrees with the nearer antecedent. If a pronoun's antecedent may be either masculine or feminine, use both the masculine and feminine pronouns to refer to it.

On the lines provided, rewrite each of the sentences or pairs of sentences to eliminate any errors in pronoun-antecedent agreement. Write "correct" if the sentence is correct. Answers may vary; sample answers given.

1. In ancient Egypt, certain animals were highly respected for its close connections to the gods.
   In ancient Egypt, certain animals were highly respected for their close connections to the gods.

2. Each of these animals had their own mythology, or collection of tales.
   Each of these animals had its own mythology, or collection of tales.

3. Through collecting exotic animals, rulers wished to advertise his or her power and wealth.
   Through collecting exotic animals, rulers wished to advertise their power and wealth.

4. The modern concept of zoos had their start in Victorian England.
   The modern concept of zoos had its start in Victorian England.

5. Neither full-grown African lions nor an adult giraffe likes its close confinement.
   correct

6. Beginning in the 1970s, ecological consciousness has had their effect on zoos.
   Beginning in the 1970s, ecological consciousness has had its effect on zoos.

7. Nowadays each zoo visitor will have to make up their minds about the animals' well-being.
   Nowadays, each zoo visitor will have to make up his or her mind about the animals' well-being.

Two-Word Completions

Circle the pair of words that best complete the meaning of each of the following passages.

See pages T38–T48 for explanations of answers.

1. After the battle, the officer who had failed to carry out his orders was arrested by the military police, charged with _____ of duty, and _____ in the stockade, pending a court-martial.

a. atrophy . . . garnered

b. dereliction . . . incarcerated

c. travesty . . . mooted

d. ignominy . . . hallowed

2. Despite the harried officer's _____ attempts to steady his troops after the left flank had been turned, they fled from the field in such _____ that their departure was more of a rout than a retreat.

a. consummate . . . ignominy

b. ludicrous . . . equity

c. intermittent . . . concord

d. frenetic . . . disarray

3. I'm extremely circumspect about what I say or do in the office because my boss is so _____ that it is easy to _____ or exasperate him.

a. mordant . . . disarray

b. abject . . . moot

c. testy . . . nettle

d. jocular . . . enervate

4. Vincent van Gogh was indeed a(n) _____ technician, able to _____ every nuance of nature's variegated panorama with a mere stroke of the brush.

a. ubiquitous . . . hallow

b. indubitable . . . enervate

c. consummate . . . delineate

d. sylvan . . . travesty

5. Although the man is certainly thought to have been involved in the crime, no _____ has yet been brought against him because the authorities have not been able to assemble enough evidence to establish his _____ beyond a reasonable doubt.

a. indictment . . . complicity

b. surveillance . . . equity

c. exigency . . . acuity

d. figment . . . perspicacity

6. Edward R. Murrow will hold a place in history as a journalist who saw in 1950s television the potential to educate, and not simply to entertain. He felt it was the _____ responsibility of all journalists to act as a(n) _____ against both zealotry and indifference.

a. consummate . . . fiat

b. plenary . . . grouse

c. overweening . . . indictment

d. incumbent . . . bastion

Choosing the Right Meaning

Read each sentence carefully. Then circle the item that best completes the statement below the sentence.

See pages T38–T48 for explanations of answers.

Many of this nation's Founding Fathers have been widely honored, but perhaps none has been so universally hallowed as its first president, George Washington. (2)

1. In line 2 the word **hallowed** most nearly means

   a. sanctified   b. emulated   c. consecrated   (d. venerated)

The real business of the convention was conducted not so much in the plenary sessions as in preliminary, backroom caucuses. (2)

2. The word **plenary** in line 1 most nearly means

   a. absolute   b. unlimited   (c. fully attended)   d. unrestricted

Although the source for the controversial story was undeniably a reputed one, the managing editor declined to print the article without independent verification of its accuracy. (2)

3. The best definition for the word **reputed** in line 1 is

   a. alleged   b. supposed   (c. reputable)   d. anonymous

The lender would agree to the loan only on the condition that the borrowers offer as security the equity they held in their home. (2)

4. In line 2 the word **equity** is used to mean

   a. impartiality   b. justice   c. furnishings   (d. financial interest)

"I, King Pericles, have lost
This Queen, worth all our mundane cost," (2)
     (Shakespeare, *Pericles*, III, 2, 70–71)

5. The word **mundane** in line 2 most nearly means

   (a. worldly)   b. ordinary   c. routine   d. humdrum

Antonyms

*In each of the following groups, circle the word or expression that is most nearly the **opposite** of the word in **boldface** type.*

1. acuity
a. orderliness
b. breadth
c. flexibility
(d. obtuseness)

2. fecund
a. fertile
b. large
(c. barren)
d. serious

3. indubitable
(a. dubious)
b. trenchant
c. surprising
d. new

4. equity
a. result
b. meaning
(c. injustice)
d. cause

5. ludicrous
a. chaotic
(b. heartrending)
c. unusual
d. lengthy

6. intermittent
a. sudden
(b. continuous)
c. seasonal
d. imminent

7. mordant
(a. gentle)
b. repellent
c. caustic
d. savage

8. neophyte
a. advocate
b. enemy
c. beginner
(d. expert)

9. inane
a. explicit
b. unexpected
c. profound
d. fatuous

11. pusillanimous
a. craven
b. ravenous
c. daring
d. corpulent

13. ignominy
a. criticism
b. publicity
c. odium
d. acclaim

15. consummate
a. report
b. initiate
c. study
d. clinch

10. sumptuous
a. open
b. meager
c. secret
d. lavish

12. frenetic
a. frantic
b. haphazard
c. relaxed
d. indolent

14. depraved
a. corrupt
b. intelligent
c. curious
d. virtuous

16. concord
a. strife
b. harmony
c. determination
d. curiosity

Word Families

A. *On the line provided, write the word you have learned in Units 4–6 that is related to each of the following nouns.*
EXAMPLE: consummation—**consummate**

1. inanity, inanition — inane
2. incarceration, incarcerator — incarcerate
3. fecundity, fecundation — fecund
4. mordancy — mordant
5. sumptuousness — sumptuous
6. depravity, depravedness, depraver, depravation — depraved
7. enervation — enervate
8. jocularity — jocular
9. testiness — testy
10. delineation, delineator — delineate
11. frenzy — frenetic
12. ubiquity, ubiquitousness — ubiquitous
13. ludicrousness — ludicrous
14. pusillanimity — pusillanimous
15. reputation, repute — reputed

B. *On the line provided, write the word you have learned in Units 4–6 that is related to each of the following verbs.*
EXAMPLE: sophisticate—**sophisticated**

16. doubt — indubitable
17. indict — indictment
18. deprave — depraved
19. repute — reputed
20. intermit — intermittent

In each of the following groups, circle the word that is best defined or suggested by the given phrase.

1. the woman who now represents this district in Congress
a. fiat   b. penchant   (c. incumbent)   d. derelict

2. senseless chatter
a. esoteric   b. plenary   c. sumptuous   (d. inane)

3. a strong inclination toward the outdoor life
a. travesty   (b. penchant)   c. effigy   d. fiat

4. sanctify
(a. hallow)   b. grouse   c. atrophy   d. nettle

5. the need of the moment
(a. exigency)   b. diatribe   c. travesty   d. figment

6. irritable and peevish behavior
(a. testy)   b. inane   c. depraved   d. ubiquitous

7. a plan to keep our surprise party a secret
a. equity   (b. stratagem)   c. indictment   d. acuity

8. gather knowledge bit by bit
a. enervate   b. nettle   (c. glean)   d. consummate

9. a habit of stirring coffee with a fork, rather than a spoon
a. surveillance   b. complicity   c. atrophy   (d. idiosyncrasy)

10. a matter of dollars and cents
a. abject   b. intermittent   c. moot   (d. pecuniary)

11. a cabin in a heavily wooded area
a. mordant   b. overweening   c. abject   (d. sylvan)

12. keep a round-the-clock watch on the suspect
(a. surveillance)   b. diatribe   c. fiat   d. equity

13. wreckage that was washed up on the beach
a. adversity   b. bastion   c. disarray   (d. flotsam)

14. never slows down and relaxes
(a. frenetic)   b. consummate   c. plenary   d. jocular

15. the sole defender of democracy in that part of the world
a. nuance   (b. bastion)   c. derelict   d. agnostic

16. the literary theme of a man destroyed by his own ambitions
a. sophistry   (b. motif)   c. indictment   d. complicity

17. intend to cause embarrassment or annoyance
a. incarcerate   b. enervate   c. garner   (d. nettle)

18. spent most of the summer lying on the beach
a. depraved   b. sumptuous   c. esoteric   (d. recumbent)

19. possesses a remarkable keenness of insight into human nature
a. concord   b. neophyte   c. diatribe   (d. perspicacity)

20. the product of a fevered brain or overactive imagination
a. travesty   b. flotsam   (c. figment)   d. ignominy

gno(s)—to know

Building with Classical Roots

This Greek root appears in **agnostic** (page 65). Note that in some words based on the root **gno-**, the **o** in the base may not appear in the final form of the word; this is the case in **cognate**. Some other words based on this root are listed below.

cognate	cognizant	gnostic	prognosis
cognition	diagnose	ignore	recognize

From the list of words above, choose the one that corresponds to each of the brief definitions below. Write the word in the blank space in the illustrative sentence below the definition.

1. related by family or origin; related in nature, character, quality, or function; a person or thing related to another

The Sanskrit word for king—*rajah*—is a _____**cognate**_____ of the Latin *rex*.

2. to disregard deliberately; to pay no attention to; to refuse to consider

If we just _____**ignore**_____ Rover, he will eventually stop begging for food at the table.

3. a prediction of the probable course of a disease; a probable forecast or estimate

With modern treatment options, patients who contract this once-fatal disease now have an excellent _____**prognosis**_____ for full recovery.

4. the broad mental process by which knowledge is acquired, including aspects of awareness, perception, reasoning, judgment, memory, and intuition; knowledge

After a serious blow to the head, her _____**cognition**_____ was impaired for several weeks.

5. to identify a disease or condition based on observation, examination, and analysis

A podiatrist is trained to _____**diagnose**_____ and treat a range of problems of the foot.

6. to know, identify, or show awareness of something from past experience or knowledge; to accept as a fact; to acknowledge a thing's existence, validity, or authority; to approve of or appreciate

The school board has come to _____**recognize**_____ the positive impact of art and music classes.

7. of, relating to, or possessing intellectual or spiritual knowledge

Many religions observe a _____**gnostic**_____ doctrine, where emphasis is placed on the pursuit of spiritual and intellectual knowledge.

8. fully informed; conscious; aware

As a result of a 1966 court decision, all arrested suspects must be made _____**cognizant**_____ of their Miranda rights.

From the list of words on page 79, choose the one that best completes each of the following sentences. Write the word in the blank space provided.

1. High-speed Internet connections and extensive medical databases make it possible for doctors to _____**diagnose**_____ certain conditions without actually seeing the patient.

2. Had she been _____**cognizant**_____ of the rugged terrain, she'd have avoided that route.

3. Ignoring her doctor's pessimistic _____**prognosis**_____, grandmother insisted on inviting the entire family to her home for a festive holiday party.

4. "I'd like this august body to _____**recognize**_____ my esteemed colleague from Iowa," boomed the senior senator from Arkansas.

5. Poet Richard Wilbur once described the Garden of Eden as the "_____**cognate**_____ splendor [from which] all things came. . . ."

6. Although they may respond to certain sensations, comatose individuals do not experience _____**cognition**_____ in the way that fully conscious people do.

7. A flourishing society must not _____**ignore**_____ its failings, but instead address and try to fix them.

8. In a short book of poetry published in 1891, Herman Melville included an eight-line fragment from a lost _____**gnostic**_____ poem believed to have been written in the twelfth century.

---

*Circle the **boldface** word that more satisfactorily completes each of the following sentences.*

1. To devise a meaningful survey, an astute pollster must be (**cognizant,** **gnostic**) of the current issues most likely to influence respondents.

2. Dedicated (**ignorant,** **gnostic**) believers sought to understand the nature of the soul and its relationship to the world.

3. One fascinating branch of neuroscience examines and analyzes the physical characteristics of (**prognosis,** **cognition**) and related brain function.

4. Clever teachers have written funny (**cognate,** **cognizant**) poems to help students learn foreign words by using the vocabulary they already know in their own language.

5. Salmon who swim upstream to spawn in the fresh waters where they were born are believed to (**recognize,** **diagnose**) their original home by some primal sense of smell.

6. I've finally learned to (**recognize,** **ignore**) those annoying messages that tell me that my computer has committed a fatal error; I just reboot and start over.

7. A good business plan should include a reasoned (**prognosis,** **cognition**) for future growth.

8. It's never easy to (**cognate,** **diagnose**) a baby's illness because an infant cannot describe his or her symptoms or provide a medical history.

Analogies

In each of the following, circle the item that best completes the comparison.

See pages T38–T48 for explanations of answers.

1. intransigent is to **compromise** as
a. dour is to carp
b. honest is to dissemble
c. friendly is to oblige
d. irresolute is to temporize

2. acquisitive is to **garner** as
a. perspicacious is to glean
b. agnostic is to dissemble
c. depraved is to belabor
d. distraught is to cavort

3. consummate is to **perfection** as
a. myopic is to perspicacity
b. esoteric is to accessibility
c. plenary is to completeness
d. taciturn is to propriety

4. pejorative is to **disparaging** as
a. jocular is to ludicrous
b. moot is to indubitable
c. abject is to lofty
d. pusillanimous is to craven

5. inane is to **acuity** as
a. overt is to brevity
b. unwonted is to status
c. banal is to originality
d. feckless is to allure

6. articulate is to **mouth** as
a. taste is to lip
b. scan is to eye
c. grouse is to heel
d. accost is to foot

7. germane is to **relevance** as
a. coherent is to consistency
b. derelict is to genuineness
c. piquant is to humanity
d. utopian is to practicality

8. diatribe is to **animadversions** as
a. eulogy is to rebukes
b. harangue is to accolades
c. encomium is to compliments
d. panegyric is to reprimands

9. detective is to **surveillance** as
a. saint is to sacrilege
b. scout is to reconnaissance
c. witch is to appropriation
d. artist is to travesty

10. testy is to **nettle** as
a. serene is to disturb
b. callous is to move
c. articulate is to numb
d. sensitive is to hurt

 Choosing the Right Meaning

Read each sentence carefully. Then circle the item that best completes the statement below the sentence.

See pages T38–T48 for explanations of answers.

"What judgment shall I dread, doing no wrong?
You have among you many a purchased slave,   (2)
Which, like your asses and your dogs and mules,
You use in abject and in slavish parts   (4)
Because you bought them. . . ." (Shakespeare, *The Merchant of Venice,* IV, 1, 89–93)

1. In line 4 the word **abject** most nearly means
a. servile   b. unrelieved   c. wretched   d. cringing

The Transcontinental Treaty of 1819, a territorial concord between Spain and
America that for the first time drew the boundary of the United States from   (2)
ocean to ocean, was chiefly the work of future President John Quincy Adams.

2. The word **concord** in line 1 is used to mean
a. harmony   b. unanimity   c. pact   d. misunderstanding

George Eliot introduces the hero of her 1861 novel *Silas Marner* as a miserly, avid weaver who cares for nothing on earth so much as his hoard of gold coins. (2)

3. The word **avid** in line 1 is best defined as

a. enthusiastic   b. keen   c. eager   (d. grasping)

The chief incumbency of the President is, in the succinct words of the inaugural oath, "to preserve, protect, and defend the Constitution of the United States." (2)

4. The best definition for the word **incumbency** in line 1 is

a. term   b. officeholder   c. aide   (d. duty)

In the comedies—especially those that involve mistaken identity—Shakespeare often hinges a turn of plot on the appearance of a character in travesty. (2)

5. In line 2 the word **travesty** is used to mean

a. burlesque   (b. disguise)   c. farce   d. caricature

Two-Word Completions

Circle the pair of words that best complete the meaning of each of the following sentences.

See pages T38–T48 for explanations of answers.

1. Even after the last _____ of enemy resistance had fallen to our troops, the sound of _____ sniper fire occasionally broke the stillness of the summer evening.

(a. bastion . . . intermittent)   c. maelstrom . . . incendiary
b. gambit . . . pejorative   d. nuance . . . recumbent

2. So much industrial waste has been dumped into that once clear lake that it has now become a _____ cesspool covered with all kinds of unsightly and potentially dangerous _____ .

a. primordial . . . concord   c. fecund . . . verbiage
b. verdant . . . largesse   (d. murky . . . flotsam)

3. Though most Northerners were not _____ proponents of war with the South, many of them responded to President Lincoln's call to arms with exemplary _____ .

a. mordant . . . ignominy   c. primordial . . . exigency
(b. avid . . . celerity)   d. reputed . . . disarray

4. It is a truly sad commentary on modern city life that bag ladies and other homeless _____ are becoming as _____ as traffic lights on the streets of our larger urban centers.

a. suppliants . . . histrionic   (c. derelicts . . . ubiquitous)
b. agnostics . . . hallowed   d. incumbents . . . overweening

5. Since the Roman emperors were autocrats who ruled their vast empire by _____ , the democratic institutions of the Republic slowly _____ and died.

a. complicity . . . dissembled   (c. fiat . . . atrophied)
b. penchant . . . evinced   d. sophistry . . . groused

Enriching Your Vocabulary

Read the passage below. Then complete the exercise at the bottom of the page.

Stepping Up to the Plate

When baseball batters step up to home plate, they ready themselves—physically and mentally—to face the opposing pitcher whose job it is to strike them out. The expression *step up to the plate,* taken from the terminology of baseball, has become a part of everyday language. People who step up to the plate take their turn putting their skill, talent, experience, or reputation on the line as they accept their unique moment of competitive confrontation.

Many words, phrases, and colorful expressions that enrich the English language have their origins in sports and games. This should come as no surprise, since athletics and recreation play such important roles in our daily lives. One such word, *gambit* (Unit 2), is derived from an opening move in chess. In standard usage, gambit has come to mean any early move made at the cost of something minor that will hopefully lead to future advantage. What does it mean to describe a political candidate as the *front-runner?* This term, from racing, refers to the competitor who clearly holds the lead.

Chess was invented in Asia centuries ago, and many words and expressions associated with it have been incorporated into the English language.

In Column A below are 8 more words and phrases that come from the world of sports and games. With or without a dictionary, match each sports word or phrase to its meaning in Column B.

Column A

_____f_____ **1.** have an ace up one's sleeve

_____c_____ **2.** kick off

_____b_____ **3.** long shot

_____d_____ **4.** Monday-morning quarterback

_____a_____ **5.** par for the course

_____g_____ **6.** pinch-hit

_____e_____ **7.** showboating

_____h_____ **8.** throw in the towel

Column B

a. what is expected according to an accepted standard, common sense, or previous experience (golf)

b. a bet or venture that has only a slight chance of success (horse racing)

c. to start, initiate, or commence (football)

d. person who is prepared to explain, *after* a defeat or disappointment, what should have been done to achieve success (football)

e. seeking to impress by acting in an ostentatious manner; grandstanding (baseball)

f. to have an effective resource held in reserve for use at a strategic point (card playing)

g. to serve as a substitute (baseball)

h. to give up, surrender, or admit defeat (boxing)

Definitions

Note carefully the spelling, pronunciation, part(s) of speech, and definition(s) of each of the following words. Then write the word in the blank space(s) in the illustrative sentence(s) following. Finally, study the lists of synonyms and antonyms given at the end of each entry.

1. allay
(ə lā′)

(*v.*) to calm or pacify, set to rest; to lessen or relieve

The politician made a speech in order to _____**allay**_____ his constituents' fears.

SYNONYMS: reduce, alleviate, moderate
ANTONYMS: aggravate, exacerbate, intensify

2. bestial
(bes′ chəl)

(*adj.*) beastlike; beastly, brutal; subhuman in intelligence and sensibility

In beating their prisoner, the guards were guilty of a truly _____**bestial**_____ act.

SYNONYMS: animal, depraved, loathsome
ANTONYMS: human, humane, clement, virtuous, upright

3. convivial
(kən viv′ ē əl)

(*adj.*) festive, sociable, having fun together, genial

Thanksgiving dinner at Grandmother's house is always a _____**convivial**_____ family gathering.

SYNONYMS: fun-loving, jovial, merry
ANTONYMS: dour, grim, sullen, unsociable

4. coterie
(kō′ tə rē)

(*n.*) a circle of acquaintances; a close-knit, often exclusive, group of people with a common interest

Robert Browning and his _____**coterie**_____ had ideas about poetry that seemed revolutionary in their day.

SYNONYMS: clique, set

5. counterpart
(kaúnt′ ər pärt)

(*n.*) a person or thing closely resembling or corresponding to another; a complement

I have to admit I was frightened of my _____**counterpart**_____ on the other team because she held the high-jump record.

SYNONYM: match

6. demur
(di mər′)

(*v.*) to object or take exception to; (*n.*) an objection

The rank and file will _____**demur**_____ if they are not consulted regularly by the union leadership.

The speech in favor of the proposal was drowned out by a chorus of _____**demurs**_____ from the senate floor.

SYNONYMS: (*v.*) protest, object to
ANTONYMS: (*v.*) assent to, consent to, accept, agree to

7. effrontery
(ə frən′ tə rē)

(*n.*) shameless boldness, impudence

After having been suspended for disrespectful behavior, the student had the _____ **effrontery** _____ to talk back to his teacher again.

SYNONYMS: gall, chutzpah, nerve, impertinence, cheek
ANTONYMS: shyness, diffidence, timidity

8. embellish
(em bel′ ish)

(*v.*) to decorate, adorn, touch up; to improve by adding details

The best storytellers _____ **embellish** _____ their tales in ways that help readers visualize the setting.

SYNONYMS: ornament, garnish
ANTONYMS: strip, mar, disfigure

9. ephemeral
(i fem′ ər əl)

(*adj.*) lasting only a short time, short-lived

Only the greatest of writers and artists achieve anything other than _____ **ephemeral** _____ popularity.

SYNONYMS: fleeting, transient, evanescent, transitory
ANTONYMS: durable, long-lasting, permanent, perpetual

10. felicitous
(fə lis′ ə təs)

(*adj.*) appropriate, apt, well chosen; marked by well-being or good fortune, happy

In view of the high prices for home heating oil, the mild winter was a _____ **felicitous** _____ turn of events.

SYNONYMS: fortunate, well-put
ANTONYMS: inappropriate, inept, graceless, unhappy

11. furtive
(fər′ tiv)

(*adj.*) done slyly or stealthily, sneaky, secret, shifty; stolen

The girl was caught taking a _____ **furtive** _____ glance at the test paper of the student sitting next to her.

SYNONYMS: clandestine, covert, surreptitious
ANTONYMS: forthright, aboveboard, open

12. garish
(gar′ ish)

(*adj.*) glaring; tastelessly showy or overdecorated in a vulgar or offensive way

The storefront was painted in _____ **garish** _____ colors so that it would attract the attention of passersby.

SYNONYMS: gaudy, flashy, tawdry
ANTONYMS: subdued, muted, understated, quiet

13. illusory
(i lü′ sə rē)

(*adj.*) misleading, deceptive; lacking in or not based on reality

Police state tactics provide an _____ **illusory** _____ sense of security in an unjust society.

SYNONYMS: specious, spurious, fanciful, imaginary
ANTONYMS: actual, real, factual, objective

14. indigent
(in′ də jənt)

(*adj.*) needy, impoverished

The number of homeless and _____ indigent _____ persons has increased since the economy took a downturn.

SYNONYMS: penniless, poverty-stricken, destitute
ANTONYMS: wealthy, affluent, prosperous

15. inordinate
(in ôr′ də nət)

(*adj.*) far too great, exceeding reasonable limits, excessive

The press showered the popular actor with _____ inordinate _____ praise for what seemed a rather ordinary performance.

SYNONYMS: exorbitant, extravagant
ANTONYMS: moderate, reasonable, equitable

16. jettison
(jet′ ə sən)

(*v.*) to cast overboard, get rid of as unnecessary or burdensome

The captain ordered the crew to _____ jettison _____ the ballast so the ship could move more quickly through the water.

SYNONYMS: cast off, discard, dump, junk, abandon
ANTONYMS: conserve, retain, hold on to, keep

17. misanthrope
(mis′ ən thrōp)

(*n.*) a person who hates or despises people

The millionaire _____ misanthrope _____ left all her money to an animal shelter and not a penny to a single human being.

SYNONYMS: people-hater

18. pertinacious
(pər tə nā′ shəs)

(*adj.*) very persistent; holding firmly to a course of action or a set of beliefs; hard to get rid of, refusing to be put off or denied

The defense attorney was as _____ pertinacious _____ as a bulldog in his cross-examination of the witness.

SYNONYMS: stubborn, dogged, determined

19. picayune
(pik ē yün′)

(*adj.*) of little value or importance, paltry, measly; concerned with trifling matters, small-minded

A supervisor who fusses about every _____ picayune _____ fault of the workers will lower morale and productivity.

SYNONYMS: inconsequential, piddling, trifling
ANTONYMS: important, significant, huge, gigantic

20. raiment
(rā′ mənt)

(*n.*) clothing, garments

When the chorus in the Greek tragedy hears that the king has died, they tear their _____ raiment _____ in anguish.

SYNONYMS: apparel, attire

Completing the Sentence

From the words for this unit, choose the one that best completes each of the following sentences. Write the word in the space provided.

1. A busy administrator in today's high-pressure business world just doesn't have time to deal with such **picayune** concerns as making coffee.

2. Recent developments in that part of the world have intensified rather than **allayed** our fears of a renewed conflict.

3. He is entitled to reasonable compensation for the damage to his car, but the demands he has made are totally **inordinate**.

4. The "Old 400" was a very small and exclusive **coterie** of prominent families that dominated East Coast society for decades.

5. When Charles V retired to a Spanish monastery, he exchanged the costly **raiment** of a king for the simple habit of a monk.

6. The crew of the freighter **jettisoned** most of its cargo in a desperate effort to keep the sinking ship afloat.

7. A good deal of sad experience has taught me that my youthful hopes of getting something for nothing are entirely **illusory**.

8. Who wouldn't have had fun among such a(n) **convivial** group of people?

9. In the Victorian era, designers **embellished** women's dresses with all sorts of elaborate frills and flounces.

10. Since we all agreed that the proposal seemed to offer the best solution to our problem, it was accepted without **demur**.

11. The disastrous stock market crash of 1929 left many a wealthy speculator as **indigent** as the proverbial church mouse.

12. Though I don't consider myself much of a diplomat, I think I handled that delicate situation in a particularly **felicitous** manner.

13. The **furtive** manner in which he sidled into the room and tried to avoid being noticed actually drew attention to his presence.

14. "If at first you don't succeed, try, try again" seems to be the motto of that **pertinacious** young woman.

15. Jonathan Swift so came to loathe human folly, vice, and hypocrisy that he died a virtual **misanthrope**.

16. At the Casablanca Conference in 1943, President Roosevelt and his military aides met with their British **counterparts** to map military strategy for the Western Allies.

17. The man's features suddenly contorted into a(n) **bestial** mask, more reminiscent of a hobgoblin than a human being.

18. The _____garish_____ movie palaces of an earlier era have given way to smaller theaters, decorated in a simpler, more austere style.

19. Many a now-forgotten "movie great" has discovered to his or her chagrin that fame may indeed be as _____ephemeral_____ as a passing shower.

20. He had the _____effrontery_____ to come into my own home to tell me what I should do to help him.

Synonyms

*Choose the word from this unit that is **the same** or **most nearly the same** in meaning as the **boldface** word or expression in the given phrase. Write the word on the line provided.*

1. the **dogged** researcher   pertinacious

2. donned fashionable **attire**   raiment

3. an influential **set** of friends   coterie

4. willingly **abandoned** their prejudices   jettisoned

5. their **apt** meeting   felicitous

6. had the **gall** to demand an apology   effrontery

7. prone to **fanciful** get-rich-quick schemes   illusory

8. will surely **relieve** his anxiety   allay

9. her **complement** at the rival company   counterpart

10. condemned the militia's **depraved** behavior   bestial

11. **protested** when asked to leave   demurred

12. a well-known **people-hater**   misanthrope

13. **ornamented** with high-sounding phrases   embellished

14. ignore those **inconsequential** objections   picayune

15. the **fleeting** nature of power   ephemeral

Antonyms

*Choose the word from this unit that is **most nearly opposite** in meaning to the **boldface** word or expression in the given phrase. Write the word on the line provided.*

16. their **forthright** attempt to withdraw   furtive

17. **moderate** increases in profits   inordinate

18. the **wealthy** inhabitants of the big cities   indigent

19. a very **grim** lunch meeting   convivial

20. **understated** taste in home furnishings   garish

Choosing the Right Word

Circle the **boldface** word that more satisfactorily completes each of the following sentences.

1. The Presidency is the "toughest job in the world" because it makes such (**bestial, inordinate**) demands on a person's time, energy, and ingenuity.

2. The famous sleuth pursued his investigation with all the (**pertinacity, conviviality**) of a lion stalking its dinner.

3. "You mean you had the (**effrontery, demur**) to ask for a raise when everyone knows you've been goofing off lately?" I asked in amazement.

4. An emotion so fickle and (**ephemeral, pertinacious**) does not deserve to be categorized as "love."

5. The kind of (**garish, picayune**) theatrical makeup used by circus clowns is not suitable for an elegant fashion model.

6. Nothing we could say seemed to (**demur, allay**) her grief over the loss of her dog.

7. The proofreader didn't notice any significant flaws in the writing, but he did find a few (**ephemeral, picayune**) defects in the typesetting.

8. To anyone as fond of horses as I am, the stable and the tack room provide as (**indigent, convivial**) an atmosphere as one could wish for.

9. If installment buying is not carefully controlled, the benefits that can accrue from it may prove wholly (**illusory, inordinate**).

10. I am flattered that you want me to chair the meeting, but I must (**demur, embellish**) on the grounds of my youth and inexperience.

11. I can always come up with the crushing rejoinder, the dazzling witticism, or the (**furtive, felicitous**) phrase—about an hour after I need it!

12. When the facts of a matter speak so plainly for themselves, we shouldn't seek to (**jettison, embellish**) them.

13. Somehow, it depresses me to think that with the approach of winter this magnificent old tree will surrender all its leafy (**effrontery, raiment**).

14. She has neither the starry-eyed optimism of the idealist nor the mordant cynicism of the (**coterie, misanthrope**).

15. Though the Federal government does much to help the (**indigent, illusory**), private charities play no small part in their welfare.

16. Often the antonym of a given English word is not so much its opposite as its (**embellishment, counterpart**)—for example, *actor* and *actress*.

17. Every dynamic and successful society must be able to (**jettison, allay**) ideas and institutions that have outlived their usefulness.

18. As the rock star's popularity began to skyrocket, what had been a small (**coterie, raiment**) of admirers became an unruly mob.

19. The atrocities committed by the (**garish, bestial**) commanders of such concentration camps as Auschwitz appalled the civilized world.

20. When I returned to the office earlier than expected, I caught the little snoop (**felicitously, furtively**) going through the papers on my desk.

Read the following passage, in which some of the words you have studied in this unit appear in **boldface** type. Then complete each statement given below the passage by circling the letter of the item that is **the same** or **almost the same** in meaning as the highlighted word.

Hello Dolley!

(Line)

Dolley Madison (1768–1849), wife of the fourth President of the United States, James Madison, was the first great Washington hostess and an outstanding First Lady. In 1794 she married then Congressman James Madison of Virginia. Despite their differences (he was seventeen years older), their marriage was a long and **felicitous** one. In fact, her warmth (5) and personal grace seemed the perfect **counterpart** to Madison's formality and social awkwardness. After Madison became President, Mrs. Madison proved a political and social asset as well. Her letters to him (10) reveal her shrewd evaluation of the issues of the day, and an ease of communication between husband and wife on matters beyond the domestic and social.

As First Lady, Dolley Madison was best (15) known for her **convivial** Wednesday evening receptions at the White House, where influential politicians and dignitaries met and mingled. At a time of intense rivalry between political parties, these gatherings helped to **allay** some of the (20) festering bitterness between the Federalists and the Republicans, making it easier for Madison to handle a divided Congress.

Dolley Madison also brought a new sense of informality and individualism to prim and (25) proper Washington society. She set tongues wagging, for example, when she wore a buff-colored velvet dress with a very **garish** purple bonnet, trimmed in white satin and feathers, to the Inaugural Ball. Misgivings about her unusual **raiment**, however, always gave way to pleasure at her ability to put others at ease. (30)

The state dining room of the White House where Dolley Madison entertained statesmen and socialites alike

---

1. Felicitous (line 5) most nearly means
a. prosperous   c. happy
b. peaceful   d. miserable

2. The meaning of **counterpart** (line 7) is
a. complement   c. contrast
b. response   d. tribute

3. Convivial (line 16) is best defined as
a. controversial   c. fashionable
b. genial   d. famous

4. The meaning of **allay** (line 20) is
a. sharpen   c. publicize
b. hide   d. moderate

5. Garish (line 28) most nearly means
a. stylish   c. large
b. expensive   d. gaudy

6. Raiment (line 29) most nearly means
a. attire   c. speech
b. ancestry   d. personality

Definitions

Note carefully the spelling, pronunciation, part(s) of speech, and definition(s) of each of the following words. Then write the word in the blank space(s) in the illustrative sentence(s) following. Finally, study the lists of synonyms and antonyms given at the end of each entry.

1. allege
(ə lej′)

(*v.*) to assert without proof or confirmation

The newspaper tabloid _____**alleged**_____ that the movie star and the director were having creative differences.

SYNONYMS: claim, contend
ANTONYMS: prove, deny

2. arrant
(ar′ ənt)

(*adj.*) thoroughgoing, out-and-out; shameless, blatant

In Shakespeare's tragedy the audience sees clearly that Iago is an _____**arrant**_____ scoundrel, but Othello is blind to his treachery.

SYNONYMS: egregious, unmitigated

3. badinage
(bad ə näzh′)

(*n.*) light and playful conversation

I enjoy the delightful _____**badinage**_____ between stars like Spencer Tracy and Katherine Hepburn in 1940s movies.

SYNONYMS: banter, persiflage, repartee
ANTONYM: sermon

4. conciliate
(kən sil′ ē āt)

(*v.*) to overcome the distrust of, win over; to appease, pacify; to reconcile, make consistent

Because of the weakness of our army, we had to try to _____**conciliate**_____ the enemy.

SYNONYM: placate, mollify, propitiate
ANTONYMS: antagonize, alienate, estrange

5. countermand
(kaün′ tər mand)

(*v.*) to cancel or reverse one order or command with another that is contrary to the first

Today's directive clearly _____**countermanded**_____ all previous instructions on how to exit the building in case of fire.

SYNONYMS: recall, revoke
ANTONYMS: reaffirm, reassert

6. echelon
(esh′ ə län)

(*n.*) one of a series of grades in an organization or field of activity; an organized military unit; a steplike formation or arrangement

Although the civil servant began in the lower _____**echelon**_____ of government service, he rose quickly through the ranks.

SYNONYMS: level, rank

7. exacerbate
(eg zas′ ər bāt)

(*v.*) to make more violent, severe, bitter, or painful

Shouting and name-calling are sure to _____ exacerbate _____ any quarrel.

SYNONYMS: aggravate, intensify, worsen
ANTONYMS: alleviate, mitigate, ameliorate

8. fatuous
(fach′ ü əs)

(*adj.*) stupid or foolish in a self-satisfied way

In order to discredit the candidate, the columnist quoted some of his more _____ fatuous _____, self-serving remarks.

SYNONYMS: silly, vapid, inane, doltish, vacuous
ANTONYMS: sensible, intelligent, perceptive, bright

9. irrefutable
(ir i fyü′ tə bəl)

(*adj.*) impossible to disprove; beyond argument

The jury felt the prosecution presented them with _____ irrefutable _____ evidence of the defendant's guilt.

SYNONYMS: indisputable, incontrovertible, undeniable
ANTONYMS: disputable, indefensible, untenable

10. juggernaut
(jəg′ ər nôt)

(*n.*) a massive and inescapable force or object that crushes whatever is in its path

Any population that has experienced the _____ juggernaut _____ of war firsthand will not easily forget its destructive power.

11. lackadaisical
(lak ə dā′ zə kəl)

(*adj.*) lacking spirit or interest, halfhearted

The team's performance in the late innings was _____ lackadaisical _____ because they were so far ahead.

SYNONYMS: listless, indolent, indifferent, lax
ANTONYMS: energetic, vigorous, wholehearted

12. litany
(lit′ ə nē)

(*n.*) a prayer consisting of short appeals to God recited by the leader alternating with responses from the congregation; any repetitive chant; a long list

Whenever she talks about her childhood, she recites an interminable _____ litany _____ of grievances.

SYNONYMS: rigmarole, catalog, megillah

13. macabre
(mə käb′ rə)

(*adj.*) grisly, gruesome; horrible, distressing; having death as a subject

The continuing popularity of horror movies suggests that one way to score at the box office is to exploit the _____ macabre _____.

SYNONYMS: grotesque, grim, ghoulish

14. paucity
(pô′ sə tē)

(*n.*) an inadequate quantity, scarcity, dearth

The senate campaign was marred by a _____**dearth**_____ of original ideas.

SYNONYM: lack
ANTONYMS: abundance, glut, plenitude, deluge

15. portend
(por tənd′)

(*v.*) to indicate beforehand that something is about to happen; to give advance warning of

In Shakespeare's plays, disturbances in the heavens usually _____**portend**_____ disaster or trouble in human affairs.

SYNONYMS: bode, foretell, foreshadow, suggest

16. raze
(rāz)

(*v.*) to tear down, destroy completely; to cut or scrape off or out

The town _____**razed**_____ the old schoolhouse to make room for a larger, more modern school complex.

SYNONYMS: pull down, demolish, shave off
ANTONYMS: build, construct, raise, erect

17. recant
(ri kant′)

(*v.*) to withdraw a statement or belief to which one has previously been committed, renounce, retract

On the stand, the defendant _____**recanted**_____ the guilty admissions she had made in her confession to the police.

SYNONYMS: repudiate, disavow
ANTONYMS: reaffirm, reassert

18. saturate
(sach′ ə rāt)

(*v.*) to soak thoroughly, fill to capacity; to satisfy fully

A sponge that is _____**saturated**_____ with water swells up but does not drip.

SYNONYMS: permeate, drench, flood, imbue
ANTONYM: drain

19. saturnine
(sat′ ər nīn)

(*adj.*) of a gloomy or surly disposition; cold or sluggish in mood

Ebenezer Scrooge, the main character of Dickens's *A Christmas Carol*, has a decidedly _____**saturnine**_____ temperament.

SYNONYMS: sullen, morose
ANTONYMS: lighthearted, cheerful, vivacious

20. slough
(sləf)

(*v.*) to cast off, discard; to get rid of something objectionable or unnecessary; to plod through as if through mud; (*n.*) a mire; a state of depression

At New Year's time, many people resolve to _____**slough**_____ off bad habits and start living better, healthier lives.

The advancing line of tanks became bogged down in a _____**slough**_____.

SYNONYMS: (*v.*) shed, slog
ANTONYMS: (*v.*) take on, acquire, assume

Completing the Sentence

From the words for this unit, choose the one that best completes each of the following sentences. Write the word in the space provided.

1. However much it may cost me, I will never _____ **recant** _____ the principles to which I have devoted my life.

2. No sooner had the feckless tsar decreed a general mobilization than he _____ **countermanded** _____ his order, only to reissue it a short time later.

3. Though some "home remedies" appear to alleviate the symptoms of a disease, they may in fact _____ **exacerbate** _____ the condition.

4. Ms. Ryan's warnings to the class to "review thoroughly" seemed to me to _____ **portend** _____ an usually difficult examination.

5. The men now being held in police custody are _____ **alleged** _____ to have robbed eight supermarkets over the last year.

6. Her friendly manner and disarming smile helped to _____ **conciliate** _____ those who opposed her views on the proposal.

7. The service in honor of the miners trapped in the underground collapse included prayers and _____ **litanies** _____.

8. We object to the policy of _____ **razing** _____ historic old buildings to make way for unsightly parking lots.

9. You are not going to do well in your job if you continue to work in such a(n) _____ **lackadaisical** _____ and desultory manner.

10. The enemy's lines crumpled before the mighty _____ **juggernaut** _____ of our attack like so much wheat before a harvester.

11. As a snake _____ **sloughs** _____ off its old skin, so he hoped to rid himself of his weaknesses and develop a new and better personality.

12. My shirt became so _____ **saturated** _____ with perspiration on that beastly day that I had to change it more than once during the match.

13. After he made that absurd remark, a(n) _____ **fatuous** _____ grin of self-congratulation spread like syrup across the lumpy pancake of his face.

14. "I find it terribly depressing to be around people whose dispositions are so _____ **saturnine** _____ and misanthropic," I remarked.

15. The breaking news story concerned corruption among the highest _____ **echelons** _____ of politics.

16. Only someone with a truly _____ **macabre** _____ sense of humor would decide to use a hearse as the family car or a coffin as a bed.

17. "It seems to me that such _____ **arrant** _____ hypocrisy is indicative of a thoroughly opportunistic approach to running for office," I said sadly.

18. The seriousness of the matter under discussion left no room for the type of lighthearted _____**badinage**_____ encountered in the locker room.

19. At first I thought it would be easy to shoot holes in their case, but I soon realized that their arguments were practically _____**irrefutable**_____ .

20. His four disastrous years in office were marked by a plenitude of promises and a(n) _____**paucity**_____ of performance.

Synonyms

*Choose the word from this unit that is **the same** or **most nearly the same** in meaning as the **boldface** word or expression in the given phrase. Write the word on the line provided.*

1. the **indisputable** evidence — irrefutable

2. the **banter** of the morning talk show hosts — badinage

3. the **egregious** corruption of the officials — arrant

4. **claimed** that a crime had been committed — alleged

5. **foreshadows** dangers to come — portends

6. an idea that **permeates** all aspects of society — saturates

7. will **aggravate** tensions between the rivals — exacerbate

8. a long **rigmarole** of questions and answers — litany

9. a **listless** response from voters — lackadaisical

10. the upper **levels** of power — echelons

11. tried to **placate** both sides in the dispute — conciliate

12. **revoked** the outgoing President's orders — countermanded

13. wore a very **grotesque** mask — macabre

14. crushed by the **force** of progress — juggernaut

15. **slog** through the seemingly endless files — slough

Antonyms

*Choose the word from this unit that is **most nearly opposite** in meaning to the **boldface** word or expression in the given phrase. Write the word on the line provided.*

16. a growing **abundance** of cheap labor — paucity

17. given to **lighthearted** predictions — saturnine

18. known for his **sensible** opinions — fatuous

19. has **reaffirmed** her support of free trade — recanted

20. **constructed** a downtown shopping district — razed

Circle the **boldface** word that more satisfactorily completes each of the following sentences.

1. By (**portending, sloughing**) off the artificiality of her first book, the novelist arrived at a style that was simple, genuine, and highly effective.

2. By denying your guilt without offering any explanation of your actions, you will only (**recant, exacerbate**) an already bad situation.

3. Not surprisingly, the committee's final report was an incongruous mixture of the astute and the (**irrefutable, fatuous**).

4. Stephen King's book *Danse* (**Macabre, Lackadaisical**) surveys popular and obscure horror fiction of the twentieth century.

5. With incredible unconcern, the nobles of Europe immersed themselves in social frivolities as the fearful (**juggernaut, litany**) of World War I steamrolled ineluctably toward them.

6. She excused herself from lending me the money I so desperately needed by (**conciliating, alleging**) that she had financial troubles of her own.

7. Over the years, hard work and unstinting devotion to duty have raised me from one (**echelon, paucity**) of company management to the next.

8. Economists believe that the drop in automobile sales and steel production (**countermands, portends**) serious problems for business in the future.

9. We have many capable and well-meaning people in our organization, but it seems to me that there is a (**paucity, juggernaut**) of real leadership.

10. It is a good deal easier to (**raze, allege**) an old building than it is to destroy a time-honored social institution.

11. I never ask anyone "How are you?" anymore because I am afraid I will be treated to an endless (**litany, badinage**) of symptoms and ailments.

12. His attempts at casual (**badinage, echelon**) did not conceal the fact that he was acutely embarrassed by his blunder.

13. What possible purpose will be served by setting up yet another hamburger stand in an area already (**saturated, sloughed**) with fast-food shops?

14. His debating technique is rooted in the firm belief that anything bellowed in a loud voice is absolutely (**saturnine, irrefutable**).

15. Our excitement at visiting the world-famous ruins was dampened by the (**lackadaisical, arrant**) attitude of the bored and listless guide.

16. In earlier times, people whose views conflicted with "received opinion" often had to (**recant, portend**) their ideas or face the consequences.

17. Only a(n) (**arrant, macabre**) knave would be capable of devising such an incredibly underhanded and treacherous scheme.

18. The authority of the Student Council is not absolute because the principal can (**countermand, exacerbate**) any of its decisions.

19. Someone with such a (**fatuous, saturnine**) outlook on life doesn't make an agreeable traveling companion, especially on a long journey.

20. The views of the two parties involved in this dispute are so diametrically opposed that it will be almost impossible to (**conciliate, saturate**) them.

Read the following passage, in which some of the words you have studied in this unit appear in **boldface** type. Then complete each statement given below the passage by circling the letter of the item that is **the same** or **almost the same** in meaning as the highlighted word.

(Line)

The Grass Might Be Greener

In December 2000 President Bill Clinton signed the historic Comprehensive Everglades Restoration Plan, a 7.8 billion-dollar project to rescue a unique natural habitat that was **irrefutably** on the brink of destruction. Before the twin **juggernauts** of development and agriculture transformed Florida's landscape,
(5)   the seasonally **saturated** lands known as the Everglades stretched from just south of Orlando to the Florida Keys. This 60-mile wide ecosystem was comprised of sawgrass marshes, wet prairies, muddy **sloughs**, and hardwood swamps. What made the region unique was the unpredictable changes in weather patterns that
(10)   created very wet and very dry periods. Indigenous wildlife adapted to these changes over the centuries, but the growing human population of South Florida wanted to control the flooding and secure a reliable water supply.
(15)   In 1947 ten feet of rain fell on South Florida, flooding most of the region, including parts of Miami. The residents agitated for government assistance, and to **conciliate** them, the Army Corps of Engineers initiated a massive flood
(20)   control project. Beginning in 1948, and for the next thirty years, an intricate network of canals and levees was built across the region, managing water flow for the benefit of farmers and the general population. These canals effectively cut
(25)   off the northern Everglades from the southern wetlands. This **exacerbated** conditions in the southern region not only because water flow was reduced, but also because fertilizers contaminated what water remained.

The bill President Clinton signed is meant to reverse these trends and restore as
(30)   much as 1.7 billion gallons of fresh water to the Everglades ecosystem.

This Everglades alligator may live as long as 35 years and weigh as much as 500 pounds.

---

1. Irrefutably (line 3) most nearly means
   a. remarkably   c. arguably
   b. indisputably   d. irreversibly

2. The meaning of **juggernauts** (line 4) is
   a. engines   c. benefits
   b. forces   d. industries

3. Saturated (line 5) is best defined as
   a. flooded   c. neglected
   b. cultivated   d. varied

4. The meaning of **sloughs** (line 7) is
   a. fields   c. ponds
   b. trails   d. mires

5. Conciliate (line 18) most nearly means
   a. silence   c. placate
   b. reward   d. divert

6. Exacerbated (line 26) most nearly means
   a. changed   b. improved
   b. favored   d. worsened

Definitions

Note carefully the spelling, pronunciation, part(s) of speech, and definition(s) of each of the following words. Then write the word in the blank space(s) in the illustrative sentence(s) following. Finally, study the lists of synonyms and antonyms given at the end of each entry.

1. acclamation
(ak lə mā′ shən)

(*n.*) a shout of welcome; an overwhelming verbal vote of approval

It is very rare for a presidential candidate to be nominated by _____ **acclamation** _____ from the convention floor.

SYNONYMS: ovation, cheering, plaudits
ANTONYMS: booing, hissing, jeers, catcalls

2. bucolic
(byü käl′ ik)

(*adj.*) characteristic of the countryside, rural; relating to shepherds and cowherds, pastoral

The Elizabethans who wrote of shepherds in ideal country settings were imitating the Greek _____ **bucolic** _____ poets.

SYNONYM: rustic
ANTONYMS: urban, metropolitan

3. calumniate
(kə ləm′ nē āt)

(*v.*) to slander; to accuse falsely and maliciously

Not only did the artist's enemy seek to discredit her while she was alive but tried to _____ **calumniate** _____ her memory as well.

SYNONYMS: defame, libel
ANTONYMS: flatter, whitewash, praise

4. chary
(châr′ ē)

(*adj.*) extremely cautious, hesitant, or slow (to); reserved, diffident

Since so many funds had been spent with so few results, they were _____ **chary** _____ about appropriating more money.

SYNONYMS: wary, skittish
ANTONYMS: heedless, reckless, incautious

5. collusion
(kə lü′ zhən)

(*n.*) secret agreement or cooperation

Years later, it was discovered that senior members of the company had been in _____ **collusion** _____ with the enemy.

SYNONYMS: conspiracy, plot, connivance, cahoots

6. dilettante
(dil′ ə tänt)

(*n.*) a dabbler in the arts; one who engages in an activity in an amateurish, trifling way; (*adj.*) superficial

Many people dismissed the poster artists of the 1960s as mere _____ **dilettantes** _____ with nothing serious to say about life or art.

SYNONYMS: amateur, trifler
ANTONYM: professional

7. imperturbable
(im pər tər' bə bəl)

(*adj.*) not easily excited; emotionally steady

The witness remained _____**imperturbable**_____ throughout the grueling cross-examination.

SYNONYMS: unflappable, unexcitable, serene, unruffled
ANTONYM: excitable

8. increment
(in' krə mənt)

(*n.*) an enlargement, increase, addition

Employees were added to the work force in ___**increments**___ of five to save money on training costs.

SYNONYMS: accretion, gain
ANTONYMS: loss, reduction, decrease

9. mandate
(man' dāt)

(*n.*) an authoritative command, formal order, authorization; (*v.*) to issue such an order

The peacekeepers were sent into the war-torn country under a UN _____**mandate**_____ to protect minority populations.

The environmental protection agency has ___**mandated**___ that all automobiles pass an annual emissions test.

SYNONYM: (*n.*) directive
ANTONYMS: (*v.*) forbid, ban, outlaw

10. paltry
(pôl' trē)

(*adj.*) trifling, insignificant; mean, despicable; inferior, trashy

The billionaire was so greedy that he contributed only a _____**paltry**_____ sum of money to charity each year.

SYNONYMS: measly, meager, piddling, trivial
ANTONYMS: gigantic, immense, colossal

11. paroxysm
(par' ək siz əm)

(*n.*) a sudden outburst; a spasm, convulsion

The children greeted the clown with a ___**paroxysm**___ of laughter when he began making his funny faces.

SYNONYMS: fit, seizure

12. pedantry
(ped' ən trē)

(*n.*) a pretentious display of knowledge; overly rigid attention to rules and details

The fussy music professor was distinguished more for her _____**pedantry**_____ than her true scholarship.

SYNONYMS: nit-picking, hairsplitting, pettifoggery

13. peregrination
(per ə grə nā' shən)

(*n.*) the act of traveling; an excursion, especially on foot or to a foreign country

After returning from my _____**peregrination**_____ throughout South America, I began writing a book about my experiences.

SYNONYMS: journey, wandering, odyssey

14. redolent
(red′ ə lənt)

(*adj.*) fragrant, smelling strongly; tending to arouse memories or create an aura

My grandmother's kitchen was always _____ **redolent** _____ with the smells of baking.

SYNONYMS: evocative, reminiscent, aromatic
ANTONYMS: unevocative, odorless

15. refulgent
(ri fəl′ jənt)

(*adj.*) shining, radiant, resplendent

The swift-flowing stream beside our house was _____ **refulgent** _____ in the morning light.

SYNONYMS: luminous, splendid
ANTONYMS: dim, dark, obscure, dingy, dull, murky

16. shibboleth
(shib′ ə leth)

(*n.*) a word, expression, or custom that distinguishes a particular group of persons from all others; a commonplace saying or truism

By the time Election Day finally rolls around, most voters are tired of hearing the same old slogans and ____ **shibboleths** ____.

SYNONYMS: catchphrase, password, slogan

17. tyro
(tī′ rō)

(*n.*) a beginner, novice; one with little or no background or skill

You cannot expect a mere _____ **tyro** _____ to perform like a veteran in his first season of major league play.

SYNONYM: neophyte
ANTONYMS: veteran, past master, expert

18. unremitting
(ən ri mit′ iŋ)

(*adj.*) not stopping, maintained steadily, never letting up, relentless

The social laws in Edith Wharton's novels are _____ **unremitting** _____.

SYNONYMS: constant, incessant, unrelenting
ANTONYMS: desultory, intermittent

19. vacillate
(vas′ ə lāt)

(*v.*) to swing indecisively from one idea or course of action to another; to waver weakly in mind or will

Someone who _____ **vacillates** _____ in a crisis should not be in a position of leadership.

SYNONYMS: seesaw, fluctuate, oscillate
ANTONYM: persevere

20. vituperative
(vī tü′ pər ə tiv)

(*adj.*) harshly abusive, severely scolding

That _____ **vituperative** _____ speech in which she blamed others for her own mistakes may have cost her the election.

SYNONYMS: abusive, scurrilous, insulting
ANTONYMS: complimentary, laudatory, flattering

Completing the Sentence

From the words for this unit, choose the one that best completes each of the following sentences. Write the word in the space provided.

1. As we waited through the long night for the arrival of the rescue party, we _____**vacillated**_____ between hope and despair.

2. However long and hard the struggle, we must be _____**unremitting**_____ in our efforts to wipe out racism in this country.

3. She may have great musical talents, but she will get nowhere so long as she has the casual attitude of the _____**dilettante**_____.

4. The painting shows a restfully _____**bucolic**_____ scene, with some cows grazing placidly in a meadow as their shepherd dozes under a bush.

5. I had expected a decent tip from the party of six that I waited on early that evening, but all I got was a(n) _____**paltry**_____ two bucks!

6. The scene may seem ordinary to you, but I find it _____**redolent**_____ with memories of happy summers spent in these woods.

7. Since Lincoln is now considered a great national hero, it is hard to believe that he was bitterly _____**calumniated**_____ when he was President.

8. The contractor was suspected of having acted in _____**collusion**_____ with a state official to fix the bids on certain public works contracts.

9. "The overwhelming victory I have won at the polls," the Governor-elect said, "has given me a clear _____**mandate**_____ to carry out my program."

10. As a(n) _____**refulgent**_____ summer sun sank slowly in the west, the skies were ablaze with color.

11. In a series of searing orations, filled with the most _____**vituperative**_____ language, Cicero launched the full battery of political invective against the hapless Mark Antony.

12. Every time I sign a new lease on my apartment, my rent goes up, though the _____**increments**_____ are not usually very large.

13. I thought I was unexcitable, but she is as _____**imperturbable**_____ as the granite lions in front of the public library.

14. Even the merest _____**tyro**_____ in the use of firearms knows that a gun should never be pointed at another person.

15. Since Lucy had expected no more than polite applause, she was delighted by the _____**acclamation**_____ she received from the audience.

16. The Pledge of Allegiance is no mere _____**shibboleth**_____ to be recited mechanically and without understanding like some advertising jingle.

17. In my various _____**peregrinations**_____ through that vast metropolis, I ran across many curious old buildings that the ordinary tourist never sees.

18. I have learned from long experience to be extremely _____ chary _____ about offering advice when it has not been requested.

19. Seized by a(n) _____ paroxysm _____ of rage, he began to beat the bars of his cell with his bare hands.

20. It is sheer _____ pedantry _____ to insist upon applying the rules of formal literary composition to everyday speech and writing.

Synonyms

*Choose the word from this unit that is **the same** or **most nearly the same** in meaning as the **boldface** word or expression in the given phrase. Write the word on the line provided.*

1. evocative of old memories _____ redolent _____

2. in **cahoots** with the competition _____ collusion _____

3. kept up the **constant** pressure to surrender _____ unremitting _____

4. greeted with an overwhelming **ovation** _____ acclamation _____

5. bored us with his **hairsplitting** _____ pedantry _____

6. overcome by a **fit** of anger _____ paroxysm _____

7. reluctantly ended her **journeys** _____ peregrinations _____

8. seesawed in their commitments _____ vacillated _____

9. keeps repeating the tired old **catchphrases** _____ shibboleths _____

10. slandered his rivals at every opportunity _____ calumniated _____

11. labeled a mere **trifler** by the experts _____ dilettante _____

12. an urgent **directive** from the President _____ mandate _____

13. a **scurrilous** response to the question _____ vituperative _____

14. wary of flattery and favor-seekers _____ chary _____

15. painted a charming **rustic** scene _____ bucolic _____

Antonyms

*Choose the word from this unit that is **most nearly opposite** in meaning to the **boldface** word or expression in the given phrase. Write the word on the line provided.*

16. is **excitable** when challenged _____ imperturbable _____

17. a **colossal** amount of unpaid debts _____ paltry _____

18. reported a steady **loss** in annual sales _____ increment _____

19. looked up at the **murky** dawn sky _____ refulgent _____

20. an **expert** in the art of fencing _____ tyro _____

Choosing the Right Word

*Circle the **boldface** word that more satisfactorily completes each of the following sentences.*

1. Not satisfied with the slow (**increment,** peregrination) of his savings in a bank account, he turned to speculation in the stock market.

2. Are we to try to make a realistic analysis of our alternatives or let ourselves be distracted by slogans and (tyros, **shibboleths**)?

3. Perhaps he would be less lyrical about the delights of the (**bucolic,** redolent) life if, like me, he had grown up on a farm in Kansas.

4. It has long been known that some twisted and unhappy people derive a kind of satisfaction from (**calumniating,** colluding) others.

5. Once the senator's nomination became a certainty, all opposition to him evaporated, and he was named by (vituperation, **acclamation**).

6. During the course of my (**peregrinations,** paroxysms) through the world of books, I have picked up all kinds of useful information.

7. The phrase "We the people" in the Constitution indicates that the ultimate (**mandate,** vacillation) of our government comes from the popular will.

8. Since she comes from a rural area, she expresses herself in language that is (**redolent,** paltry) of the farm and of country life in general.

9. It is easy to criticize him, but how can we overlook the fact that for 20 years he has worked (**unremittingly,** charily) to help the homeless?

10. Although he has been in this business for 20 years, he still has the sublime innocence of the most helpless (**tyro,** shibboleth).

11. A (**paroxysm,** pedantry) of indignation flashed though the community, and the streets filled with angry people ready to protest the proposal.

12. Clad in the (**refulgent,** dilettante) armor of moral rectitude, he sallied forth to do battle with the forces of evil.

13. How do you have the nerve to offer such a(n) (**paltry,** unremitting) sum for this magnificent "antique" car!

14. Isn't it sheer (**pedantry,** refulgence) on his part to use terms like *Proustian* and *Kafkaesque*, when he knows they mean nothing to his audience?

15. The same difficulties that serve as a challenge to the true professional will be a crushing discouragement to the typical (mandate, **dilettante**).

16. If we (**vacillate,** increment) now at adopting a tough energy policy, we may find ourselves in a desperate situation in the future.

17. I'm not sure if Tom's (**imperturbable,** collusive) spirit is due to toughness or to an inability to understand the dangers of the situation.

18. I am perfectly willing to listen to a reasonable complaint, but I will not put up with that kind of (bucolic, **vituperative**) backbiting.

19. The gambler's predictions of the game scores were so incredibly accurate that we suspected some form of (acclamation, **collusion**).

20. Because my teacher is usually so (**chary,** imperturbable) of giving compliments, I felt especially good when she spoke well of my essay

*Read the following passage, in which some of the words you have studied in this unit appear in **boldface** type. Then complete each statement given below the passage by circling the letter of the item that is **the same** or **almost the same** in meaning as the highlighted word.*

At Home in the Woods

(Line)

A lifelong lover of the outdoors and one of America's most distinguished nature essayists, John Burroughs (1837–1921) was born on a farm near Roxbury, New York, in the **bucolic** Catskill Mountain region. After a **paltry** early education, Burroughs, at 17, became a country schoolteacher in a small Catskill (5) town, and eventually managed to finance some advanced study at the Ashland Collegiate Institute and the Cooperstown Seminary.

John Burroughs at home in Roxbury, N.Y., 1910

In 1860 Burroughs began writing on (10) natural and philosophical subjects for some of the leading periodicals of the day. The young **tyro** learned the essayist's art quickly and became a frequent contributor to the *Atlantic Monthly*, which he later referred to as (15) his "university." While some of his readers appreciated the echoes of Emerson in these early essays, others responded negatively to what they experienced as Burroughs' dry **pedantry**. (20)

In 1863 Burroughs took a job as a clerk in Washington, D.C. While there, he became a close friend of the poet Walt Whitman, and this relationship provided him with material for his first book: *Notes on Walt Whitman as Poet and Person.* In 1872 Burroughs (25) returned to his native Catskills and began writing more concretely about the wonders he encountered during his **peregrinations** in the local woodlands. His writings from this period show the influence of Whitman's expansive style. **Redolent** of a more leisurely time, his works are still remembered today for their appreciation of the simple. (30)

---

1. Bucolic (line 3) most nearly means
a. backward
b. distant
c. rugged
d. rustic

2. The meaning of **paltry** (line 3) is
a. meager
b. sterling
c. conventional
d. boring

3. Tyro (line 13) is best defined as
a. fighter
b. neophyte
c. invalid
d. scholar

4. The meaning of **pedantry** (line 20) is
a. style
b. wit
c. nit-picking
d. propaganda

5. Peregrinations (line 27) means
a. dwellings
b. speeches
c. wanderings
d. writings

6. Redolent (line 29) most nearly means
a. reminiscent
b. stinking
c. composed
d. proud

Vocabulary for Comprehension

*Read the following passage, in which some of the words you have studied in Units 7–9 appear in **boldface** type. Then answer questions 1–12 on page 106 on the basis of what is <u>stated</u> or <u>implied</u> in the passage and in the introductory statement.*

As this passage shows, the central goal of the League of Women Voters is good citizenship.

(Line)

The League of Women Voters is a citizen advocacy organization that was developed as a result of the women's suffrage movement. It was
(5) founded in 1920 by the suffragist Carrie Chapman Catt, an **unremitting** champion of women's rights and social reform. Its immediate mission was to help inform and empower the
(10) 20 million American women who were enfranchised as a result of the passage in 1920 of the Nineteenth Amendment to the U.S. Constitution.

Over the years, however, the League
(15) has advocated issues less directly related to the women's movement. It has supported programs as diverse as assistance to the **indigent** during the Great Depression, civil rights in the
(20) 1960s, and environmental conservation and campaign finance reform today. Though the League vigorously champions its causes, it sees itself as staunchly nonpartisan. In other words,
(25) the League supports programs and policies but **demurs** when asked to endorse specific parties or candidates. This stance has led critics on both the left and the right to **allege** that the
(30) League is a **coterie** of activists with a hidden agenda concealed behind a banner of nonpartisanship. The

League replies that it is undeniably political but definitely not partisan.
(35) The League also takes great pride in its grassroots style of organization. Policy decisions are not made by a few leaders in the upper **echelons** of the organization, but rather are arrived
(40) at by intense study, debate, and consensus building among the rank-and-file membership at the chapter level. This reflects the League's attitude toward the power of well-
(45) informed citizens in a democracy, who ideally will make choices that will lead to a better life for all.

1. The main purpose of the first paragraph (lines 1–13) is to
   a. show how the League of Women Voters got its name
   b. discuss the origins of the League
   c. highlight the career of Carrie Chapman Catt
   d. analyze the opposition to the Nineteenth Amendment
   e. explain why women had to wait so long for the vote

2. According to the passage, the League's original mission was to
   a. lobby for passage of the Nineteenth Amendment
   b. advise Republican candidates in the 1920 election
   c. inform and empower newly enfranchised women voters
   d. lobby for campaign finance reform
   e. create a grassroots organization of local chapters

3. The meaning of **unremitting** (line 6) is
   a. undefeated
   b. intolerant
   c. unrelenting
   d. incomparable
   e. controversial

4. **Indigent** (line 18) most nearly means
   a. handicapped
   b. despondent
   c. penniless
   d. homeless
   e. oppressed

5. **Demurs** (line 26) is best defined as
   a. objects
   b. rethinks
   c. consents
   d. waffles
   e. debates

6. The meaning of **allege** (line 29) is
   a. imply
   b. dispute
   c. refute
   d. deny
   e. claim

7. **Coterie** (line 30) most nearly means
   a. clique
   b. party
   c. conspiracy
   d. family
   e. gang

8. From the details the author provides in paragraph 2 (lines 14–34), you may reasonably infer that the League has at times been
   a. partisan
   b. inconsistent
   c. unsuccessful
   d. controversial
   e. undemocratic

9. Which of the following best identifies the comparison/contrast the writer makes in paragraph 2?
   a. the Great Depression vs. the Civil Rights movement
   b. Republicans vs. Democrats
   c. national issues vs. local issues
   d. political vs. partisan
   e. critics on the left vs. critics on the right

10. The author identifies all of the following as activities of the League EXCEPT
    a. informing citizens
    b. supporting environmental conservation
    c. advocating campaign finance reform
    d. assisting the indigent
    e. lobbying for tax cuts

11. **Echelons** (line 38) most nearly means
    a. salaries
    b. levels
    c. offices
    d. classes
    e. floors

12. The author's attitude toward the League may best be described as
    a. hostile
    b. skeptical
    c. romantic
    d. admiring
    e. reflective

Grammar in Context

In the sentence "The League of Women Voters is a citizen advocacy organization that was developed as a result of the women's suffrage movement (lines 1–4 on page 105), the relative pronoun *that* has a clear antecedent, the noun *organization*. If a pronoun does not have a clear antecedent, however, ambiguity or confusion may result. Clear writers avoid faulty **pronoun reference and shift**.

Ambiguous pronoun reference occurs when a pronoun can refer to either of two antecedents, as in the sentence "Harriet supported Clare because she was convinced the chapter needed new leadership." *General reference* occurs when a pronoun refers to a general idea rather than to a specific word or phrase, as in the sentence "The League does not endorse individual candidates; this has led to criticism." *Weak reference* occurs when a pronoun refers to an antecedent that has not been expressed, as in the sentence "We attended the candidates' debates but did not endorse a single one." *Indefinite or illogical pronoun shift* occurs when there is an unexpected shift in number or person between a pronoun and its antecedent, as in the sentence "Members of the League study the issues, and you also need patience to educate voters.

On the lines provided, rewrite each of the following sentences, correcting errors in pronoun reference or shift. Write "correct" if the sentence is correct.
Answers may vary; sample answers given.

1. Carrie Chapman Catt founded the League of Women Voters in 1920. It was a historic action.

Carrie Chapman Catt founded the League of Women Voters in 1920. Her action was historic.

2. The League embarked on its immediate mission, which was to inform 20 million women voters.

correct

3. In that magazine article, it describes the League's assistance to the indigent during the Great Depression.

That magazine article describes the League's assistance to the indigent during the Great Depression.

4. The people want good leaders, but many voters do not think that is a strong point of any of the candidates.

The people want good leadership, but many voters do not think that it is a strong point of any of the candidates.

5. The rivalry between Caroline and Sandra ended when she was elected chapter president.

The rivalry between Caroline and Sandra ended when Sandra was elected chapter president.

6. A grassroots style of organization is where you make decisions among the rank-and-file membership.

In a grassroots style of organization, decisions are made among the rank-and-file membership.

Two-Word Completions

Circle the pair of words that best complete the meaning of each of the following passages.

See pages T38–T48 for explanations of answers.

1. Only a thoroughgoing _____ would enjoy castigating other people's behavior in such unremittingly harsh and _____ language.
a. pedant . . . felicitous
b. misanthrope . . . vituperative
c. tyro . . . arrant
d. dilettante . . . convivial

2. The speed with which the Kaiser issued, then _____, then reissued orders during the crisis was indicative of his essentially weak and _____ personality.
a. embellished . . . pertinacious
b. recanted . . . imperturbable
c. demurred . . . fatuous
d. countermanded . . . vacillating

3. The _____ rains had so _____ the ground over which we passed that it actually squished and gurgled in protest as we trod on it, and our attack had to be postponed until the sun came out again.
a. inordinate . . . razed
b. ephemeral . . . embellished
c. unremitting . . . saturated
d. bestial . . . jettisoned

4. At the June 1961 summit meetings in Vienna, President John Kennedy met with his Soviet _____, Nikita Khrushchev, in an effort to deal with sources of friction between the two superpowers and _____ international fears that the so-called cold war was heating up.
a. counterpart . . . allay
b. raiment . . . mandate
c. coterie . . . exacerbate
d. shibboleth . . . conciliate

5. Though the official is _____ to have been in cahoots with the swindlers, so far no substantive evidence has been brought forward to prove _____.
a. portended . . . acclamation
b. demurred . . . peregrination
c. alleged . . . collusion
d. calumniated . . . badinage

6. In Chaucer's *Canterbury Tales*, twenty-nine travelers from various _____ of society set out for Canterbury on a pilgrimage to the shrine of Saint Thomas Beckett. At night the _____ of travelers share their stories in order to help time pass.
a. mandates . . . collusion
b. litanies . . . raiment
c. echelons . . . coterie
d. shibboleths . . . paucity

Choosing the Right Meaning

Read each sentence carefully. Then circle the item that best completes the statement below the sentence.

See pages T38–T48 for explanations of answers.

The prodigious sums advanced to best-selling authors for tales of murder and mayhem would seem to put the lie to the old shibboleth "Crime doesn't pay." (2)

1. The best definition for the word **shibboleth** in line 2 is

   a. password   b. custom   c. slogan   (d. truism)

"Canst thou not minister to a mind diseased,
Pluck from the memory a rooted sorrow, (2)
Raze out the written troubles of the brain . . . ?"
    (Shakespeare, *Macbeth,* V, 3, 40–42)

2. The phrase **Raze out** in line 3 most nearly means

   a. tear down   c. destroy completely
   (b. cut out)   d. demolish

When the jeep broke down in the middle of the bog, there was nothing left for us but to slough through the mud on foot. (2)

3. In line 2 the phrase **slough through** is used to mean

   a. cast off   b. shed   (c. slog through)   d. slither over

Though computers have long since eclipsed human beings in the ability to perform complex mathematical calculations, as reasoning entities they are (2) still comparatively bestial.

4. The word **bestial** in line 3 most nearly means

   (a. subhuman in intelligence)   c. depraved and brutal
   b. beastlike   d. inferior

Antonyms

*In each of the following groups, circle the word or expression that is most nearly the **opposite** of the word in **boldface** type.*

1. ephemeral
a. scheduled
b. infallible
(c. perpetual)
d. deleterious

2. garish
a. inventive
b. exciting
c. tasteless
(d. understated)

3. fatuous
a. conceited
b. vapid
(c. perceptive)
d. surprised

4. calumniate
(a. flatter)
b. introduce
c. defame
d. debate

5. indigent
(a. wealthy)
b. ethnic
c. poor
d. segregated

6. irrefutable
a. startling
(b. disputable)
c. unbiased
d. undeniable

7. badinage
a. persiflage
b. raillery
(c. sermon)
d. exception

8. convivial
(a. grim)
b. salutary
c. sociable
d. mysterious

9. furtive
(a. open)
b. sneaky
c. sorrowful
d. ghostly

11. razed
a. inspected
(b. erected)
c. destroyed
d. criticized

13. recant
(a. reaffirm)
b. refute
c. condemn
d. forget

15. felicitous
a. apt
b. witty
(c. inappropriate)
d. negative

10. acclamation
a. bias
b. cheers
(c. jeers)
d. departure

12. alleged
a. novice
b. veteran
c. bungling
(d. proven)

14. jettison
a. eliminate
b. improve
(c. retain)
d. grasp

16. paucity
a. dearth
(b. abundance)
c. destruction
d. arrival

Word Families

A. *On the line provided, write the word you have learned in Units 7–9 that is related to each of the following nouns.*
EXAMPLE: allegation—**allege**

1. portent, portentousness	portend
2. bestiality, beast	bestial
3. saturation, saturator, saturant	saturate
4. indigence	indigent
5. exacerbation	exacerbate
6. refulgence	refulgent
7. conviviality	convivial
8. felicity, felicitousness, felicitation	felicitous
9. illusoriness, illusion	illusory
10. conciliator, conciliation	conciliate
11. vituperation, vituperator	vituperative
12. embellishment, embellisher	embellish
13. pertinacity	pertinacious
14. vacillation, vacillator	vacillate
15. paltriness	paltry

B. *On the line provided, write the word you have learned in Units 7–9 that is related to each of the following verbs.*
EXAMPLE: acclaim—**acclamation**

16. felicitate	felicitous
17. collude	collusion
18. perturb	imperturbable
19. vituperate	vituperative
20. refute	irrefutable

Word Associations

In each of the following groups, circle the word that is best defined or suggested by the given phrase.

1. just a beginner at tennis
a. counterpart   b. dilettante   c. misanthrope   (d. tyro)

2. She fills her time with inconsequential work.
(a. picayune)   b. saturnine   c. pertinacious   d. unremitting

3. "Why does he have to show off by quoting from Latin poets!"
a. coterie   (b. pedantry)   c. badinage   d. paucity

4. laughed until our stomachs hurt
a. shibboleth   b. acclamation   c. misanthrope   (d. paroxysm)

5. indications that we may find ourselves in bad trouble
a. calumniate   b. conciliate   c. saturate   (d. portend)

6. a brazen request not warranted by circumstances
a. raiment   (b. effrontery)   c. badinage   d. paucity

7. kept us laughing with their interchange of jokes and quips
a. paucity   (b. badinage)   c. dilettante   d. litany

8. cancel the legislation of the previous commissioner
a. vacillate   b. slough   c. allege   (d. countermand)

9. the equivalent of our President in a foreign government
a. misanthrope   b. shibboleth   c. tyro   (d. counterpart)

10. a nightly bedtime story that calmed the child's fears
a. countermand   b. demur   (c. allay)   d. portend

11. a mirage or a will-o'-the-wisp
(a. illusory)   b. chary   c. convivial   d. garish

12. "He seems to do everything in a halfhearted, uninterested way."
a. refulgent   b. arrant   c. macabre   (d. lackadaisical)

13. gloomy, serious, and with little to say
a. convivial   (b. saturnine)   c. bucolic   d. imperturbable

14. a force of nature as unstoppable as the changing of the seasons
a. paroxysm   b. litany   c. slough   (d. juggernaut)

15. "Unfortunately, we had to get rid of him to protect our interests."
(a. jettison)   b. demur   c. portend   d. embellish

16. a long list of grievances
a. collusion   b. badinage   (c. litany)   d. peregrination

17. look forward to the annual salary increase
a. collusion   (b. increment)   c. shibboleth   d. dilettante

18. flowers that emit a strong, sweet smell
a. refulgent   b. illusory   (c. redolent)   d. chary

19. a mire
a. paroxysm   b. acclamation   c. misanthrope   (d. slough)

20. a car alarm that sounded for what seemed like an eternity
(a. unremitting)   b. portending   c. bucolic   d. chary

Building with Classical Roots

clam, claim—to cry out, shout, call

This root appears in **acclamation** (page 98). The literal meaning of acclamation is "shouting at," but it now suggests "applause" or "an overwhelmingly favorable oral vote." Some other words based on the same root are listed below.

acclaim	clamorous	disclaimer	proclamation
claimant	declaim	irreclaimable	reclamation

From the list of words above, choose the one that corresponds to each of the brief definitions below. Write the word in the blank space in the illustrative sentence below the definition.

1. to speak like an orator; to recite in public, make a public speech; to speak bitterly against

The actor would _____**declaim**_____ lines from Shakespeare in response to any comment.

2. an official or formal public announcement

The clerk posted the latest mayoral _____**proclamation**_____ at the entrance to City Hall.

3. a denial or disavowal of responsibility or connection; a formal refusal of one's rights or claims

The manufacturer issued a swift _____**disclaimer**_____ after mediocre reviews of its new product.

4. incapable of being reformed; incapable of being rendered useful

That region of the park is nothing more than _____**irreclaimable**_____ swampland.

5. the act of bringing back or restoring to a normal or useful condition (*"to call back"*)

Innovative irrigation techniques have resulted in the _____**reclamation**_____ of much of the desert.

6. to applaud; to indicate strong approval; noisy and enthusiastic applause

The winning team enjoyed vigorous public _____**acclaim**_____ in a ticker-tape parade.

7. a person who asserts a right or title

After many years, the estranged son resurfaced as the last _____**claimant**_____ to the estate.

8. marked by loud confusion or outcry; noisily insistent (*"crying out"*)

The protesters outside the White House made _____**clamorous**_____ demands for reform.

From the list of words on page 112, choose the one that best completes each of the following sentences. Write the word in the blank space provided.

1. "By spurning every opportunity to turn away from a life of crime," the judge said to the repeat offender, "you have proven yourself ____**irreclaimable**____."

2. Is there anything in literature to match the eloquence of the funeral speech that William Shakespeare has Mark Antony ____**declaim**____ over the body of Caesar!

3. Throughout the realm, the queen's subjects gathered to hear the ____**proclamation**____ announcing the birth of an heir to the throne.

4. For legal purposes, the film carried a brief ____**disclaimer**____ stating that any resemblance between the characters portrayed and real persons was purely coincidental.

5. The primary objective of our penal system should be the ____**reclamation**____ of the great majority of inmates, so that they will have a chance to lead productive lives.

6. Though some people denounced the man as a fraud, others ____**acclaimed**____ him as a saint.

7. Although he was a legitimate ____**claimant**____ to the throne of France, he lived for years as an exile in poverty and obscurity.

8. A good baby-sitter won't yield to the ____**clamorous**____ demands of spoiled children.

---

*Circle the **boldface** word that more satisfactorily completes each of the following sentences.*

1. The estimated time set aside for completing the lakeshore (**disclaimer**, **reclamation**) project is between two and three years.

2. Abraham Lincoln issued the Emancipation (**Proclamation**, **Reclamation**) on January 1, 1863.

3. Following the toxic spill at the chemical plant, civic leaders feared that the land would be (**irreclaimable**, **clamorous**); but recent environmental tests document a successful cleanup.

4. The special effects are so realistic that audiences may find it hard to believe the (**acclaim**, **disclaimer**) that no animals were harmed in the making of the adventure film.

5. Firefighters earned widespread (**proclamation**, **acclaim**) for their many courageous and selfless acts of heroism during the disaster.

6. If you intend to become a (**claimant**, **declaimer**) in the class-action lawsuit, you must file your legal documents by the end of the month.

7. "What famous speech or poem have you chosen to (**acclaim**, **declaim**) at Friday's school assembly?" asked the principal.

8. The (**clamorous**, **irreclaimable**) crowds that line the entire race route are famous for spurring on thousands of weary runners in the annual New York City Marathon.

Analogies

In each of the following, circle the item that best completes the comparison.

See pages T38–T48 for explanations of answers.

1. furtive is to **overt** as
- a. intermittent is to continuous ⟵
- b. testy is to irascible
- c. indigent is to indignant
- d. sumptuous is to lavish

2. juggernaut is to **steamroller** as
- a. talisman is to record player
- b. maelstrom is to washing machine ⟵
- c. coterie is to hair dryer
- d. echelon is to vacuum cleaner

3. tyro is to **neophyte** as
- a. dilettante is to cadaver
- b. suppliant is to recluse
- c. misanthrope is to philanthropist
- d. agnostic is to skeptic ⟵

4. inane is to **fatuous** as
- a. plenary is to limited
- b. incumbent is to obligatory ⟵
- c. convivial is to somber
- d. utopian is to practical

5. carping is to **picayune** as
- a. sophistry is to irrefutable
- b. exigency is to optional
- c. verbiage is to inordinate ⟵
- d. nuance is to egregious

6. nettle is to **conciliate** as
- a. raze is to allay
- b. exacerbate is to belabor
- c. embellish is to portend
- d. mandate is to countermand ⟵

7. increment is to **more** as
- a. deduction is to less ⟵
- b. debit is to more
- c. asset is to less
- d. decrease is to more

8. vacillate is to **temporize** as
- a. calumniate is to slander ⟵
- b. eschew is to embrace
- c. hallow is to desecrate
- d. jettison is to salvage

9. badinage is to **jocular** as
- a. acclamation is to pejorative
- b. effrontery is to circumspect
- c. sarcasm is to mordant ⟵
- d. sophistry is to felicitous

10. reputed is to **alleged** as
- a. articulate is to tongue-tied
- b. viscous is to dog-tired
- c. myopic is to shortsighted ⟵
- d. arrant is to old-fashioned

Choosing the Right Meaning

Read each sentence carefully. Then circle the item that best completes the statement below the sentence.

See pages T38–T48 for explanations of answers.

Bowing to the unbending realities of political deal making, the freshman legislator abandoned his hard-line stance and pronounced himself ready to temporize. (2)

1. The word **temporize** in line 2 most nearly means
- a. stall
- b. filibuster
- c. compromise ⟵
- d. procrastinate

"Do not embrace me till each circumstance
Of peace, time, fortune, do cohere and jump
That I am Viola. . . ."   (Shakespeare, *Twelfth Night*, V, 1, 256–260) (2)

2. The word **cohere** in line 2 is used to mean
- a. stick together
- b. make a whole ⟵
- c. have meaning
- d. recognize one another

Behind the facade of a respectable repair shop there hid a fencing operation, and what passed for customers were in fact petty thieves bringing their furtive goods to barter for cash. (2)

3. In line 2 the word **furtive** most nearly means

a. sneaky   b. stealthy   c. shifty   (d. stolen)

"Still to ourselves in every place consigned,
Our own felicity we make or find, (2)
With secret course, which no loud storms annoy,
Glides the smooth current of domestic joy." (4)
        (Samuel Johnson, "Lines Added to Goldsmith's Traveller")

4. The word **felicity** in line 2 is best defined as

a. apposition   (b. happiness)   c. good taste   d. aptness

Two-Word Completions

Circle the pair of words that best complete the meaning of each of the following sentences.

See pages T38–T48 for explanations of answers.

1. As the speaker grew more heated, his address began to turn into an intemperate _____, chock-full of the most scathing and _____ abuse I have ever been "privileged" to hear.

(a. diatribe . . . vituperative)
b. eulogy . . . incendiary
c. encomium . . . taciturn
d. indictment . . . halcyon

2. Even though he had been educated by the foremost philosopher of his age, the emperor Nero possessed the _____ mind and _____ appetites of a monster like Count Dracula or the Marquis de Sade.

a. meretricious . . . refulgent
b. fecund . . . piquant
c. murky . . . abject
(d. depraved . . . bestial)

3. Any trial that is being conducted by people with absolutely no sense of _____ can only be considered a _____ of justice.

(a. equity . . . travesty)
b. propriety . . . figment
c. concord . . . counterpart
d. collusion . . . bastion

4. I realized that my theory about how the crime had been committed was no longer _____ when I accidentally stumbled across _____ evidence of a quite different scenario.

a. coherent . . . moot
(b. tenable . . . irrefutable)
c. ludicrous . . . esoteric
d. abject . . . indubitable

5. In my various _____ through the forest that bordered on my childhood home, I often came quite unexpectedly upon birds, insects, and other _____ creatures that I had never before encountered.

a. paroxysms . . . bucolic
b. gambits . . . macabre
(c. peregrinations . . . sylvan)
d. pedantries . . . mundane

Enriching Your Vocabulary

Read the passage below. Then complete the exercise at the bottom of the page.

Abbondanza from Italy

The rousing Broadway show tune "Abbondanza" by Frank Loesser describes the great abundance of food guests will enjoy at a banquet celebrating a bride-to-be. Fortunately, the English language has reaped its own abundant vocabulary from Italy. The word *dilettante* (Unit 9) meaning "amateur, or dabbler in the arts" is borrowed directly from Italian.

Leonardo Ferri throws pizza dough in the air, as chef Claudio Marchesan displays plates of food at Prego restaurant in San Francisco.

One way that English speakers pay homage to Italy is to acknowledge some of its many mouth-watering foods such as *pizza, spaghetti, espresso, salami, pasta, parmesan, macaroni, ravioli,* and *zucchini.* The realm of music also brings the Italian language to the American tongue with such terms as *tempo, soprano, solo, aria, madrigal, piano, duet, opera,* and *trio.* If your school choir presents a piece without instrumental accompaniment, that piece is said to be performed *a cappella.* This phrase derives from the Italian words that mean "in the manner of the chapel," referring to the church, where musical instruments were not originally used. Do you know your school's *motto*—a saying that expresses its goals or ideals? The original Italian meaning of *motto* is "a word."

In Column A below are 8 more words and phrases that come from the Italian heritage. With or without a dictionary, match each word or phrase with its meaning in Column B.

Column A

c	**1.**	cognoscenti
f	**2.**	finale
h	**3.**	imbroglio
a	**4.**	manifesto
d	**5.**	prima donna
b	**6.**	sotto voce
g	**7.**	squadron
e	**8.**	tempo

Column B

a. a public declaration of intentions or principles (from the Italian for "a manifestation")

b. very softly or quietly (from the Italian for "under one's breath")

c. persons of outstanding knowledge or taste, connoisseurs (from the Italian for "those in the know")

d. the lead female singer in an opera; a temperamental person (from the Italian for "first lady")

e. the speed at which a musical composition is played; pace (from the Italian for "time")

f. the end or climax of a theatre piece or other work (from the Italian for "final" or "end")

g. a large military or naval unit; any organized multitude (from the Italian for "a big square" or "formation of troops")

h. a complicated situation (from the Italian for "a tangle")

Definitions

Note carefully the spelling, pronunciation, part(s) of speech, and definition(s) of each of the following words. Then write the word in the blank space(s) in the illustrative sentence(s) following. Finally, study the lists of synonyms and antonyms given at the end of each entry.

1. askance
(ə skans')

(*adv.*) with suspicion, distrust, or disapproval

The English teacher looked _____ **askance** _____ at the suggestion that students read compendiums of Dickens's novels.

SYNONYMS: distrustfully, suspiciously, skeptically

2. attenuate
(ə ten' yü āt)

(*v.*) to make thin or slender; to weaken or lessen in force, intensity, or value

After making sure the wound was clean, the doctor took steps to _____ **attenuate** _____ the victim's pain.

SYNONYMS: thin out, dilute, water down
ANTONYMS: thicken, strengthen, bolster

3. benign
(bi nīn')

(*adj.*) gentle, kind; forgiving, understanding; having a favorable or beneficial effect; not malignant

Abraham Lincoln's sensitive stepmother had a _____ **benign** _____ influence on the lonely boy who had lost his mother.

SYNONYMS: benevolent, salutary, salubrious, harmless
ANTONYMS: malevolent, deleterious

4. cavil
(kav' əl)

(*v.*) to find fault in a petty way, carp; (*n.*) a trivial objection or criticism

I suggest you do not _____ **cavil** _____ over small things but instead focus on what is important.

Despite a few _____ **cavils** _____ I might make, I still find her to be an excellent poet.

SYNONYMS: (*v.*) nitpick, quibble

5. charlatan
(shär' lə tən)

(*n.*) one who feigns knowledge or ability; a pretender, impostor, or quack

The reporter exposed the real estate agent as a _____ **charlatan** _____ who routinely deceived her customers.

SYNONYMS: fraud, mountebank

6. decimate
(des' ə māt)

(*v.*) to kill or destroy a large part of

Again and again, Napoleon was able to _____ **decimate** _____ the armies of his enemies and lead his men on to further victories.

SYNONYMS: ravage, devastate

7. foible
(foi' bəl)

(*n.*) a weak point, failing, minor flaw

Backbiting is one human _____ **foible** _____ not likely to be eradicated.

SYNONYMS: shortcoming, defect, quirk
ANTONYMS: forte, virtue

8. forgo
(fôr go')

(*v.*) to do without, abstain from, give up

One of the best, if not the easiest, ways to lose weight is to _____ **forgo** _____ dessert.

SYNONYMS: refrain from, renounce
ANTONYMS: indulge in, partake of

9. fraught
(frôt)

(*adj.*) full of or loaded with; accompanied by

Even with the most advanced equipment, expeditions to the top of Mt. Everest are still _____ **fraught** _____ with danger.

SYNONYM: charged with
ANTONYMS: devoid of, lacking, deficient in

10. inure
(in yür')

(*v.*) to toughen, harden; to render used to something by long subjection or exposure

The Inuit have become _____ **inured** _____ to the hardships of the long Arctic winters through years of experience.

SYNONYMS: accustom, acclimate

11. luminous
(lü' mə nəs)

(*adj.*) emitting or reflecting light, glowing; illuminating

Walking under that _____ **luminous** _____ night sky induced in me weighty thoughts not often pondered.

SYNONYMS: radiant, bright, refulgent, lustrous
ANTONYMS: dark, opaque, dim, murky

12. obsequious
(əb sē' kwē əs)

(*adj.*) marked by slavish attentiveness; excessively submissive, often for purely self-interested reasons

Jane Austen ridiculed characters who were _____ **obsequious** _____ to the aristocracy but condescending to their social inferiors.

SYNONYMS: fawning, servile, sycophantic, mealymouthed
ANTONYMS: assertive, bumptious, overbearing, candid, frank, independent

13. obtuse
(äb tüs')

(*adj.*) blunt, not coming to a point; slow or dull in understanding; measuring between 90° and 180°; not causing a sharp impression

The lieutenant was too _____ **obtuse** _____ to see the danger and led his company right into the hands of the enemy.

SYNONYMS: stupid, dumb, thick, mild, dull-witted
ANTONYMS: acute, perceptive, quick-witted

14. oscillate
(äs′ ə lāt)

(v.) to swing back and forth with a steady rhythm; to fluctuate or waver

The terrified narrator in Poe's story *The Pit and the Pendulum* watches the dreaded instrument _____ oscillate _____ as it slowly moves toward him.

SYNONYMS: vibrate, vacillate

15. penitent
(pen′ ə tənt)

(adj.) regretful for one's sins or mistakes; (n.) one who is sorry for wrongdoing

The thief was sincerely _____ penitent _____.

In the Middle Ages, _____ penitents _____ often confessed their sins publicly and were publicly punished.

SYNONYMS: (adj.) remorseful, regretful, rueful, sorry
ANTONYMS: (adj.) unrepentant, remorseless

16. peremptory
(pə remp′ tə rē)

(adj.) having the nature of a command that leaves no opportunity for debate, denial, or refusal; offensively self-assured, dictatorial; determined, resolute

The board members resented the director's _ peremptory _ tone of voice.

SYNONYMS: high-handed, unconditional
ANTONYMS: irresolute, tentative, mild, unassuming

17. rebuff
(ri bəf′)

(v.) to snub; to repel, drive away; (n.) a curt rejection, a check

The old man _____ rebuffed _____ his neighbors by refusing all offers of friendship.

Her _____ rebuff _____ of my invitation was quite rude.

SYNONYMS: (v.) spurn, repulse, reject; (n.) setback
ANTONYMS: (v.) accept, welcome

18. reconnoiter
(rē kə noit′ ər)

(v.) to engage in reconnaissance; to a make a preliminary inspection

Infantry officers often ask for volunteers to _ reconnoiter _ the terrain ahead before ordering their soldiers to advance.

SYNONYM: scout

19. shambles
(sham′ bəlz)

(n.) a slaughterhouse; a place of mass bloodshed; a state of complete disorder and confusion, mess

The burglars made a complete _____ shambles _____ of the apartment in their search for money and jewelry.

20. sporadic
(spô rad′ ik)

(adj.) occurring at irregular intervals, having no set plan or order

The soldiers heard _____ sporadic _____ gunfire from the other side of the river.

SYNONYMS: intermittent, spasmodic
ANTONYMS: constant, steady, continuous, uninterrupted

Completing the Sentence

From the words for this unit, choose the one that best completes each of the following sentences. Write the word in the space provided.

1. Life on the family farm has _____**inured**_____ me to hard physical labor and long hours of unremitting toil.

2. The general sent scouts on ahead of the army to _____**reconnoiter**_____ the area for a suitable site to pitch camp.

3. Although there had been some _____**sporadic**_____ fighting earlier, the real battles of the Civil War did not begin until Bull Run in July, 1861.

4. Unless the title Special Aide to the Assistant Section Manager involves a salary increase, I would just as soon _____**forgo**_____ it.

5. The riot converted the quiet streets of that suburban community into a ghastly _____**shambles**_____ .

6. Although the moon appears to be a(n) _____**luminous**_____ body, the fact is that it only reflects light received from the sun.

7. As all kinds of wild rumors ran rampant through the besieged city, the mood of the populace _____**oscillated**_____ between hope and despair.

8. Good supervisors know that they can get more cooperation from their staff by making polite requests than by issuing _____**peremptory**_____ orders.

9. The man's personality was a strange mixture of strengths and weaknesses, fortes and _____**foibles**_____ .

10. I was totally taken aback when they _____**rebuffed**_____ my kind offers of assistance so rudely and nastily.

11. No doubt he's very sorry he got caught, but that does not mean that he's at all _____**penitent**_____ about what he did.

12. Any "investment counselor" who promises to double your money overnight must be regarded as a(n) _____**charlatan**_____ or a crook.

13. Though my childhood recollections have been _____**attenuated**_____ by the passage of time, they have not been totally effaced from my memory.

14. In a typical James Bond movie, Agent 007 has a series of adventures that are _____**fraught**_____ with tongue-in-cheek peril.

15. His statements have been so uniformly _____**obtuse**_____ that I get the impression that he is wearing a permanent pair of mental blinders.

16. Though critics _____**caviled**_____ at minor faults in the new Broadway show, the general public loved it.

17. I was relieved to learn that the tumor on my arm was _____**benign**_____ and my worst fears groundless.

18. We look _____**askance**_____ at any program that makes it harder for city dwellers to get out and enjoy the beauties of nature.

19. During the 14th century, the Black Death suddenly swept across Europe, _____**decimating**_____ the population and paralyzing everyday life.

20. During imperial times, the Roman Senate was little more than a collection of _____**obsequious**_____ yes-men, intent upon preserving their own lives by gratifying the emperor's every whim.

Synonyms

*Choose the word from this unit that is **the same** or **most nearly the same** in meaning as the **boldface** word or expression in the given phrase. Write the word on the line provided.*

1. **quibble** over who is at fault — cavil
2. exposed him as a complete **fraud** — charlatan
3. **vacillated** between two choices — oscillated
4. looked **skeptically** at their proposals — askance
5. **accustomed** to extremes of temperature — inured
6. a storm that **ravaged** the countryside — decimated
7. an attempt to **scout** the interior — reconnoiter
8. unwilling to **renounce** her inheritance — forgo
9. shocked by the **mess** they had created — shambles
10. a **salutary** effect on consumer confidence — benign
11. **full of** suspense and tension — fraught with
12. willing to overlook its **defects** — foibles
13. will **spurn** his offer of marriage — rebuff
14. his **high-handed** challenge to our authority — peremptory
15. in the **radiant** circle of the spotlight — luminous

Antonyms

*Choose the word from this unit that is **most nearly opposite** in meaning to the **boldface** word or expression in the given phrase. Write the word on the line provided.*

16. measures that may **strengthen** the economy — attenuate
17. an entirely **unrepentant** gambler and thief — penitent
18. her **acute** handling of the issue — obtuse
19. assumed an **overbearing** manner — obsequious
20. his **constant** attention to detail — sporadic

Choosing the Right Word

Circle the **boldface** word that more satisfactorily completes each of the following sentences.

1. We must never allow our passion for justice to be (**inured, attenuated**) to mere halfhearted goodwill.

2. I have learned that (**sporadic, peremptory**) sessions of intense "cramming" can never take the place of a regular study program.

3. Somehow or other, a bull got into the china shop and turned it into a complete (**shambles, foibles**).

4. The (**decimated, penitent**) youths agreed to work without pay until they could make restitution for the damage their carelessness had caused.

5. When I found that people I admired were looking (**askance, sporadic**) at my unconventional clothing, I resolved to remedy the situation.

6. How could you have the heart to (**rebuff, cavil**) those people's piteous appeals for aid?

7. Since he didn't want to give me credit for having done a good job, he took refuge in endless (**foibles, cavils**) about my work.

8. Imagine the general disappointment when the so-called "miracle cure" was exposed as a fraud promoted by a (**charlatan, cavil**).

9. Over the years, her (**luminous, obtuse**) descriptions and scintillating wit have helped her students master the difficult subject she taught.

10. Their relationship has been so (**fraught, benign**) with strife and malice that I don't see how they can ever patch things up.

11. Though I admire the woman's strong points, I find her (**rebuffs, foibles**) comic.

12. All angles are classified as acute, right, (**obtuse, benign**), or straight, according to the number of degrees they contain.

13. Though the small nation was always ready to settle a conflict peacefully, it was not afraid to use (**luminous, peremptory**) force when necessary.

14. At an autocrat's court, free speech is usually replaced by the (**penitent, obsequious**) twaddle of self-serving flunkies and toadies.

15. Do you want to be a ballet dancer badly enough to (**oscillate, forgo**) all other activities?

16. Bank robbers often spend a good deal of time (**reconnoitering, rebuffing**) the neighborhood in which the bank they intend to rob is located.

17. During the Civil War the ranks of both armies were (**decimated, rebuffed**) as much by disease as by enemy action.

18. Even though my experiences in battle have (**inured, caviled**) me to scenes of suffering, I was horrified by the devastation wrought by the tornado.

19. Since he is not guided by firm principles, he (**attenuates, oscillates**) between the rival factions, looking for support from both of them.

20. We believe that classes taught by teachers with specialized training will have a (**sporadic, benign**) effect on the troubled children.

Vocabulary in Context

*Read the following passage, in which some of the words you have studied in this unit appear in **boldface** type. Then complete each statement given below the passage by circling the letter of the item that is **the same** or **almost the same** in meaning as the highlighted word.*

Squirrel It Away!

(Line)

With 260 known species, squirrels are found worldwide. Some are tree-dwelling, others (flying squirrels) glide from tree to tree by means of furry flaps of skin that connect their front and hind legs, and still others (chipmunks) are terrestrial. Most often when we think of squirrels, we envision the gray ones indigenous to North

(5)   America that collect nuts from tree to tree, **reconnoitering** the local neighborhoods in search of new sources of food.

Like rats and mice, squirrels are classified in the rodent family. Some might look **askance** at their behavior,

(10)   **peremptorily** condemning these creatures who notoriously **decimate** bird feeders and, along with the less comely members of their rodent family, make a **shambles** of garbage

(15)   bags left for collection on city streets.

But the squirrel has some **benign** attributes as well, and people have been known to keep them as pets, or feed them in parks and

(20)   backyards. It has learned to live with humans in cities, but can also survive in places as rural as the North American tundra. It is an important part of

Like bats, flying squirrels are nocturnal.

the ecosystem, and its digestion of such things as hard shells of nuts, seeds,

(25)   and pine cones helps renew soil and scatter seeds. While it may be tempting to allow familiarity to breed contempt, one should consider the fact that squirrels might even be capable of communication. Some infer that the pitch and duration of the shrill sounds they make have meanings, and that even tail gestures are a form of communication. The most common tail gesture is the "flicking," which

(30)   means "get away!"

---

1. Reconnoitering (line 5) most nearly means
   a. showing
   b. recognizing
   c. sectioning
   d. scouting *(circled)*

2. Askance (line 9) most nearly means
   a. curiously
   b. suspiciously *(circled)*
   c. seriously
   d. fondly

3. Peremptorily (line 10) is best defined as
   a. conditionally
   b. angrily
   c. unconditionally
   d. sweepingly *(circled)*

4. The meaning of **decimate** (line 11) is
   a. ravage *(circled)*
   b. drop
   c. decorate
   d. locate

5. Shambles (line 14) most nearly means
   a. mess *(circled)*
   b. vision
   c. terrain
   d. disruption

6. The meaning of **benign** (line 16) is
   a. benevolent *(circled)*
   b. courageous
   c. endangered
   d. destructive

Definitions

Note carefully the spelling, pronunciation, part(s) of speech, and definition(s) of each of the following words. Then write the word in the blank space(s) in the illustrative sentence(s) following. Finally, study the lists of synonyms and antonyms given at the end of each entry.

1. abrogate
(ab' rə gāt)

(*v.*) to repeal, cancel, declare null and void

Often with no legal or moral grounds, the U. S. government would _____ **abrogate** _____ treaties made with Native Americans.

SYNONYMS: annul, revoke
ANTONYMS: reaffirm, renew, ratify

2. ambient
(am' bē ənt)

(*adj.*) completely surrounding, encompassing

The new filtering system is capable of cleaning and deodorizing the _____ **ambient** _____ air.

3. asperity
(a sper' ə tē)

(*n.*) roughness, severity; bitterness or tartness

The _____ **asperity** _____ of the drama critic's statements undermined the young actor's confidence.

SYNONYMS: rigor, harshness
ANTONYMS: mildness, blandness, softness, lenience

4. burnish
(bər' nish)

(*v.*) to make smooth or glossy by rubbing, polish; (*n.*) gloss, brightness, luster

The hotel manager ordered the waiters to _____ **burnish** _____ all the brass candlesticks before the formal banquet.

The _____ **burnish** _____ on the metal frame had faded with age and neglect.

SYNONYMS: (*v.*) shine, buff
ANTONYMS: (*v.*) tarnish, dull, abrade

5. cabal
(kə bäl')

(*n.*) a small group working in secret

The members of the _____ **cabal** _____ met at an unknown location for the purpose of fixing prices and stifling competition.

SYNONYMS: clique, ring, gang, plot, conspiracy

6. delectable
(di lek' tə bəl)

(*adj.*) delightful, highly enjoyable; deliciously flavored, savory; (*n.*) an appealing or appetizing food or dish

The banquet ended with a truly _____ **delectable** _____ dessert made of peaches, raspberries, and ice cream.

The eatery attracted customers with a mouth-watering display of _____ **delectables** _____ in its front window.

SYNONYMS: (*adj.*) delicious, scrumptious
ANTONYMS: (*adj.*) repugnant, repulsive, distasteful

7. deprecate
(dep′ rə kāt)

(v.) to express mild disapproval; to belittle

The administration ___**deprecated**___ such foolish practices as the hazing of new students but did not ban them outright.

SYNONYMS: deplore, frown upon
ANTONYMS: smile on, countenance, approve

8. detritus
(di trīt′ əs)

(n.) loose bits and pieces of material resulting from disintegration or wearing away; fragments that result from any destruction

Pieces of people's homes, furniture, and toys could be seen in the _____**detritus**_____ of the landslide.

SYNONYMS: debris, wreckage, ruins, rubble

9. ebullient
(i bül′ yənt)

(adj.) overflowing with enthusiasm and excitement; boiling, bubbling

After a string of very favorable reviews, the dance company was in an _____**ebullient**_____ mood for weeks.

SYNONYMS: exhilarated, elated, exuberant
ANTONYMS: gloomy, morose, sullen, apathetic, blasé

10. eclectic
(e klek′ tik)

(adj.) drawn from different sources; (n.) one whose beliefs are drawn from various sources

Stanford White developed an _____**eclectic**_____ style of architecture that made use of classic and modern elements.

The critics accused the composer of being a mere _____**eclectic**_____ with no original style of her own.

SYNONYMS: (adj.) selective, synthetic, pick-and-choose
ANTONYMS: (adj.) uniform, monolithic

11. flaccid
(flas′ əd)

(adj.) limp, not firm; lacking vigor or effectiveness

Because the injured bodybuilder had not worked out for weeks, his muscles grew _____**flaccid**_____.

SYNONYMS: soft, flabby
ANTONYMS: hard, firm, solid

12. impecunious
(im pə kyü′ nē əs)

(adj.) having little or no money

In my present _____**impecunious**_____ state, I will not be able to pay for dinner.

SYNONYMS: penniless, impoverished, indigent
ANTONYMS: affluent, wealthy, prosperous, rich

13. inexorable
(in ek′ sər ə bəl)

(adj.) inflexible, beyond influence; relentless, unyielding

In the Greek tragedies, nothing could save characters like Oedipus Rex from their _____**inexorable**_____ fates.

SYNONYMS: inescapable, ineluctable, obdurate
ANTONYMS: avoidable, yielding, pliant

14. moribund
(môr′ ə bənd)

(*adj.*) dying, on the way out

In the age of electronic communication, writing letters by hand seems to be a _____ **moribund** _____ custom.

SYNONYM: obsolescent
ANTONYMS: flourishing, thriving

15. necromancer
(nek′ rə man sər)

(*n.*) one who claims to reveal or influence the future through magic, especially communication with the dead; in general, a magician or wizard

When the stock market began to tumble, some desperate investors resorted to _____ **necromancers** _____ for financial advice.

SYNONYMS: sorcerer, conjurer

16. onerous
(än′ ər əs)

(*adj.*) burdensome; involving hardship or difficulty

Informing patients of bad news is an _____ **onerous** _____ duty that every doctor has to perform.

SYNONYMS: oppressive, weighty
ANTONYMS: light, easy, undemanding, untaxing

17. rife
(rīf)

(*adj.*) common, prevalent, widespread, happening often; full, abounding; plentiful, abundant, replete

Since rumors were _____ **rife** _____, the president announced that the company had been bought out by its major competitor.

ANTONYMS: devoid of, lacking

18. rudiments
(rüd′ ə mənts)

(*n. pl.*) the parts of any subject or discipline that are learned first; the earliest stages of anything

At a very young age, the girl learned the _____ **rudiments** _____ of chess from her father, a professional player.

SYNONYMS: fundamentals, basics

19. sequester
(si kwes′ tər)

(*v.*) to set apart, separate for a special purpose; to take possession of and hold in custody

The parties agreed to _____ **sequester** _____ the disputed funds pending a decision by the court.

SYNONYMS: seclude, segregate, isolate, closet

20. winnow
(win′ ō)

(*v.*) to get rid of something unwanted, delete; to sift through to obtain what is desirable; to remove the chaff from the wheat by blowing air on it; to blow on, fan

Spelling and grammar software programs are designed to help writers _____ **winnow** _____ inaccuracies from their documents.

SYNONYMS: sift, strain, filter, sort

Completing the Sentence

From the words for this unit, choose the one that best completes each of the following sentences. Write the word in the space provided.

1. I could tell that my boss was really "riled" by the _____ **asperity** _____ of his tone of voice when he summoned me.

2. I thought the job of revising the manuscript would be a relatively simple matter, but it proved to be a(n) _____ **onerous** _____ task.

3. She is a very private person who _____ **deprecates** _____ any attempt to honor publicly her great services to humanity.

4. Though monarchies still exist in some parts of the world, they are more or less a(n) _____ **moribund** _____ form of government.

5. Even before they said a word, I could tell from their _____ **ebullient** _____ expressions that our team had won.

6. In a sense, the man is a(n) _____ **eclectic** _____ philosopher because his ideas have been influenced by many different schools of thought.

7. All the facts and figures point to one _____ **inexorable** _____ conclusion: we are hopelessly outnumbered.

8. As air slowly seeped out through the tiny puncture, the inner tube became more and more _____ **flaccid** _____ .

9. Some superstitious Roman emperors consulted _____ **necromancers** _____ and other dabblers in black magic to find out what the future held.

10. It is often difficult to hold a conversation while walking on a busy city street because of the high level of _____ **ambient** _____ traffic noise.

11. The copper pots had been so highly _____ **burnished** _____ that I could see my face in them.

12. In order to prevent outside influences from coming into play, a jury is normally _____ **sequestered** _____ until it reaches a decision.

13. Unless you have mastered the _____ **rudiments** _____ of French grammar, you will find it difficult to speak the language fluently.

14. It was then that he began to organize the _____ **cabal** _____ that would later depose the king.

15. The conversation at dinner tables all over town was _____ **rife** _____ with speculation as to the outcome of the big game.

16. We will never allow anyone to curtail or _____ **abrogate** _____ the basic rights and liberties guaranteed to us in the Constitution.

17. The plot of the novel centers on a(n) _____ **impecunious** _____ adventurer who attempts to remedy his financial embarrassment by marrying into money.

18. One of Darwin's theories suggests that nature ensures the survival of a species by slowly _____ winnowing _____ out the less fit members.

19. Late that night, we began the heartbreaking task of sifting through the _____ detritus _____ of our ravaged home.

20. There is nothing more _____ delectable _____ on a hot day than to stretch out in a hammock with a good book and pitcher of icy lemonade!

Synonyms

*Choose the word from this unit that is **the same** or **most nearly the same** in meaning as the **boldface** word or expression in the given phrase. Write the word on the line provided.*

1. sort the good ideas from the bad   winnow

2. taught us the **fundamentals** of physics   rudiments

3. the **encompassing** sound of the drums   ambient

4. cleaned up the **debris** from the parade   detritus

5. fooled by a **sorcerer's** tricks   necromancer's

6. secluded on a remote country estate   sequestered

7. a ruthless **clique** of gangsters   cabal

8. could not miss the **harshness** in his tone   asperity

9. the **inescapable** consequences of her actions   inexorable

10. rebelled against the **oppressive** taxation   onerous

11. weeds that were **widespread** in the area   rife

12. tempted me with **delicious** treats   delectable

13. a **varied** collection of opinions   eclectic

14. the **exuberant** cheerleading squad   ebullient

15. sheltered the **penniless** immigrants   impecunious

Antonyms

*Choose the word from this unit that is **most nearly opposite** in meaning to the **boldface** word or expression in the given phrase. Write the word on the line provided.*

16. tarnish the silver   burnish

17. noticed her **firm** handshake   flaccid

18. the **flourishing** downtown area   moribund

19. will **reaffirm** his oath to the king   abrogate

20. countenanced our peaceful protest   deprecated

Choosing the Right Word

*Circle the **boldface** word that more satisfactorily completes each of the following sentences.*

1. "The (**inexorable,** moribund) march of the years," said the aged speaker, "decrees that this is the last time I will address you."

2. Writing that is so full of soggy clichés, gummy sentence structure, and excessive wordiness can best be described as (inexorable, **flaccid**).

3. What appeared to be an informal study group was in a reality a highly organized (detritus, **cabal**) determined to overthrow the establishment.

4. (Asperity, **Necromancy**) and other forms of witchcraft were punishable by death during the Middle Ages.

5. The investigating committee spent long hours trying to (burnish, **winnow**) fact from fiction in the witnesses' testimony.

6. Though she entered this country as a(n) (**impecunious,** rife) child, she eventually made a fortune in the garment industry.

7. Anyone who has the slightest acquaintance with the (**rudiments,** cabals) of economic theory understands that we cannot solve our financial problems simply by borrowing more and more money.

8. (**Eclectic,** Ambient) schools of art are typical of a period when there is little original inspiration or bold experimentation.

9. Though the presidency confers great powers on the person who holds the office, it also saddles that person with (**onerous,** eclectic) responsibilities.

10. Since archaeologists spend a lot of time rummaging through the (**detritus,** asperity) of vanished civilizations, they bear a striking resemblance to junk collectors and ragpickers.

11. As we sat in the locker room after our heartbreaking loss, the (**ambient,** impecunious) gloom was so thick you could almost cut it.

12. It is one thing to (burnish, **deprecate**) human follies and pretensions; it is quite another to correct them.

13. Though skeptics insist that patriotism is (onerous, **moribund**) in America, I believe that it is alive and well in the hearts of the people.

14. The old adage that "one man's meat is another man's poison" simply means that what is considered (**delectable,** onerous) is often quite subjective.

15. Any political party that is (**rife,** ebullient) with petty jealousies and backbiting can never hope to present a united front in an election.

16. The (moribund, **burnished**) helmets and breastplates of the warriors gleamed and twinkled in the morning sunlight.

17. As one veteran aptly observed, a soldier had to be hardy to cope with the (**asperities,** cabals) of life in the trenches during World War I.

18. The charm of this musical comedy lies in its slam-bang pacing, its sprightly music, and its generally (onerous, **ebullient**) good cheer.

19. Oliver Wendell Holmes, Jr., once observed that he did not wish to lead a(n) (**sequestered,** abrogated) life far from the conflicts of his times.

20. No one, however powerful or dominant, can (**abrogate,** sequester) the basic moral laws on which civilization rests.

*Read the following passage, in which some of the words you have studied in this unit appear in **boldface** type. Then complete each statement given below the passage by circling the letter of the item that is **the same** or **almost the same** in meaning as the highlighted word.*

Merlin the Magician

(Line)

The legend of Camelot has carried cultural resonance throughout the centuries. Modern writers have reinvented the tale, and directors have made films about it. It is a dynamic legend that changes in order to reflect the mores of the times. The one thing that has not changed, however, is the mysterious nature of Merlin, at once a fearsome **necromancer**, and at the same time, (5) a kindly protector and advisor to King Arthur.

A famous wizard from American popular culture, The Wizard of Oz (1939).

The Merlin character is **eclectic**, drawn partly from historical sources, but mostly constructed from early Celtic legends. The kernel of history that can be **winnowed** from (10) the chaff of legend relates Merlin to a wanderer with the gift of prophecy, who roamed through the forests of southern Scotland around 575 A.D. A similar figure with powers to divine the future, called Myrddin, (15) appeared in early Welsh poetry. In the twelfth century, Geoffrey of Monmouth combined the **rudiments** of the wandering prophet stories and the Myrddin legends with his own newly invented material to create the character he (20) called Merlin. Writing in Latin for a Norman French audience, Geoffrey divulged that Merlin was responsible for engineering the secret conception of Arthur by King Uther Pendragon, **sequestering** the royal offspring during his boyhood, and later giving Arthur the magical power to pull the sword from the stone and secure his kingship. (25)

Merlin's luster was further **burnished** by later medieval writers, who added new elements to his character, making him the inspiration for Arthur's foundation of the idealistic institution of the Round Table.

---

1. Necromancer (line 5) most nearly means
a. explorer
b. storyteller
c. sorcerer
d. emperor

2. Eclectic (line 7) is best defined as
a. mysterious
b. powerful
c. famous
d. synthetic

3. The meaning of **winnowed** (line 10) is
a. sifted
b. learned
c. dropped
d. made

4. The meaning of **rudiments** (line 18) is
a. riches
b. basics
c. features
d. rules

5. Sequestering (line 23) most nearly means
a. educating
b. endangering
c. misleading
d. secluding

6. Burnished (line 26) most nearly means
a. tainted
b. betrayed
c. polished
d. clouded

Definitions

Note carefully the spelling, pronunciation, part(s) of speech, and definition(s) of each of the following words. Then write the word in the blank space(s) in the illustrative sentence(s) following. Finally, study the lists of synonyms and antonyms given at the end of each entry.

1. aesthetic
(es thet' ik)

(*adj.*) pertaining to beauty; sensitive or responsive to beauty

Since the structure had no practical purpose, keeping it in place could only be justified on _____ **aesthetic** _____ grounds.

SYNONYM: artistic

2. defunct
(di fəŋkt')

(*adj.*) no longer in existence or functioning, dead

I could find no forwarding address or phone number for the _____ **defunct** _____ organization.

SYNONYMS: extinct, nonexistent
ANTONYMS: alive, extant

3. discomfit
(dis kəm' fit)

(*v.*) to frustrate, thwart, or defeat; to confuse, perplex, or embarrass

The general tried to _____ **discomfit** _____ his enemies by repeatedly beginning an advance and then pulling back.

SYNONYMS: nonplus, disconcert, foil

4. espouse
(es paüz')

(*v.*) to take up and support; to become attached to, adopt; to marry

To appeal to the large number of dissatisfied voters, the candidate _____ **espoused** _____ a strong program of reform.

SYNONYMS: embrace, wed
ANTONYMS: repudiate, disavow, renounce

5. fetish
(fet' ish)

(*n.*) an object believed to have magical powers; an object of unreasoning devotion or reverence

The rabbit's foot, once a very popular _____ **fetish** _____, seems to have lost its hold on the public imagination.

SYNONYMS: charm, talisman, obsession

6. gregarious
(grə gār' ē əs)

(*adj.*) living together in a herd or group; sociable, seeking the company of others

I would expect the recreation director of a cruise ship to be a _____ **gregarious** _____ person.

SYNONYMS: outgoing, extroverted
ANTONYMS: aloof, introverted, reclusive

7. hapless
(hap′ lis)

(*adj.*) marked by a persistent absence of good luck

Once again, my younger brother has become the _____**hapless**_____ victim of a silly practical joke.

SYNONYMS: unlucky, ill-starred, unfortunate
ANTONYMS: lucky, charmed, fortunate

8. impeccable
(im pek′ ə bəl)

(*adj.*) faultless, beyond criticism or blame

We always consulted my grandmother about what to wear because she had _____**impeccable**_____ taste in clothing.

SYNONYMS: flawless, spotless, immaculate
ANTONYMS: grimy, soiled, spotted, sullied

9. importune
(im pôr tyün′)

(*v.*) to trouble with demands; to beg for insistently

My bankrupt uncle _____**importuned**_____ my father for a loan.

SYNONYMS: implore, entreat, dun, tax

10. interpolate
(in tər′ pə lāt)

(*v.*) to insert between other parts or things; to present as an addition or correction

At the director's request, the screenwriter _____**interpolated**_____ some new lines into the script.

SYNONYMS: inject, interpose, introduce

11. irreparable
(i rep′ ər ə bəl)

(*adj.*) incapable of being repaired or rectified

The husband believed that the surgeon did _____**irreparable**_____ harm to his wife and sued the doctor and the hospital.

SYNONYM: irremediable
ANTONYMS: remediable, fixable, reversible

12. laconic
(lə kän′ ik)

(*adj.*) concise, using few words

The senator issued a _____**laconic**_____ statement declaring her innocence after the accusations of fraud were made public.

SYNONYMS: terse, succinct, pithy, compact
ANTONYMS: garrulous, prolix, loquacious, verbose

13. languish
(laŋ′ gwish)

(*v.*) to become weak, feeble, or dull; to droop; to be depressed or dispirited; to suffer neglect

Without the Constitutional guarantee of a speedy trial, the accused could _____**languish**_____ in jail for years.

SYNONYMS: flag, wilt, fade, pine

14. mendacious
(men dā ′shəs)

(*adj.*) given to lying or deception; untrue

The deputy gave a _____ **mendacious** _____ account of his employer's actions on the day of the alleged crime.

SYNONYMS: untruthful, false
ANTONYMS: truthful, veracious

15. nadir
(nā′ dər)

(*n.*) the lowest point

At the _____ **nadir** _____ of his popularity, the prime minister decided to resign his office and call for new elections.

SYNONYMS: rock bottom
ANTONYMS: apex, pinnacle, zenith

16. omnipresent
(äm ni pre′ zənt)

(*adj.*) present in all places at all times

They believed in an _____ **omnipresent** _____ deity that existed in all things.

SYNONYMS: ubiquitous, ever-present

17. perfunctory
(per fəŋk′ tə rē)

(*adj.*) done in a superficial or halfhearted manner; without interest or enthusiasm

The police made a _____ **perfunctory** _____ search for the missing handbag, but they really did not expect to find it.

SYNONYMS: slapdash, cursory, shallow
ANTONYMS: thorough, assiduous, diligent, meticulous

18. plaintive
(plān′ tiv)

(*adj.*) expressive of sorrow or woe, melancholy

The recently widowed man spoke of his loneliness in a _____ **plaintive** _____ tone of voice.

SYNONYMS: sad, doleful, lugubrious
ANTONYMS: cheerful, blithe, joyous, merry

19. requite
(ri kwīt′)

(*v.*) to make suitable repayment, as for a kindness, service, or favor; to make retaliation, as for an injury or wrong; to reciprocate

We made sure to _____ **requite** _____ the neighbors for looking after our house while we were away.

SYNONYMS: reimburse, recompense, avenge

20. tantamount
(tan′ tə maůnt)

(*adj.*) equivalent, having the same meaning, value, or effect

The armed invasion of their territory was _____ **tantamount** _____ to a declaration of war.

SYNONYM: indistinguishable from

Completing the Sentence

From the words for this unit, choose the one that best completes each of the following sentences. Write the word in the space provided.

1. No matter where candidates for high political office go these days, the _____omnipresent_____ eye of the TV camera seems focused on them.

2. As his irrepressible flow of reminiscences continued without a letup, I tried in vain to _____interpolate_____ a few observations of my own.

3. To say that he is _____mendacious_____ does not even begin to convey just how alienated he is from any regard for the truth.

4. One wall of the museum was filled with charms and _____fetishes_____ designed to ward off everything from a hangnail to the evil eye.

5. They claim to have made a thorough search of the premises, but I suspect that their efforts were no more than _____perfunctory_____.

6 Last night, Central High's Netnicks captured the basketball championship by _____discomfiting_____ the South High Slammers, 61 to 44.

7. I thought our state legislators would consider the proposal at the earliest opportunity, but they let it _____languish_____ in committee for months.

8. Responding to the melancholy note in the song of the nightingale, Keats wrote of its "_____plaintive_____ anthem."

9. Suddenly I was surrounded by a mob of street urchins loudly _____importuning_____ me for a handout.

10. I was greatly relieved to learn that the accident I had with my car last week didn't do any _____irreparable_____ damage to the motor.

11. The _____hapless_____ creature had somehow gotten its foot caught in the grate and could not extricate it without help.

12. When asked what terms he would offer the Confederate army, General Grant made the _____laconic_____ reply, "Unconditional surrender!"

13. I felt a little foolish when the librarian told me that I was asking for the current issue of a magazine that had long been _____defunct_____.

14. Every general seems to have one defeat that marks the _____nadir_____ of his military fortunes—for example, Lee at Gettysburg, or Grant at Cold Harbor.

15. It's easy enough to back a popular program, but it takes real courage to _____espouse_____ a cause that most people oppose.

16. Since extroverts are _____gregarious_____ by nature, they usually prefer not to live alone.

17. Never once has the least whiff of a scandal or impropriety tainted the man's _____impeccable_____ reputation as an upstanding member of this agency.

18. "Don't you think it's a little foolish to pursue the young lady when your warm feelings for her are clearly not _____requited_____?" I asked.

19. From a(n) _____aesthetic_____ point of view, the painting didn't appeal to me, but I kept it because it was a memento of my childhood.

20. When you get more experience on the job, you will learn that a "request" from your employer is _____tantamount_____ to an order.

Synonyms

Choose the word from this unit that is **the same** or **most nearly the same** in meaning as the **boldface** word or expression in the given phrase. Write the word on the line provided.

1. **recompensed** them for their hospitality — requited
2. **entreated** the governor for a pardon — importuned
3. clinging to a **talisman** — fetish
4. **disconcerted** the conservative audience — discomfited
5. kept repeating that **doleful** melody — plaintive
6. tried to **interject** a different opinion — interpolate
7. **wilt** under the hot sun — languish
8. the **ubiquitous** sound of cell phone chatter — omnipresent
9. no more than a **cursory** note of apology — perfunctory
10. the **unfortunate** recipient of bad advice — hapless
11. **embraced** the values of democracy — espoused
12. expressed some **artistic** objections — aesthetic
13. **equivalent** to betraying a friend — tantamount
14. an **irremediable** act of perfidy — irreparable
15. known for his **outgoing** personality — gregarious

Antonyms

Choose the word from this unit that is **most nearly opposite** in meaning to the **boldface** word or expression in the given phrase. Write the word on the line provided.

16. an **extant** species of sea turtles — defunct
17. the **apex** of her fame — nadir
18. a **truthful** account of the events — mendacious
19. gave a **verbose** tribute to his partner — laconic
20. a **sullied** reputation — impeccable

Circle the **boldface** word that more satisfactorily completes each of the following sentences.

1. Though I left the house feeling "as fit as a fiddle," my spirits began to (**requite, languish**) after only five minutes in that withering heat.

2. Though few of us today stand on ceremony to quite the extent that our ancestors did, common courtesy is by no means (**plaintive, defunct**).

3. It is one thing to be concerned about discipline; it is quite another to make a (**perfunctory, fetish**) of it.

4. A diplomat must always proceed on the assumption that no rupture between nations, no matter how serious, is (**irreparable, perfunctory**).

5. Although fate has decreed that he make his living as a stockbroker, his main interests and talents are definitely (**irreparable, aesthetic**).

6. Prehistoric peoples banded together into tribes, not only for protection, but also to satisfy their (**gregarious, mendacious**) instincts.

7. The sternness of my boss's expression so (**discomfited, languished**) me that at first I had difficulty responding to the question.

8. In our desire to improve the quality of life in America, we should not be too quick to (**importune, espouse**) an idea simply because it is new.

9. The (**omnipresent, gregarious**) threat of a nuclear holocaust that characterized the Cold War era changed many people's attitudes toward war in profound ways.

10. When the scandal broke, the man found himself the (**hapless, impeccable**) victim of other people's misdeeds.

11. One of the best-known figures of American folklore is the lean, tough, (**laconic, hapless**) cowboy.

12. Perhaps we should be overjoyed that the great man condescended to give us a(n) (**aesthetic, perfunctory**) nod as we passed by.

13. I don't know which is more painful—to have to ask someone for a favor, or to have some unfortunate (**importune, discomfit**) one for help.

14. Her sense of tact is so (**hapless, impeccable**) and unerring that she can handle the most trying situation as if it were mere child's play.

15. Fortunately, our lawyer was able to produce documents that disproved the (**mendacious, omnipresent**) assertions of our former partner.

16. I hope to (**espouse, requite**) my parents for all the care they have shown me.

17. The legal adage "Silence implies consent" means that not objecting to an action that concerns you is (**perfunctory, tantamount**) to approving to it.

18. One of the comforting things about reaching the (**fetish, nadir**) of one's career is that the only place to go from there is up.

19. She sang a (**laconic, plaintive**) little ditty about a man who yearns wistfully for the girl he left behind many years before.

20. Many scholars believe that Beaumont or Fletcher (**interpolated, requited**) a scene or two into the present text of Shakespeare's *Macbeth*.

Read the following passage, in which some of the words you have studied in this unit appear in **boldface** type. Then complete each statement given below the passage by circling the letter of the item that is **the same** or **almost the same** in meaning as the highlighted word.

The Lost Generation

(Line)

Not only did World War I (1914–1918) have profound economic and political effects on the United States, but it also changed the social and moral outlook of the generation that lived through it. American youth lost its innocence on the bloody battlefields of Europe, and when the survivors returned home, they were

(5) **discomfited** by the very values they had gone off to war to defend. In their war-weary eyes, self-sacrificing patriotism and unquestioning respect for authority were **defunct**, even dangerous, ideals. They had seen the bravery of too many young men **requited** with a violent death or a

(10) gruesome maiming, and the psychic wounds inflicted by the war seemed as **irreparable** as the physical ones.

The American novelist Ernest Hemingway (1899–1961) has become a

(15) symbol of this post-World War I generation. Wounded in Italy in 1918 while serving as an ambulance driver for the Red Cross, Hemingway returned from the war disillusioned and restless.

(20) No longer able to **espouse** the values he had grown up with, Hemingway went to Paris in 1921 in search of a new moral and **aesthetic** code by which he could

Ernest Hemingway sits at his typewriter and reads his writings during his World War II work as a war correspondent.

live and work. There he met other artists and writers engaged in a similar search. In

(25) fact, it was one of these fellow expatriates, the American writer Gertrude Stein, who applied the phrase "the lost generation" to Hemingway and his contemporaries.

In Paris, Hemingway found the new values he was looking for and created a new type of hero and prose style to express what he had discovered. The Hemingway protagonist in novels like *The Sun Also Rises* and *A Farewell to Arms* finds

(30) meaning in a shattered world by constructing a personal code of honor and remaining faithful to it against all odds.

---

1. Discomfited (line 5) most nearly means
a. shocked   c. excited
(b.) disconcerted   d. comforted

2. The meaning of **defunct** (line 7) is
a. noble   (c.) dead
b. unrealistic   d. childish

3. Requited (line 9) is best defined as
(a.) recompensed   c. erased
b. equated   d. condemned

4. The meaning of **irreparable** (line 12) is
a. deep   (c.) irremediable
b. deadly   d. invisible

5. Espouse (line 20) most nearly means
a. reject   c. proclaim
b. ignore   (d.) embrace

6. Aesthetic (line 23) most nearly means
(a.) artistic   c. superior
b. personal   d. unbreakable

Vocabulary for Comprehension

*Read the following passage, in which some of the words you have studied in Units 10–12 appear in **boldface** type. Then answer questions 1–11 on page 139 on the basis of what is <u>stated</u> or <u>implied</u> in the passage and in the introductory statement.*

This passage focuses on the brief but remarkable era of silent films.

(Line)

It may be tempting for modern viewers to **deprecate** silent films. After all, they are technically primitive compared with today's movies. Much

(5) of the acting is exaggerated and overwrought, and the plots are often melodramatic or sentimental. Also, there is no dialogue except for some **laconic** titles that appear on the

(10) screen from time to time. Yet in their day, audiences flocked to see these movies, marveling at the **luminous** images on the flickering screen. To these enthusiastic new moviegoers,

(15) there was nothing as exciting as moving pictures!

Two men, Louis Lumiere and Thomas Alva Edison, one French and one American, are usually credited

(20) with the invention of the motion picture camera. In 1895 Louis Lumiere invented what he called the *cinematographe.* This compact, versatile instrument was **tantamount**

(25) to a camera, film-processing unit, and projector all in one. Because Edison's camera was bulkier and less portable than Lumiere's, the Europeans took an early lead in the development of

(30) motion pictures. The Americans soon caught up, however, and Hollywood eventually became the capital of a vastly profitable international film industry, which began in the 1910s

(35) with the production of silent movies.

Many contemporary viewers have overlooked the masterpieces of the silent era because they find the adjustments they must make to watch

(40) these films **onerous**. Without knowing it, however, they are depriving themselves of some unparalleled pleasures. These include the brilliant physical comedy of Buster Keaton,

(45) the visual expressiveness of Charlie Chaplin, and the landmark editing, camera work, and set designs of the great pioneer filmmakers D. W. Griffith, Sergei Eisenstein, F. R.

(50) Murnau, and Fritz Lang.

1. In the first paragraph (lines 1–16), the writer's main focus is on
  a. contrasting the drawbacks of silent films with the excitement they inspired in audiences of the day
  b. describing the landmark camera work of some silent filmmakers
  c. discussing the invention of the motion picture camera
  d. comparing Keaton and Chaplin
  e. introducing some of the writer's favorite silent films

2. The meaning of **deprecate** (line 2) is
  a. underestimate
  b. belittle
  c. ignore
  d. misunderstand
  e. overpraise

3. In paragraph 1, the author mentions all of the following as drawbacks of silent films EXCEPT
  a. overwrought acting
  b. laconic captions
  c. melodramatic plots
  d. primitive technical achievements
  e. unattractive set designs

4. Laconic (line 9) most nearly means
  a. obscure
  b. humorous
  c. succinct
  d. brilliant
  e. redundant

5. Luminous (line 12) is best defined as
  a. bright
  b. shocking
  c. blurred
  d. lifelike
  e. timeless

6. From the details given in paragraph 2 (lines 17–35), one may reasonably infer that the Americans caught up with the Europeans because
  a. the Americans made more films
  b. technical refinements made film equipment less bulky and more portable

  c. most of the leading actors and filmmakers were American
  d. the climate of Hollywood was appealing
  e. Louis Lumiere's equipment often broke down

7. Tantamount (line 24) most nearly means
  a. opposed
  b. compared
  c. similar
  d. supplementary
  e. equivalent

8. According to the passage, the international film industry began in
  a. the 1880s
  b. the 1890s
  c. the 1910s
  d. the 1920s
  e. the 1930s

9. In paragraph 3 (lines 36–50), the writer most likely includes so many examples in order to
  a. display a high level of expertise
  b. persuade the reader of the claims made for silent films in the passage
  c. bolster the claim that silent moves are primitive compared with today's films
  d. prove that directors were more skilled than actors in the silent film era
  e. trace the ways in which silent film stars influenced one another

10. Onerous (line 40) most nearly means
  a. silly
  b. impossible
  c. burdensome
  d. easy
  e. annoying

11. The writer's attitude toward silent films might best be described as
  a. enthusiastic
  b. respectful
  c. neutral
  d. skeptical
  e. dismissive

Grammar in Context

In the sentence "Yet in their day, audiences flocked to see these movies, marveling at the luminous images on the flickering screen" (lines 10–14 on page 138), the participial phrase "marveling at the luminous images" clearly modifies "audiences." However, this connection would have been lost if the author of the passage had written "Marveling at the luminous images on the flickering screen, these movies were flocked to by audiences." A participial phrase that does not sensibly modify any word or group of words in a sentence is called a **dangling participle**.

You can use these techniques to correct a dangling participle: (1) Add a word or words that the phrase can logically modify. (2) Add words to the phrase so that its meaning is clear. (3) Reword the entire sentence.

On the lines provided, rewrite each of the following sentences, correcting dangling participles. Write "correct" if the sentence is correct.

Answers may vary; sample answers given.

1. Listening to my great-uncle's stories, it was interesting to hear him describe the silent film era.
   As I listened to my great-uncle's stories, it was interesting to hear him describe the silent film era.

2. Tightly constructed, all my uncle's contemporaries enjoyed silents.
   All my great-uncle's contemporaries enjoyed the tightly constructed silents.

3. When evaluating a silent film, a number of criteria should be employed.
   In the evaluation of a silent film, a number of criteria should be employed.

4. While discussing silents with some friends, the topic of titles came up.
   In my discussions of silents with some friends, the topic of titles came up.

5. After searching in several catalogs, *City Lights* with Charlie Chaplin was located.
   After searching in several catalogs, we located *City Lights* with Charlie Chaplin.

6. Contrasting the comedy of Charlie Chaplin and Buster Keaton, the lecturer enthralled the audience.
   correct

7. Sitting on the edge of their seats, the films of Fritz Lang and D. W. Griffith delighted audiences.
   The films of Fritz Lang and D. W. Griffith delighted audiences, who sat on the edge of their seats.

8. Beginning in the late 1920s, however, silents were eclipsed in popularity by talkies.
   In the late 1920s, however, silents were eclipsed in popularity by talkies.

Two-Word Completions

Circle the pair of words that best complete the meaning of each of the following passages.

See pages T38–T48 for explanations of answers.

1. As soon as I heard its _____ cries for help, I knew that the _____ animal had once again got its paw caught in the grillwork on the front porch.

  a. obsequious . . . moribund   c. onerous . . . defunct
  b. laconic . . . impeccable   (d. plaintive . . . hapless)

2. Though Seneca embraced the tenets of Stoicism in their entirety, Cicero _____ no one school of Greek philosophy but, like a true _____ , chose what he thought best from each and ignored the rest.

  a. discomfited . . . penitent   (c. espoused . . . eclectic)
  b. abrogated . . . aesthetic   d. deprecated . . . foible

3. Although many of the pioneers found it difficult at first to cope with the _____ of frontier life, they were a hardy race who quickly became _____ such rough-and-tumble living.

  a. rudiments . . . importuned by   c. detritus . . . decimated by
  (b. asperities . . . inured to)   d. shambles . . . discomfited by

4. In *Of Human Bondage,* W. Somerset Maugham's main character Philip Carey is _____ by external adversity as well as his own self-consciousness because at birth he was the _____ recipient of a club foot.

  a. rebuffed . . . sporadic   c. decimated . . . laconic
  b. requited . . . benign   (d. discomfited . . . hapless)

5. The "truth-in-advertising" laws that many states have recently passed were in part designed to discourage crooks and _____ from making _____ claims about the products they offer to the unsuspecting public.

  (a. charlatans . . . mendacious)   c. fetishes . . . laconic
  b. necromancers . . . sporadic   d. cabals . . . eclectic

6. Though the man appeared to be the most _____ pauper on the face of the earth, he had actually _____ large sums of money in various hiding places in the hovel he called home.

  a. flaccid . . . burnished   c. ambient . . . interpolated
  (b. impecunious . . . sequestered)   d. benign . . . decimated

Choosing the Right Meaning

Read each sentence carefully. Then circle the item that best completes the statement below the sentence.

See pages T38–T48 for explanations of answers.

The infamous Hatfield-McCoy feud began in earnest when, in 1882, the Hatfields requited the slaying of Ellison Hatfield by executing three McCoy brothers. (2)

1. In line 2 the word **requited** is used to mean
(a. avenged)   b. recompensed   c. reimbursed   d. witnessed

The deep hush was broken when a gust of wind billowed through the parlor window and winnowed the pages of the book that lay open on the table. (2)

2. The word **winnowed** in line 2 most nearly means
a. deleted   b. sorted out   c. tore   (d. fanned)

By 1864 Southern war-making resources were so depleted that Confederate commanders could deal only temporary rebuffs to the Union juggernaut. (2)

3. In line 2 the word **rebuffs** is best defined as
a. curt rejections   b. cease-fires   c. snubs   (d. setbacks)

"When from our better selves we have too long
Been parted by the hurrying world, and droop (2)
Sick of its business, of its pleasures tired,
How gracious, how benign, is Solitude," (Wordsworth, *The Prelude*) (4)

4. In line 4 the word **benign** is used to mean
a. forgiving   (b. salutary)   c. benevolent   d. lonely

The mad scientist, a stock character of Hollywood B movies, is often found in a dark laboratory, surrounded by a sinister array of beakers of ebullient potions. (2)

5. The best definition for the word **ebullient** in line 2 is
(a. boiling)   b. enthusiastic   c. delicious   d. poisoned

Antonyms

*In each of the following groups, circle the word or expression that is most nearly the **opposite** of the word in **boldface** type.*

1. forgo
(a. indulge)
b. concoct
c. refrain from
d. serve

2. espouse
a. devise
b. select
(c. repudiate)
d. support

3. abrogate
(a. renew)
b. debate
c. nullify
d. reveal

4. rebuff
a. spurn
b. expect
(c. welcome)
d. question

5. delectable
a. delicious
b. powerful
c. traditional
(d. repulsive)

6. impecunious
a. impoverished
b. close
(c. wealthy)
d. kindly

7. burnish
(a. tarnish)
b. melt
c. polish
d. steal

8. laconic
a. humorous
(b. verbose)
c. concise
d. sarcastic

9. mendacious
a. deceitful
b. convincing
c. unwilling
d. truthful

11. onerous
a. burdensome
b. easy
c. supplementary
d. obligatory

13. sporadic
a. fitful
b. continuous
c. bloody
d. mock

15. irreparable
a. fatal
b. instant
c. unforeseen
d. reversible

10. eclectic
a. selective
b. weird
c. creative
d. uniform

12. deprecate
a. approve
b. describe
c. contrive
d. condemn

14. moribund
a. dying
b. depressed
c. flourishing
d. controversial

16. flaccid
a. weak
b. firm
c. new
d. elected

Word Families

A. On the line provided, write the word you have learned in Units 10–12 that is related to each of the following nouns.
EXAMPLE: attenuation—**attenuate**

1. deprecation, deprecator — deprecate
2. gregariousness — gregarious
3. oscillation, oscillator — oscillate
4. mendacity, mendaciousness — mendacious
5. omnipresence — omnipresent
6. abrogation — abrogate
7. plaintiveness — plaintive
8. ebullience, ebullition — ebullient
9. requital — requite
10. espousal, espouser — espouse
11. inexorability, inexorableness — inexorable
12. discomfiture — discomfit
13. decimation — decimate
14. interpolation, interpolator — interpolate
15. sequestration — sequester
16. obtuseness — obtuse
17. impeccability — impeccable

B. On the line provided, write the word you have learned in Units 10–12 that is related to each of the following verbs.
EXAMPLE: fetishize—**fetish**

18. repent — penitent
19. repair — irreparable
20. illuminate — luminous

Word Associations

In each of the following groups, circle the word that is best defined or suggested by the given phrase.

1. humbling himself in an effort to be accepted
a. sporadic   (b. obsequious)   c. peremptory   d. mendacious

2. never happy unless she has a lot of people around her
a. peremptory   b. irreparable   c. moribund   (d. gregarious)

3. suffering an unbroken string of bad breaks and disappointments
a. delectable   b. benign   c. obtuse   (d. hapless)

4. regard his suggestions with deep suspicion
a. defunct   (b. askance)   c. plaintive   d. laconic

5. laden with
a. sporadic   (b. fraught)   c. tantamount   d. impeccable

6. a small group that plotted to oust me from the club presidency
a. necromancer   (b. cabal)   c. cavil   d. charlatan

7. getting used to cold weather before going on the camping trip
(a. inure)   b. espouse   c. winnow   d. attenuate

8. a minor, often humorous failing
a. cavil   (b. foible)   c. rebuff   d. detritus

9. "At that moment, life seemed more hopeless that it ever had before or since."
a. detritus   b. cabal   (c. nadir)   d. shambles

10. pine away
a. sequester   b. decimate   (c. languish)   d. inure

11. given to trivial and frivolous objections
a. attenuate   b. forgo   c. reconnoiter   (d. cavil)

12. lessen the impact of the economic recession
a. oscillate   b. winnow   c. rebuff   (d. attenuate)

13. how fate may sometimes be characterized
(a. inexorable)   b. charlatan   c. perfunctory   d. ambient

14. will never undertake anything without his "lucky coin" with him
(a. fetish)   b. burnish   c. detritus   d. nadir

15. a type of wizard or warlock
a. penitent   b. charlatan   (c. necromancer)   d. cabal

16. genuinely sorry for one's mistakes
a. obsequious   b. ebullient   c. moribund   (d. penitent)

17. exposed as an utter fraud
a. shambles   (b. charlatan)   c. cavil   d. detritus

18. learning the basic strokes, moves, and tactics of tennis
(a. rudiments)   b. fetishes   c. foibles   d. eclectics

19. an artillery barrage that took a heavy toll of life and limb
a. abrogate   (b. decimate)   c. sequester   d. importune

20. wreckage
(a. detritus)   b. fetish   c. shambles   d. nadir

rog—to ask, beg, call

This root appears in **abrogate** (page 124), meaning "to cancel, to abolish by authoritative action." Some other words based on the same root are listed below.

abrogation	derogation	interrogative	supererogatory
arrogance	interrogation	prorogue	surrogate

From the list of words above, choose the one that corresponds to each of the brief definitions below. Write the word in the blank space in the illustrative sentence below the definition.

1. exaggerated self-importance, haughty pride

The king was corrupted by power and, over time, exchanged his humility for _____**arrogance**_____.

2. an act or expression that detracts from reputation, value, power, etc. (*"to call down"*)

The aid workers deeply resented any _____**derogation**_____ of their motives.

3. a substitute, deputy; a judge in charge of the probate of wills, administration of estates, and appointment of guardians

While my parents were on vacation, my aunt served as a _____**surrogate**_____ guardian.

4. an act of formal or systematic questioning

The detective asked question after question during the _____**interrogation**_____ of the prime suspect.

5. a cancellation; the act of repealing or annulling (*"calling off"*)

Unfavorable evidence has emerged, forcing the _____**abrogation**_____ of the agreement between the two parties.

6. to discontinue a session of a legislative body; to defer, postpone

The prime minister was determined to _____**prorogue**_____ the legislative assembly until all members were present.

7. asking a question; having the form or character of a question; a word or sentence that asks a question

In Spanish class, we are learning how to phrase _____**interrogative**_____ sentences.

8. performed or observed beyond the degree required; demanded, or expected; unnecessary; superfluous

"We could do with fewer _____**supererogatory**_____ remarks," the teacher observed.

From the list of words on page 145, choose the one that best completes each of the following sentences. Write the word in the space provided.

1. The suspect was led into a small _____interrogation_____ room, where two police officers questioned him until the wee hours of the morning.

2. It was kind of the gas station attendant to give me directions to the next town, but to give me a map, along with written directions, was clearly _____supererogatory_____.

3. Her colossal _____arrogance_____ led her to dismiss the feelings and concerns of her "inferiors" as scarcely worth noting.

4. "Do-gooder" is occasionally used as a term of _____derogation_____, in which the meaning of the word is inverted; it actually denotes someone who performs benevolent acts, but for dubious or attention-seeking reasons.

5. It is up to the _____surrogate_____ court to ensure that the estate is given to the appropriate parties.

6. Though her comment about cleaning the room was _____interrogative_____ in form, it was clear that she was issuing an order, not asking a question.

7. Our society may need improvement, but the answer does not lie in the _____abrogation_____ of the ideals, rules, and institutions we have inherited from the past.

8. The kings of England would often abruptly _____prorogue_____ Parliament to prevent the passage of measures unwelcome to the throne.

Circle the **boldface** word that more satisfactorily completes each of the following sentences.

1. Remember to use the proper end punctuation to distinguish (**interrogative,** **supererogatory**) sentences from exclamatory statements.

2. My Great-Aunt Sylvia was like a (**derogation,** **surrogate**) grandmother to me.

3. Legislators worked as quickly as possible to complete the bill before the session could be (**interrogated,** **prorogued**).

4. Since the (**abrogation,** **interrogative**) of the international trade agreement, debts owed to the World Bank have increased.

5. The experienced trial lawyer instructed her client to stay calm during what might prove to be a grueling (**interrogation,** **surrogate**).

6. Jonathan Swift hurled (**arrogances,** **derogations**) against the British for not doing more to aid the impoverished in Ireland.

7. My father always regarded it as a mark of utter (**arrogance,** **abrogation**) to attempt to solve the devilishly difficult Sunday crossword puzzle using a pen.

8. After a delicious pear tart, cinnamon ice cream, and hot cider, we simply had no room for the (**surrogate,** **supererogatory**) chocolates the waiter brought to our table.

Analogies

In each of the following, circle the item that best completes the comparison.

See pages T38–T48 for explanations of answers.

1. surveillance is to **monitor** as
a. espionage is to overlook
b. vigilance is to sleep
c. sabotage is to pacify
d. reconnaissance is to reconnoiter ⟵

2. carp is to **cavil** as
a. decry is to deprecate ⟵
b. conciliate is to nettle
c. hallow is to travesty
d. espouse is to eschew

3. omnipresent is to **ubiquitous** as
a. moribund is to obsolescent ⟵
b. laconic is to garrulous
c. extant is to extinct
d. eclectic is to monolithic

4. pendulum is to **oscillate** as
a. clock is to temporize
b. scale is to portend
c. wave is to undulate ⟵
d. wheel is to disarray

5. hypocrite is to **dissemble** as
a. charlatan is to feign ⟵
b. suppliant is to sham
c. derelict is to simulate
d. counterpart is to conceal

6. sporadic is to **intermittent** as
a. brackish is to fresh
b. ephemeral is to transitory ⟵
c. fraught is to devoid
d. utopian is to feasible

7. indigent is to **impecunious** as
a. furtive is to overt
b. halcyon is to turbulent
c. hapless is to unfortunate ⟵
d. felicitous is to awkward

8. acuity is to **obtuse** as
a. perspicacity is to myopic ⟵
b. equity is to impartial
c. credence is to gullible
d. asperity is to harsh

9. luminous is to **refulgent** as
a. ebullient is to saturnine
b. murky is to lucid
c. verdant is to arid
d. redolent is to aromatic ⟵

10. miser is to **sequester** as
a. misanthrope is to invest
b. neophyte is to filch
c. agnostic is to embezzle
d. spendthrift is to squander ⟵

Choosing the Right Meaning

Read each sentence carefully. Then circle the item that best completes the statement below the sentence.

See pages T38–T48 for explanations of answers.

I am at a loss to judge whether her self-deprecating manner bespeaks genuine humility or false modesty. (2)

1. The word **self-deprecating** in line 1 is best defined as
a. self-belittling ⟵   b. self-satisfied   c. self-assured   d. self-serving

"Such smiling rogues as these,
Like rats, oft bite the holy cords a-twain (2)
Which are too intrise t'unloose; smooth every passion . . .
Renege, affirm, and turn their halcyon beaks (4)
With every gale, and vary of their masters,
Knowing nought, like digs, but following." (6)
      (Shakespeare, King Lear, II, 2, 79–81, 84–86)

2. In line 4 the word **halcyon** is used to mean
a. peaceful   b. kingfisher ⟵   c. prosperous   d. happy

A blockbuster movie or a best-selling novel often spawns a host of usually paltry
imitations cranked out by those opportunist hacks whose eyes are ever fixed on   (2)
the dollar.

3. The best definition for the word **paltry** in line 1 is

a. despicable   b. mean   c. measly   (d. inferior)

Physicists employ gigantic devices called particle accelerators to smash atoms
together at tremendous velocities in order to investigate the primordial nature   (2)
of matter.

4. The word **primordial** in line 2 most nearly means

a. earliest   (b. fundamental)   c. primeval   d. original

The movie is cracked up to be a scathing indictment of the fashion industry, but
I could detect very little sting in it at all. On the contrary, its effect, to my mind,   (2)
was rather obtuse.

5. In line 3 the word **obtuse** is used to mean

a. blunt   b. thick   c. dumb   (d. mild)

Two-Word Completions

*Circle the pair of words that best complete the meaning
of each of the following sentences.*

See pages T38–T48 for explanations of answers.

1. The poor man had been _____ in the Bastille and left to
_____ there without hope of reprieve for over twenty years.

a. mandated . . . demur   c. inured . . . exacerbate
(b. incarcerated . . . languish)   d. garnered . . . vacillate

2. The _____ antics of the troupe of clowns convulsed the audience.
_____ of laughter repeatedly shook the hall like salvos of musketry.

a. fatuous . . . Gambits   c. feckless . . . Bastions
(b. ludicrous . . . Paroxysms)   d. inane . . . Litanies

3. After the bulldozers and wrecking balls had completed the lengthy task of
_____ the building, a convoy of dump trucks began the job of
carting off the resultant _____.

a. embellishing . . . flotsam   (c. razing . . . detritus)
b. belaboring . . . murk   d. exhuming . . . largesse

4. For two solid hours, our artillery kept up an _____ barrage
of cannon fire. It _____ the enemy's ranks with such deadly
accuracy that barely one man in ten was left standing after it was over.

(a. unremitting . . . decimated)   c. inexorable . . . atrophied
b. intermittent . . . winnowed   d. illusory . . . enervated

5. Since all the members of my little _____ of friends truly enjoy each other's
company, our weekly get-togethers are remarkably _____ affairs.

a. echelon . . . vituperative   c. shambles . . . gregarious
b. cabal . . . laconic   (d. coterie . . . convivial)

Enriching Your Vocabulary

Read the passage below. Then complete the exercise at the bottom of the page.

Borrowings from Arabic

In 1095, Pope Urban II appealed to the Christian knights and lords of Western Europe to undertake the First Crusade. He wanted to liberate the Holy Land from Arab Moslems, who had been living there since the 7th century. Subsequently, and for more than a century, additional crusades were launched. These expeditions brought Europeans into contact with Arabic civilization. As a result of these and other encounters, some Arabic words were eventually incorporated into the English language. One such word is *nadir* (Unit 12), meaning the lowest point.

Prior to the Crusades, Moslem armies had conquered most of the lands that comprise the Iberian Peninsula. Europeans and Arabs met and mingled in thriving commercial and artistic centers like Cordova and Granada. Some English words borrowed from Arabic at this time include: *caraway, jasmine, lilac, lime, orange, saffron,* and *tamarind*. Europeans also learned to understand the *salaam,* or respectful salutation that involves a deep bow and placement of the right hand on the forehead. This formal Arabic greeting is literally a wish for peace.

Marrakech street fairs serve as a mecca for cultural exchange between Europeans, Americans, Asians, and Africans.

In Column A below are 7 more words and phrases that have entered English from the Arabic. With or without a dictionary, match each word or phrase with its meaning in Column B.

Column A

e	**1.** alcove
g	**2.** algebra
c	**3.** cipher
b	**4.** sherbet
a	**5.** sofa
f	**6.** tariff
d	**7.** zenith

Column B

a. a long upholstered piece of furniture designed to seat several people at once (from the Arabic for "divan")

b. a sweet kind of ice cream made from water or milk and egg white, fruit juice, or gelatin (from the Arabic for "a drink")

c. a person or thing without value or influence; a kind of code; a coded message (from the Arabic for "zero")

d. the highest point above the horizon attained by a celestial body; any summit (from the Arabic for "road over head")

e. a partly enclosed recess forming part of a room or garden (from the Arabic for "the vault")

f. a duty on imported or exported goods; a system of such duties (from the Arabic for "information")

g. the branch of mathematics dealing with the properties of quantities (from the Arabic for "the science of calculating")

Definitions

Note carefully the spelling, pronunciation, part(s) of speech, and definition(s) of each of the following words. Then write the word in the blank space(s) in the illustrative sentence(s) following. Finally, study the lists of synonyms and antonyms given at the end of each entry.

1. abstruse
(ab strüs')

(*adj.*) extremely difficult to understand

The physicist tried to explain her _____ **abstruse** _____ research in the field of quantum mechanics.

SYNONYMS: esoteric, arcane, recondite, occult
ANTONYMS: simple, straightforward

2. affront
(ə frənt')

(*n.*) an open or intentional insult; a slight; (*v.*) to insult to one's face; to face in defiance, confront

The prisoner felt that being referred to by number rather than by name was an _____ **affront** _____ to her dignity.

In the nineteenth century, Irish immigrants to the United States were _____ **affronted** _____ by signs reading: No Irish Need Apply.

SYNONYMS: (*n.*) offense; (*v.*) offend
ANTONYMS: (*n., v.*) compliment, praise

3. canard
(kə närd')

(*n.*) a false rumor, fabricated story

The tabloid journalist was responsible for spreading the _____ **canard** _____ about the candidate's mental health.

SYNONYM: hoax

4. captious
(kap' shəs)

(*adj.*) excessively ready to find fault; given to petty criticism; intended to trap, confuse, or show up

She is an invariably _____ **captious** _____ critic.

SYNONYMS: faultfinding, nit-picking, carping
ANTONYM: uncritical

5. cognizant
(käg' ni zənt)

(*adj.*) aware, knowledgeable, informed; having jurisdiction

Police officers must make sure that crime suspects are made _____ **cognizant** _____ of their rights before they are questioned.

SYNONYMS: conscious, acquainted
ANTONYMS: unaware, unconscious, oblivious

6. contrite
(kən trīt')

(*adj.*) regretful for some misdeed or sin; plagued by a sense of guilt; thoroughly penitent

The convicted felon had the look of someone who was truly _____ **contrite** _____ and ready to pay for his crimes.

SYNONYMS: remorseful, rueful
ANTONYMS: unrepentant, unapologetic, impenitent

7. cynosure
(sī′ nə shür)

(*n.*) the center of attraction, attention, or interest; something that serves to guide or direct

For over a century, the Statue of Liberty has been the _____ cynosure _____ for millions of immigrants entering New York Harbor.

SYNONYM: focus

8. decorous
(dek′ ər əs)

(*adj.*) well behaved, dignified, socially proper

On formal occasions, like weddings and graduations, participants are expected to behave in a _____ decorous _____ manner.

SYNONYMS: seemly, becoming, tasteful
ANTONYMS: unseemly, unbecoming, improper, tasteless

9. deign
(dān)

(*v.*) to think it appropriate or suitable to one's dignity to do something; to condescend

The enlisted men were surprised that the four-star general _____ deigned _____ to speak to them as he toured the camp.

SYNONYMS: deem, stoop

10. desiccated
(des′ ə kā tid)

(*adj., part.*) thoroughly dried out; divested of spirit or vitality; arid and uninteresting

The cornfield was _____ desiccated _____ by the scorching sun after the long, hot summer without rain.

SYNONYMS: dehydrated, shriveled, parched
ANTONYMS: sodden, soggy, waterlogged, drenched

11. efficacy
(ef′ ə kə sē)

(*n.*) the power to produce a desired result

The pharmaceutical company has done extensive research to prove the _____ efficacy _____ of the new drug they are marketing.

SYNONYMS: effectiveness, potency, reliability
ANTONYMS: ineffectiveness, impotence

12. engender
(in jen′ dər)

(*v.*) to bring into existence, give rise to, produce; to come into existence, assume form

The university has made an appealing videotape in order to _____ engender _____ student interest in studying abroad.

SYNONYMS: beget, generate, cause, form
ANTONYMS: stop, deter

13. ethereal
(i thēr′ ē əl)

(*adj.*) light, airy, delicate; highly refined; suggesting what is heavenly (rather than earthbound)

The Renaissance painter Fra Angelico captured the
_____ **ethereal** _____ beauty of angels in his
famous frescoes.
SYNONYMS: heavenly, celestial, gossamer
ANTONYMS: infernal, hellish, thick, heavy

14. facade
(fə säd′)

(*n.*) the front or face of a building; a surface appearance (as
opposed to what may lie behind)
After years of neglect, the sooty _____ **facade** _____
of the cathedral is finally getting a much needed cleaning.
SYNONYMS: exterior, surface, mask, pretense
ANTONYM: interior

15. ghoulish
(gül′ ish)

(*adj.*) revolting in an unnatural or morbid way; suggestive of
someone who robs graves or otherwise preys on the dead
The _____ **ghoulish** _____ practice of grave robbing is
sometimes motivated by the desire to find and sell valuables.
SYNONYMS: fiendish, barbarous, monstrous

16. incongruous
(in kän′ grü əs)

(*adj.*) not in keeping, unsuitable, incompatible
Abraham Lincoln, the backwoods lawyer, and Mary Todd,
the rich socialite, seemed an _____ **incongruous** _____ couple.
SYNONYMS: discordant, jarring
ANTONYMS: compatible, harmonious, consistent

17. machination
(mak ə nā′ shən)

(*n.*) a crafty, scheming, or underhanded action designed to
accomplish some (usually evil) end
Shakespeare's Othello was the victim not only of Iago's evil
_____ **machinations** _____ but also of his own jealous nature.
SYNONYMS: plot, scheme, maneuver

18. mesmerize
(mez′ mə rīz)

(*v.*) to hypnotize, entrance; to fascinate, enthrall, bewitch
The magician was able to _____ **mesmerize** _____ the
audience with his fast-moving hands and distracting chatter.

19. opprobrium
(ə prō′ brē əm)

(*n.*) disgrace arising from shameful conduct; contempt, reproach
Despite the passage of centuries, _____ **opprobrium** _____
is still attached to the name of the traitor Benedict Arnold.
SYNONYMS: infamy, dishonor, odium, shame
ANTONYMS: acclaim, honor, glory, renown

20. putative
(pyü′ tə tiv)

(*adj.*) generally regarded as such; reputed; hypothesized, inferred
Ancient Celtic rituals and ceremonies are the
_____ **putative** _____ origins of some of our
modern Halloween customs.
SYNONYMS: supposed, presumed
ANTONYMS: known, corroborated, confirmed

Completing the Sentence

From the words for this unit, choose the one that best completes each of the following sentences. Write the word in the space provided.

1. The longer I study this country's history, the more ___**cognizant**___ I become of my rich heritage of freedom.

2. Some historians question whether Benedict Arnold really deserves all the ___**opprobrium**___ he has been accorded as America's arch-traitor.

3. At the risk of appearing a trifle ___**captious**___ , I would like to raise a few small objections to the wording of this proposal.

4. After the battle, camp followers began the ___**ghoulish**___ process of stripping the dead of whatever valuables they possessed.

5. Some teachers are able to present the most ___**abstruse**___ subjects in terms that are crystal-clear to even the dullest of students.

6. The ___**machinations**___ of the unscrupulous wheeler-dealers involved in that unsavory scandal boggle the imagination.

7. I didn't really believe that he was sorry for what he had done until I saw the ___**contrite**___ expression on his sad little face.

8. The pages of the old book were so ___**desiccated**___ that they began to crumble as soon as we touched them.

9. There is not a vast body of evidence that supports the idea that poverty tends to ___**engender**___ crime.

10. To be the ___**cynosure**___ of all eyes could be the joyous fulfillment of a dream or the unhappy realization of a nightmare.

11. The only surefire way to establish the ___**efficacy**___ of a new drug in treating a disease is to test it "in the field."

12. For more than five minutes she stared at the telegram containing the bad news, as if she were ___**mesmerized**___ .

13. His fantastic stories about his academic, athletic, financial, and romantic achievements are a(n) ___**affront**___ to common sense.

14. Am I supposed to feel honored simply because that arrogant lout sometimes ___**deigns**___ to nod vaguely in my direction?

15. Except for a balcony built during the Truman administration, the ___**facade**___ of the White House has remained virtually unchanged since it was constructed.

16. What could be more ___**incongruous**___ than the 6-foot, 7-inch center on the basketball team dolled up in a baby clothes for the class play!

17. No one knows for sure who really wrote the scene, but Shakespeare is generally regarded as its ___**putative**___ author.

18. Only a thoroughly naive and gullible person would actually believe every preposterous _____ canard _____ that circulates in this school.

19. The child's conduct during the ceremony may not have been appropriately _____ decorous _____, but it wasn't horrendous either.

20. The cherubic faces and _____ ethereal _____ voices of the choristers almost made me believe that the music they were singing was coming from heaven.

Synonyms

*Choose the word from this unit that is **the same** or **most nearly the same** in meaning as the **boldface** word or expression in the given phrase. Write the word on the line provided.*

1. a **fiendish** interest in death _____ ghoulish _____

2. exposed as a total **hoax** _____ canard _____

3. **bewitched** by the speaker's soothing voice _____ mesmerized _____

4. **esoteric** concepts developed by experts _____ abstruse _____

5. **stooped** to give a few interviews _____ deigned _____

6. the **focus** of a dazzled audience _____ cynosure _____

7. **conscious** of our mutual responsibilities _____ cognizant _____

8. disliked for his **nit-picking** tendencies _____ captious _____

9. an **offense** to an entire group of people _____ affront _____

10. the **jarring** reunion of longtime rivals _____ incongruous _____

11. foiled the **schemes** of the villain _____ machinations _____

12. **begets** distrust by covering up mistakes _____ engenders _____

13. paintings of women with **heavenly** qualities _____ ethereal _____

14. showed a mere **pretence** of gratitude _____ facade _____

15. brought **shame** on the whole family _____ opprobrium _____

Antonyms

*Choose the word from this unit that is **most nearly opposite** in meaning to the **boldface** word or expression in the given phrase. Write the word on the line provided.*

16. the **known** whereabouts of the fugitive _____ putative _____

17. the **ineffectiveness** of our foreign policy _____ efficacy _____

18. the **unrepentant** ringleaders of the riot _____ contrite _____

19. looked over the **soggy** farmland _____ desiccated _____

20. the **unseemly** appearance of the judge _____ decorous _____

Choosing the Right Word

*Circle the **boldface** word that more satisfactorily completes each of the following sentences.*

1. If you had listened to my warnings in the first place, there would be no need for you to feel (**contrite,** desiccated) now.

2. A government that fails to bring about peaceful reform (**engenders,** deigns) the kind of social unrest that makes violent revolution inevitable.

3. "Do we have sufficient evidence at hand," I asked, "to judge the (**efficacy,** cognizance) of the new method of teaching reading?"

4. In my youthful folly, I inadvertently (**affronted,** engendered) the very people whose aid I was attempting to enlist.

5. The (efficacy, **opprobrium**) of history forever attaches itself to the name of Lee Harvey Oswald, the assassin of President Kennedy.

6. For any actor, it is a unique thrill to know that when you are alone on stage, you are the (facade, **cynosure**) of hundreds of pairs of eyes.

7. He tried to conceal his lack of scholarship and intellectual depth by using unnecessarily (efficacious, **abstruse**) language.

8. The book describes in great detail the odious (**machinations,** facades) involved in Adolf Hitler's rise to power in Germany.

9. The President must always be on his toes because a careless answer to a (contrite, **captious**) question could land him in political hot water.

10. The candidate's "shocking revelation" about his opponent was later shown to be nothing more than a malicious (**canard,** cynosure).

11. I resent your nasty question about whether or not I will "(**deign,** affront) to speak to ordinary students" after I'm elected class president.

12. The audience was so quiet after the curtain fell that I couldn't tell whether they were bored or (deigned, **mesmerized**) by her artistry.

13. Like many people who are completely wrapped up in themselves, she simply isn't (**cognizant,** decorous) of the larger world around her.

14. His unmistakable interest in the gruesome details of the tragedy revealed that he possessed the sensibilities of a (canard, **ghoul**).

15. The play is so peopled with spirits and other incorporeal beings that it has the (**ethereal,** captious) quality of a dream.

16. Her quiet speech, subdued clothes, and (**decorous,** desiccated) manner made it hard to believe that she was a famous rock star.

17. He acts like someone whose vital juices have long since dried up, leaving only a drab and (**desiccated,** contrite) shell behind.

18. It has been said that humor is essentially the yoking of (**incongruous,** ethereal) elements within a familiar or recognizable framework.

19. Philologists believe that many Western languages can be traced back to a (**putative,** decorous) parent tongue known as Indo-European.

20. It wasn't at all hard of recognize signs of extreme uneasiness beneath her (canard, **facade**) of buoyant optimism.

*Read the following passage, in which some of the words you have studied in this unit appear in **boldface** type. Then complete each statement given below the passage by circling the letter of the item that is **the same** or **almost the same** in meaning as the highlighted word.*

Portrait of a Lady

(Line)

At the Louvre, the famous art museum in Paris, the **cynosure** for many is the *Mona Lisa*. This portrait was painted in the early sixteenth century by the Renaissance genius Leonardo da Vinci, and it has been fascinating viewers ever since.

The subject is an aristocratic woman with a **mesmerizing** gaze and the tantalizing hint of a smile. Contrary to popular opinion, the word "Mona" is not (5) part of the woman's name but a title of respect similar to "madam" or "my lady." The identity of Leonardo's sitter is not absolutely certain, but she is generally believed to be Lisa di Antonio Maria Gherardini, the wife of a (10) prominent Florentine named Francesco del Giocondo. It is on the basis of this **putative** identification that the painting is sometimes referred to as *La Gioconda*. Whoever the lady was, Leonardo placed her amidst an amazing (15) landscape of rocks, roads, water, and trees that were more a product of his imagination than a realistic depiction of the Tuscan countryside near where he was born and spent most of his life. (20)

The Mona Lisa, on display at the Louvre in Paris, is painted with such subtle brush strokes that they are almost invisible to the naked eye.

Why this painting has **engendered** so much public and professional interest over the centuries is hard to pinpoint. The sitter is not beautiful by most conventional standards, and yet she exerts a powerful allure. Perhaps it is (25) the contrast between her **decorous** posture and her direct, almost challenging, gaze that so captivates. Or maybe it is the way her mysterious smile suggests both the **ethereal** and earthly dimensions of feminine attractiveness. But whatever the allure, the *Mona Lisa* is certain to captivate for years to come. (30)

---

1. Cynosure (line 1) most nearly means
a. confusion
b. focus
c. excitement
d. assurance

2. The meaning of **mesmerizing** (line 4) is
a. entrancing
b. myopic
c. deadly
d. inspiring

3. Putative (line 12) is best defined as
a. careful
b. positive
c. shameful
d. presumed

4. The meaning of **engendered** (line 21) is
a. produced
b. devoured
c. satisfied
d. disappointed

5. Decorous (line 26) most nearly means
a. careless
b. casual
c. dignified
d. slack

6. Ethereal (line 28) most nearly means
a. excellent
b. formal
c. sensitive
d. heavenly

Definitions

Note carefully the spelling, pronunciation, part(s) of speech, and definition(s) of each of the following words. Then write the word in the blank space(s) in the illustrative sentence(s) following. Finally, study the lists of synonyms and antonyms given at the end of each entry.

1. beatific
(bē ə tif′ ik)

(*adj.*) blissful; rendering or making blessed

During the awards ceremony, the Gold Medal winner had a positively _____**beatific**_____ expression on her face.

SYNONYMS: rapturous, ecstatic, transcendent
ANTONYMS: disconsolate, dejected, doleful

2. behemoth
(bi hē′ məth)

(*n.*) a creature of enormous size, power, or appearance

The Loch Ness monster is a famous _____**behemoth**_____.

SYNONYMS: mammoth, whale, elephant, colossus
ANTONYMS: dwarf, pygmy, midget

3. blandishment
(blan′ dish mənt)

(*n., often pl.*) anything designed to flatter or coax; sweet talk, apple-polishing

The king was often influenced by subtle _____**blandishments**_____.

SYNONYMS: allurement, enticement, cajolery
ANTONYMS: threat, intimidation

4. cacophonous
(kə käf′ ə nəs)

(*adj.*) harsh-sounding, raucous, discordant, dissonant

The scene opened with _____**cacophonous**_____ laughter coming from three witches gathered around a steaming cauldron.

ANTONYMS: harmonious, melodious, mellifluous

5. chicanery
(shi kā′ nə rē)

(*n.*) trickery, deceptive practices or tactics, double-dealing

The accountants used legal _____**chicanery**_____ to cover up the company's shaky financial position.

ANTONYM: fair dealing

6. consign
(kən sīn′)

(*v.*) to give over to another's care, charge, or control; to entrust, deliver; to set apart for a special use

The ship's captain _____**consigned**_____ many duties to her trusted first mate.

SYNONYMS: transfer, remit, convey

7. coup
(kü)

(*n.*) a highly successful stroke, masterstroke, tour de force, act, plan, or stratagem; a sudden takeover of power or leadership

The surprise _____**coup**_____ by high-ranking military officers toppled the weak government in a matter of hours.

ANTONYMS: blunder, faux pas, gaffe

8. euphemism
(yü' fə miz əm)

(*n.*) a mild or inoffensive expression used in place of a harsh or unpleasant one; a substitute

Common _____ euphemisms _____ for *die* include the expressions *pass away* and *go to the other side*.

9. febrile
(feb' ril)

(*adj.*) feverish; pertaining to or marked by fever; frenetic

The journalist wrote with _____ febrile _____ intensity.

ANTONYMS: leisurely, relaxed

10. gainsay
(gān' sā)

(*v.*) to deny, contradict, controvert; to dispute, oppose

Some wished to _____ gainsay _____ the conclusions of the US Supreme Court in the matter of the 2000 Presidential election.

ANTONYMS: confirm, corroborate, support, admit

11. imminent
(im' ə nənt)

(*adj.*) about to happen, threatening

An _____ imminent _____ hurricane forced the islanders back to the mainland.

SYNONYMS: impending, looming
ANTONYMS: distant, remote, faraway

12. innate
(i nāt')

(*adj.*) natural, inborn, inherent; built-in

Musical excellence often comes from _____ innate _____ ability.

SYNONYMS: intrinsic, congenital
ANTONYMS: learned, acquired, extrinsic, accidental

13. loath
(lōth)

(*adj.*) unwilling, reluctant, disinclined

My hard-working grandfather was _____ loath _____ to retire.

SYNONYMS: averse, indisposed
ANTONYMS: willing, eager, inclined

14. manifest
(man' ə fest)

(*adj.*) clear, evident to the eyes or mind; (*v.*) to show plainly, exhibit, evince; (*n.*) a list of cargo and/or passengers

It was _____ manifest _____ to many nineteenth-century Americans that the nation was destined to extend to the Pacific Ocean.

When the man began to _____ manifest _____ signs of hearing loss, he went to a specialist.

The passenger _____ manifest _____ helps investigators find out who is on board a plane.

SYNONYMS: (*adj.*) apparent; (*v.*) reveal, disclose
ANTONYMS: (*adj.*) unrevealed, hidden; (*v.*) hide, conceal

15. minutiae
(mə nü′ shē ə)

(*pl. n.*) small or trivial details, trifling matters

Because the researcher was too concerned with
_____minutiae_____, she was unlikely to make an original discovery.

SYNONYMS: trivia, trifles
ANTONYM: essentials

16. moratorium
(môr ə tōr′ ē əm)

(*n.*) a suspension of activity; an official waiting period; an authorized period of delay

The conference was held to try to negotiate a
_____moratorium_____ on arms sales to both sides of the conflict.

SYNONYMS: postponement, stoppage
ANTONYMS: acceleration, escalation

17. nostrum
(näs′ trəm)

(*n.*) an alleged cure-all; a remedy or scheme of questionable effectiveness

The federal Food and Drug Administration was created in part to keep unsavory characters from peddling
_____nostrums_____ to the public.

SYNONYMS: panacea, elixir

18. pariah
(par ī′ ə)

(*n.*) one who is rejected by a social group or organization

In most of the world today, those who are suffering from the disease of leprosy are no longer treated as
_____pariahs_____.

SYNONYMS: outcast, untouchable, persona non grata

19. visionary
(vizh′ ə ner ē)

(*adj.*) not practical, lacking in realism; having the nature of a fantasy or dream; (*n.*) one given to far-fetched ideas; a dreamer or seer characterized by vision or foresight

Ideas that once were considered _____visionary_____ often become widely accepted over time.

The Reverend Martin Luther King, Jr., was a
_____visionary_____ whose dreams inspired the American civil rights movement.

SYNONYMS: (*adj.*) utopian, idealistic, impractical
ANTONYMS: (*adj.*) realistic, practical

20. wizened
(wiz′ ənd)

(*adj., part.*) dry, shrunken, and wrinkled (often as the result of aging)

The _____wizened_____ old woman walked with the aid of a cane.

SYNONYMS: withered, shriveled
ANTONYMS: bloated, distended

Completing the Sentence

From the words for this unit, choose the one that best completes each of the following sentences. Write the word in the space provided.

1. However much I may dispute your views, I will never _____**gainsay**_____ your right to hold them.

2. Just when it seemed that defeat was inevitable, she pulled off a dazzling _____**coup**_____ that totally discomfited her opponent.

3. When it became clear just how shamelessly he had treated his brother, he became a virtual _____**pariah**_____ in his own family.

4. In a touching ceremony, the soldiers _____**consigned**_____ the body of their fallen leader to the grave and his memory to their hearts.

5. On the first play, our diminutive quarterback was "sacked" by a veritable _____**behemoth**_____ of a linebacker, ominously nicknamed "Bone Crusher."

6. When the swollen river threatened to overflow its banks, a devastating flood seemed _____**imminent**_____.

7. Since I was brought up in a sleepy country town, I found it very hard to adjust to the _____**febrile**_____ pace of big-city life.

8. You may be, as you say, "_____**loath**_____ to leave such a fascinating book," but I'm telling you right now to take out the garbage!

9. If you spend all your time on _____**minutiae**_____, you won't have any left for really important matters.

10. The nation's economic ills call for a variety of remedies; they cannot be cured by any single, miraculous _____**nostrum**_____.

11. Suddenly I was overcome by such a feeling of _____**beatific**_____ peace that I began to wonder whether I was on earth or in heaven.

12. One way to bring relief to small farmers who cannot meet their mortgage payments is to declare a temporary _____**moratorium**_____ on foreclosures.

13. Before you dismiss him as just another impractical _____**visionary**_____, think of how many great inventors were once regarded as mere "cranks."

14. Though the ability to paint is probably a(n) _____**innate**_____ gift, it can certainly be improved by training and practice.

15. Some Civil War generals weren't professional soldiers and got their jobs through wire-pulling and other forms of political _____**chicanery**_____.

16. Though her body had become bent and _____**wizened**_____ with age, her mind was as alert and active as ever.

17. No matter what _____**euphemism**_____ you use to describe his conduct, you can't disguise the fact he betrayed his best friend.

160 ■ *Unit 14*

18. Some people enjoy the type of atonal music written by such composers as Arnold Schoenberg; others find it _____cacophonous_____.

19. We were all surprised that someone with the reputation of a frivolous playboy could _____manifest_____ such courage and determination.

20. Only a fool would have succumbed to the cloying _____blandishments_____ of that smooth-talking rascal!

Synonyms

*Choose the word from this unit that is **the same** or **most nearly the same** in meaning as the **boldface** word or expression in the given phrase. Write the word on the line provided.*

1. a **substitute** for the word *fired* _____euphemism_____

2. considered an **outcast** by her neighbors _____pariah_____

3. delivered a well-timed **masterstroke** _____coup_____

4. fooled by a worthless **panacea** _____nostrum_____

5. when **mammoths** roamed the Earth _____behemoths_____

6. accused of outright **double-dealing** _____chicanery_____

7. an **intrinsic** capacity for learning _____innate_____

8. dared to **controvert** the scientific evidence _____gainsay_____

9. without the **withered** look of advanced age _____wizened_____

10. fascinated by the **trivia** of celebrity gossip _____minutiae_____

11. transcendent vision of another world _____beatific_____

12. the **raucous** roar from the trading floor _____cacophonous_____

13. transferred to an underground facility _____consigned_____

14. warned of an **impending** investigation _____imminent_____

15. open to the **enticement** of lobbyists _____blandishments_____

Antonyms

*Choose the word from this unit that is **most nearly opposite** in meaning to the **boldface** word or expression in the given phrase. Write the word on the line provided.*

16. a **realistic** blueprint for change _____visionary_____

17. proceeded at a **relaxed** pace _____febrile_____

18. was **willing** to make a compromise _____loath_____

19. demanded an immediate **acceleration** _____moratorium_____

20. the **hidden** cause of the problem _____manifest_____

Choosing the Right Word

Circle the **boldface** word that more satisfactorily completes each of the following sentences.

1. Although I play a fair hand of bridge, I'm not capable of the brilliant (**coups,** **manifests**) that mark a true master of the game.

2. Only when we tried to implement the plan did its (**innate,** **imminent**) defects become clear to us.

3. The (**wizened,** **febrile**) tempo of the symphony's opening movement gives way to a placid and stately largo in the next.

4. Accidents at nuclear power plants have prompted some people to agitate for a (**moratorium,** **nostrum**) on the construction of such facilities.

5. When he took his first bite of Mother's famous coconut custard pie, a look of (**visionary,** **beatific**) joy spread over his face.

6. The plan is certainly ingenious, but it strikes me as far too (**visionary,** **imminent**) to serve as the basis for practical legislation.

7. It is a rare leader indeed who can tell the public unpleasant truths without evasions or (**pariahs,** **blandishments**).

8. Someone who "can't see the forest for the trees" is usually too concerned with (**minutiae,** **nostrums**) to be aware of the overall picture.

9. "As soon as we received the order," I said, "we crated the equipment and (**gainsaid,** **consigned**) it to the buyer in Atlanta."

10. The kind of financial (**minutiae,** **chicanery**) involved in bringing off that deal may not have been illegal, but it was certainly unethical.

11. No one who knows the facts would venture to (**gainsay,** **consign**) your claim to have done your utmost to improve this community.

12. The solution to our problems is to be found in long-term programs of social planning, not in easy (**pariahs,** **nostrums**).

13. Although I am (**febrile,** **loath**) to boast, I must acknowledge my superior qualities as a student, athlete, financier, and all-round social luminary.

14. "How much of a chance do you suppose a 98-pound weakling like me actually stands against that 320-pound (**coup,** **behemoth**)?" I asked incredulously.

15. After it had been left to rot in the sun for a few days, the plump little apple began to take on the (**visionary,** **wizened**) appearance of a prune.

16. (**Imminent,** **Loath**) disaster stared us in the face when we were thrown for a loss and then fumbled the ball on our own five-yard line.

17. After he killed Alexander Hamilton in a duel, Aaron Burr found himself no longer a respected statesman, but a social and political (**coup,** **pariah**).

18. The (**cacophony,** **moratorium**) that suddenly greeted my ears made me suspect that a fox had somehow gotten into the henhouse.

19. "The evidence that we will present in this trial," the prosecutor told the jury, "will make the defendant's guilt abundantly (**beatific,** **manifest**)."

20. It didn't make me any happier to learn that my firing was being referred to (**euphemistically,** **cacophonously**) as a "termination."

*Read the following passage, in which some of the words you have studied in this unit appear in **boldface** type. Then complete each statement given below the passage by circling the letter of the item that is **the same** or **almost the same** in meaning as the highlighted word.*

Meet the Maestro

(Line)

Few will **gainsay** the fact that Arturo Toscanini was one of the great conductors of the twentieth century, a **manifest** musical genius of extraordinary temperament, aspiration, and energy. Born in Parma, Italy in 1867, Toscanini began his musical career as a cellist but soon moved to

(5) conducting, making his debut in a performance of Verdi's opera *Aida* in Rio de Janeiro in 1886. After returning to Italy, he premiered Puccini's *La Boheme*.

His first major assignment was as the

(10) musical director of La Scala, the great opera house in Milan. Here Toscanini launched a **visionary** program to purify and ennoble the operatic art, which had degenerated into a social entertainment for

(15) Italian society. Toscanini was determined to restore seriousness to the opera, and he largely succeeded, but not without gaining a reputation as a single-minded purist. His admirers, perhaps **euphemistically**, called

(20) him uncompromising. His detractors took the more blatant road, describing him as dictatorial. Once, the maestro even stopped conducting a performance because he could not rid the audience of their annoying (to him) habit of breaking into lengthy and **cacophonous** demands for encores.

The exacting maestro conducting the NBC Symphony Orchestra in New York

(25) The last twenty-five years of Toscanini's great career were spent mostly in New York City. He was principal conductor of the combined Philharmonic and Symphony orchestras, where he performed with great clarity, precision, and intensity. Then in 1937, he took the reins of the newly formed orchestra of the National Broadcasting Company, where he conducted and recorded in his

(30) characteristically **febrile** style until his death in 1954.

---

1. Gainsay (line 1) most nearly means
a. detract
b. examine
c. confirm
d. deny ⟵

2. The meaning of **manifest** (line 2) is
a. exceptional
b. latent
c. evident ⟵
d. possible

3. Visionary (line 12) is best defined as
a. intangible
b. idealistic ⟵
c. mundane
d. hypothetical

4. The meaning of **euphemistically** (line19) is
a. without knowledge
b. with respect
c. with a substitute ⟵
d. with hostility

5. Cacophonous (line 24) means
a. colossal
b. discordant ⟵
c. unsightly
d. harmonious

6. Febrile (line 30) most nearly means
a. frenetic ⟵
b. dominating
c. placid
d. impending

Definitions

Note carefully the spelling, pronunciation, part(s) of speech, and definition(s) of each of the following words. Then write the word in the blank space(s) in the illustrative sentence(s) following. Finally, study the lists of synonyms and antonyms given at the end of each entry.

1. amenity
(ə men' ə tē)

(*n.*) that which is pleasant or agreeable; (*pl.*) attractive features, customs, etc.

When I backpack there are certain basic ___**amenities**___, such as clean sheets and a dry tent, that I will not go without.

ANTONYMS: unpleasantness, disagreeableness

2. aperture
(ap' ər chər)

(*n.*) an opening, gap, hole; orifice

After the earthquake, rain and cold came through the ___**aperture**___ in the wall of the damaged house.

ANTONYMS: closure, blockage, occlusion

3. dissidence
(dis' ə dəns)

(*n.*) a difference of opinion; discontent

When the commanding officer announced that all leave was cancelled, there was widespread ___**dissidence**___ in the ranks.

SYNONYMS: disagreement, dissent, disaffection
ANTONYMS: agreement, harmony, concord

4. epicurean
(ep ə kyü' rē ən)

(*adj.*) devoted to the pursuit of pleasure; fond of good food, comfort, and ease; with discriminating tastes; (*n.*) a person with discriminating tastes

The chef took an ___**epicurean**___ delight in presenting the most delicious dishes to his demanding clientele.

Even the most fervent ___**epicurean**___ should not expect fine dining in a poor, war-torn country.

SYNONYMS: (*adj.*) hedonistic, sybaritic, discriminating
ANTONYMS: (*adj.*) ascetic, self-denying, abstemious

5. improvident
(im präv' ə dənt)

(*adj.*) not thrifty; failing to plan ahead

Some people are so ___**improvident**___ that despite high incomes they struggle to make ends meet.

SYNONYMS: prodigal, spendthrift, extravagant
ANTONYMS: thrifty, frugal, economical, cautious

6. iniquity
(i nik' wə tē)

(*n.*) wickedness, sin; a grossly immoral act

English Puritans looked upon the court that surrounded King Charles I as a den of ___**iniquity**___.

SYNONYMS: evil, crime
ANTONYMS: probity, rectitude, uprightness

7. inviolable
(in vī′ ə lə bəl)

(*adj.*) sacred; of such a character that it must not be broken, injured, or profaned

Safeguarding the retirement income of millions of Americans is an _____**inviolable**_____ trust of the federal government.

SYNONYMS: sacrosanct, unassailable
ANTONYMS: vulnerable, assailable

8. mutable
(myü′ tə bəl)

(*adj.*) open to or capable of change, fickle

Most people would agree that one's principles and moral values should not be as _____**mutable**_____ as fashion.

SYNONYMS: changeable, variable
ANTONYMS: changeless, steadfast, constant

9. nascent
(nā′ sənt)

(*adj.*) just beginning to exist or develop; having just come into existence

Recent public opinion polls registered _____**nascent**_____ opposition to the proposed tax increase.

SYNONYMS: budding, incipient, embryonic
ANTONYMS: dying, moribund, senescent

10. obeisance
(ō bē′ səns)

(*n.*) a deep bow or other body movement indicating respect or submission; deference, homage

Upon entering the throne room, each courtier made a respectful _____**obeisance**_____ before the king and queen.

SYNONYMS: respect, honor
ANTONYMS: disrespect, irreverence, disregard

11. panegyric
(pan ə ji′ rik)

(*n.*) formal or elaborate praise; a tribute

The speaker delivered a _____**panegyric**_____ in honor of the award-winning author.

SYNONYMS: tribute, encomium, testimonial
ANTONYMS: diatribe, tirade, philippic

12. pillory
(pil′ ə rē)

(*n.*) a device for publicly punishing offenders; a means for exposing one to public contempt or ridicule; (*v.*) to expose to public contempt or ridicule

The _____**pillory**_____ was placed in the center of town so that everyone could view the outlaws and their shame.

The candidate tried to _____**pillory**_____ her political opponent by suggesting that he had ties to organized crime.

ANTONYMS: (*v.*) praise, extol, laud, acclaim

13. pittance
(pit′ əns)

(*n.*) a woefully meager allowance, wage, or portion

In comparison to the overwhelming need for food and medicine, the shipment was a mere _____ pittance _____.

SYNONYMS: modicum, trifle
ANTONYM: fortune

14. presage
(pres′ ij)

(*v.*) to foreshadow or point to a future event; to predict; (*n.*) a warning or indication of the future

The skirmishes at the border _____ presaged _____ a war.

The fall in stock prices and retail sales may be a _____ presage _____ of hard economic times to come.

SYNONYMS: (*v.*) augur, portend, foretell

15. progeny
(präj′ ə nē)

(*n.*) descendants, offspring, children, followers, disciples

The Bill of Rights guarantees certain civil rights and protections to ourselves and our _____ progeny _____.

SYNONYMS: issue, posterity
ANTONYMS: ancestors, forebears, antecedents

16. promulgate
(präm′ əl gāt)

(*v.*) to proclaim or issue officially; to make known far and wide

The School Board _____ promulgated _____ a new approach to education that emphasized phonics.

SYNONYM: announce
ANTONYMS: withdraw, retract, abrogate, nullify

17. rectitude
(rek′ tə tüd)

(*n.*) uprightness, righteousness; correctness

The mayor is a person of unquestionable _____ rectitude _____.

SYNONYMS: probity, integrity
ANTONYMS: iniquity, heinousness

18. restive
(res′ tiv)

(*adj.*) restless, hard to manage, balky

The _____ restive _____ horse had not been taken out of the stable for five days.

SYNONYMS: uneasy, fidgety, recalcitrant
ANTONYMS: serene, unruffled, docile

19. seraphic
(sə raf′ ik)

(*adj.*) angelic, heavenly, celestial

The artist painted the children with _____ seraphic _____ smiles to suggest their innocence.

SYNONYM: cherubic
ANTONYMS: devilish, impish

20. subsist
(səb sist′)

(*v.*) to have existence; to remain alive, manage to make a living or maintain life; to persist or continue

Peasants in nineteenth-century Ireland were able to _____ subsist _____ almost exclusively on potatoes.

SYNONYMS: last, survive, sustain

Completing the Sentence

From the words for this unit, choose the one that best completes each of the following sentences. Write the word in the space provided.

1. We are sure that their vow is _____**inviolable**_____ because their sense of moral obligation will prevent them from ever breaking it.

2. Conscientious parents will do everything they can to foster and develop the _____**nascent**_____ intellectual curiosity of a small child.

3. Imagine someone with my _____**epicurean**_____ tastes having to live for a week on that watery mush!

4. The biography is a pretty evenhanded appraisal of the man's strengths and weaknesses, not just another _____**panegyric**_____ to a great hero.

5. I see no reason to question the _____**rectitude**_____ of her dealings with us since I know her to be "as honest as the day is long."

6. He inveighs against the sins of society with all the stridency of an Old Testament prophet castigating the _____**iniquities**_____ of the ungodly.

7. The wranglers suspected that there were wolves or mountain lions nearby when the herd suddenly grew nervous and _____**restive**_____.

8. The Bible tells us that visitors to the court of Solomon, the great Hebrew king, willingly paid him _____**obeisance**_____.

9. For many ancient peoples, the appearance of a comet was a fearful omen that _____**presaged**_____ great social upheaval.

10. After a few days in which everything went my way, I suddenly learned just how _____**mutable**_____ Lady Luck can be.

11. Am I to be _____**pilloried**_____ before the entire student body because I made a few minor mistakes as a member of the Student Council?

12. The liberties that we have inherited from our forefathers are a sacred trust that we must pass on undiminished to our _____**progeny**_____.

13. Authoritarian governments often resort to violence and coercion in their efforts to repress political _____**dissidence**_____.

14. Our financial situations are so different that what she considers a mere _____**pittance**_____ seems a fortune to me.

15. It was the _____**amenity**_____ of its natural setting on those rolling hills that led the architect to dub the estate "Mount Pleasant."

16. The President has _____**promulgated**_____ a policy that commits the nation to curbing pollution.

17. "I'm afraid that the child's _____**seraphic**_____ countenance belies the devilry in his heart," I observed sadly.

18. The _____ aperture _____ on most cameras can be adjusted to admit more or less light, as required.

19. Nutritionists say that most of us could _____ subsist _____ on a great deal less food than we actually consume.

20. Though I'm by no means _____ improvident _____ with my money, I don't hoard it either.

Synonyms

Choose the word from this unit that is **the same** or **most nearly the same** in meaning as the **boldface** word or expression in the given phrase. Write the word on the line provided.

1. tried to **survive** in a desert — subsist

2. dark clouds **portending** rain — presaging

3. the **angelic** tones of the choir — seraphic

4. challenged the **integrity** of the judge — rectitude

5. a **hedonistic** display of luxury — epicurean

6. stuffed the **orifice** with old newspapers — aperture

7. showed a **budding** interest in politics — nascent

8. paid **respect** to those who came before her — obeisance

9. the **pleasantness** of a quiet garden — amenity

10. the **sacrosanct** principle of equality — inviolable

11. will be punished for their **crimes** — iniquities

12. repaid a mere **modicum** of what is owed — pittance

13. **announced** by the public health authorities — promulgated

14. **fidgety** after the caffeine — restive

15. a **fickle** disposition — mutable

Antonyms

Choose the word from this unit that is **most nearly opposite** in meaning to the **boldface** word or expression in the given phrase. Write the word on the line provided.

16. insulted the king's **ancestors** — progeny

17. always **praises** those in authority — pillories

18. gave a long **diatribe** on the military — panegyric

19. widespread political **agreement** — dissidence

20. a **thrifty** manager — improvident

Choosing the Right Word

Circle the **boldface** word that more satisfactorily completes each of the following sentences.

1. Religious (**obeisance, dissidence**) was one of the motives that led many people to leave their homes and found colonies in North America.

2. Writers often regard their works as their (**dissidence, progeny**) in much the same way as other people regard their pets as family members.

3. The resounding victory we scored at the polls is an eloquent tribute to the (**rectitude, dissidence**) of her approach as campaign manager.

4. As the speaker's remarks became more inflammatory, the crowd grew more sullen and (**nascent, restive**).

5. The novel centers on a(n) (**improvident, seraphic**) young man who squanders his inheritance on riotous living and dies in the poorhouse.

6. I realize the official made a serious mistake, but that is no reason to (**pillory, subsist**) him so unmercifully in the press.

7. We would like to believe that the intensifying fear of ecological catastrophe (**subsists, presages**) an era of environmental harmony in the near future.

8. The cost of living has risen so sharply that a salary that was adequate a decade ago is now no more than a mere (**panegyric, pittance**).

9. The new "gourmet" deli features delicacies that are bound to delight even the most exacting of (**epicurean, nascent**) palates.

10. No matter how well defended, no boundary is (**inviolable, restive**) unless the people on either side of it respect each other.

11. "Angelica" is indeed an apt name for one whose (**mutable, seraphic**) beauty is complemented by such sweetness of temper and gentleness of spirit.

12. One cannot expect a(n) (**epicurean, nascent**) democracy to go through its early years without experiencing serious growing pains.

13. Recently, the Principal (**promulgated, presaged**) a new dress code that abolished some of the unnecessary strictness of the old rules.

14. Liberty (**subsists, presages**) only so long as people have the intelligence to know their rights and the courage to defend them.

15. There was a loophole in the law, and through this (**aperture, obeisance**) the defendant escaped the legal consequences of his crime.

16. Instead of being so concerned with the (**iniquities, apertures**) of others, they would do well to concentrate on correcting their own shortcomings.

17. The study of government shows us that many political institutions thought to be unchanging are in fact highly (**inviolable, mutable**).

18. Specific customs vary widely in different lands, but the basic (**affectations, amenities**) of civilized living are much the same everywhere.

19. Like so many others of his generation, he paid unquestioning (**iniquity, obeisance**) to the accepted symbols of material success.

20. Instead of mouthing empty (**panegyrics, apertures**) to the Bill of Rights, let's strive to make this great document a reality in our lives.

Read the following passage, in which some of the words you have studied in this unit appear in **boldface** type. Then complete each statement given below the passage by circling the letter of the item that is **the same** or **almost the same** in meaning as the highlighted word.

The Scarlet Woman

(Line)

One of the most vivid female characters in American fiction is Hester Prynne, the protagonist of Nathaniel Hawthorne's *The Scarlet Letter.* Published in 1850, the novel is set in Puritan New England in the mid-seventeenth century and deals with two major Puritan preoccupations: sin and redemption.

The particular **iniquity** of which Hester is (5) guilty is adultery. She has broken what her Puritan neighbors view as the **inviolable** bond of matrimony, and, therefore, must be publicly exposed and punished for her sin. To that end, she is forced to wear a scarlet (10) *A* for adultery on the bodice of her dress, and to stand **pilloried** in the town square with her illegitimate **progeny** Pearl in her arms. Hester is a strong-willed woman, however, and although she acknowledges (15) her own guilt and accepts her punishment, she will not cooperate in punishing others. Repeatedly, she refuses to reveal the identity of the father of her child, choosing to leave her former lover, the young minister (20) Arthur Dimmesdale, to wrestle with his own conscience. And wrestle he does. A model of apparent **rectitude**, the Reverend Dimmesdale is torn between his inner sense of guilt and the fear of losing his good name in the community.

Old-fashioned pillory in Colonial Williamsburg

After years of self-defeating struggle, Dimmesdale finally confesses and dies (25) in Hester's arms, **presaging** the fate of those who hide away their guilt and fail to acknowledge their wrongdoings. Hester alone forgives herself and others, and she alone goes on, with renewed strength, to live and love generously.

1. Iniquity (line 5) most nearly means
a. misstatement   c. evil
b. prejudice   d. disturbance

2. The meaning of **inviolable** (line 7) is
a. loving   c. fragile
b. sacrosanct   d. eternal

3. Pilloried (line 12) is best defined as
a. exposed   c. compelled
b. protected   d. exonerated

4. The meaning of **progeny** (line 13) is
a. ancestry   c. name
b. issue   d. gains

5. Rectitude (line 23) most nearly means
a. selflessness   c. courage
b. gentleness   d. integrity

6. Presaging (line 26) most nearly means
a. mocking   c. defying
b. confusing   d. foretelling

Vocabulary for Comprehension

Read the following passage, in which some of the words you have studied in Units 13–15 appear in **boldface** *type. Then answer questions 1–12 on page 172 on the basis of what is* <u>stated</u> *or* <u>implied</u> *in the passage and in the introductory statement.*

This passage focuses on one of the most famous American novelists of the twentieth century, F. Scott Fitzgerald.

(Line)

Few writers have been as identified with an age as F. Scott Fitzgerald (1896–1940). Not only is his best fiction set in the 1920s, but he helped

(5) define that era as the Jazz Age, an **epicurean** decade of fevered pleasure-seeking, **improvident** spending, and gaudy excess.

Born in St. Paul, Minnesota,

(10) Francis Scott Key Fitzgerald (named after his famous ancestor) was a restless young man full of romantic dreams. In 1917 he left Princeton University before receiving

(15) his degree, to train as an Army officer, but he never made it overseas. While stationed at Camp Sheridan near Montgomery, Alabama, Fitzgerald fell for a local southern

(20) beauty, Zelda Sayre. By dint of sheer charm and persistence, Fitzgerald got Zelda to agree to marry him, but she was too **cognizant** of his poverty to succumb

(25) permanently to his **blandishments**. When the novel he was writing was rejected for a second time, she broke off the engagement.

Scott, however, was not deterred.

(30) He went back to St. Paul and rewrote the novel again. Upon its third submission to the Scribners publishing house, the manuscript was

accepted. It was published in 1920

(35) as *This Side of Paradise* and became an instant success. Scott and Zelda were married within a week. Like the characters in Fitzgerald's Jazz Age novels, the couple spent the next

(40) decade shuttling between New York and Europe, living the high life and spending lavishly. Behind the frothy **facade**, however, lay a darker reality that Fitzgerald depicted in his most

(45) famous novel, *The Great Gatsby* (1925). In *Gatsby*, Fitzgerald examines the moral decadence **engendered** by the American dream of wealth and success. When

(50) Fitzgerald died of a heart attack at the age of 44 (Zelda died in a fire only a few years later), his works that chronicled such a discrete period of American history seemed on their

(55) way to obscurity. In the 1950s, however, critics revived such classics as *Gatsby* and *Tender Is the Night* (1934), securing a place for him in the canon of American writers.

1. According to the author, which era did Fitzgerald help to define?
a. the Age of Discovery
b. the Jazz Age
c. the Great Depression
d. the Civil Rights era
e. the Information Age

2. The meaning of **epicurean** (line 6) is
a. impoverished
b. turbulent
c. idyllic
d. uneventful
e. hedonistic

3. Improvident (line 7) most nearly means
a. prudent
b. extravagant
c. intermittent
d. frugal
e. impressive

4. In paragraph 2 (lines 9–28), it may be inferred that when Scott was courting Zelda, her values were
a. idealistic
b. literary
c. patriotic
d. materialistic
e. romantic

5. Cognizant (line 24) is best defined as
a. proud
b. ashamed
c. aware
d. scornful
e. oblivious

6. The meaning of **blandishments** (line 25) is
a. enticements
b. threats
c. fantasies
d. apologies
e. tantrums

7. You can reasonably infer that an important factor responsible for Scott and Zelda's marriage was
a. his repeated pleas to her
b. the instant success of *This Side of Paradise*
c. the intervention of Zelda's parents

d. the couple's admiring European friends
e. Scott's promise to leave New York for Europe

8. According to the author, the main focus in the novel *The Great Gatsby* is on which of the following?
a. the complex rhythms of jazz
b. the moral decadence flowing from the American dream
c. contrasts between American and European society
d. the pitfalls of romance
e. the corruption of American politics

9. Facade (line 43) most nearly means
a. costume
b. mask
c. attitude
d. lifestyle
e. celebration

10. Engendered (line 48) most nearly means
a. generated
b. baffled
c. offended
d. deterred
e. enraged

11. The primary purpose of the passage is to
a. analyze contrasts between Fitzgerald's early novels and his later works
b. show how the Fitzgeralds epitomized the Jazz Age lifestyle
c. survey the highlights of Fitzgerald's life and literary career
d. support the claim that *The Great Gatsby* is Fitzgerald's masterpiece
e. emphasize the irony in Fitzgerald's handling of the theme of illusion vs. reality

12. For the most part, what organizational scheme does the author use in the passage?
a. order of importance
b. spatial order
c. order of impression
d. chronological order
e. comparison and contrast

Grammar in Context

In the sentence "When the novel he was writing was rejected for the second time, she broke off the engagement" (lines 26–28 on page 171), the independent clause "she broke off the engagement" expresses the main idea. However, if the author had written "Before she broke off the engagement, the novel he was writing was rejected for the second time," the independent clause would have misleadingly stressed a subordinate idea, rather than the main idea. This error is known as **faulty subordination**.

To avoid faulty subordination, review your sentences for logical emphasis and balance of ideas. For example, make sure that your sentences reflect the relative importance of ideas. Do not use a coordinating conjunction to join ideas of unequal importance. Be careful to link ideas clearly and accurately. Be sure to express cause and effect logically.

On the lines provided, rewrite each of the following sentences to correct faulty subordination. Write "correct" if the sentence is correct.
Answers may vary; sample answers given.

1. F. Scott Fitzgerald was born in St. Paul, Minnesota, and he is identified with a particular era in American history.
   Born in St. Paul, Minnesota, F. Scott Fitzgerald is identified with a particular era in American history.

2. Fitzgerald's fiction is set in the 1920s, but he helped define that era as the Jazz Age.
   Fitzgerald, whose fiction is set in the 1920s, helped define that era as the Jazz Age.

3. Fitzgerald was a restless young man full of romantic dreams, and he studied for a while at Princeton University.
   A restless young man full of romantic dreams, Fitzgerald studied for a while at Princeton University.

4. Fitzgerald trained as an army officer, but he never made it overseas in World War I.
   correct

5. He was stationed at an army camp in Alabama, yet he fell for a local southern beauty, Zelda Sayre.
   While he was stationed at an army camp in Alabama, he fell for a local southern beauty, Zelda Sayre.

6. The couple lived the high life in New York and Europe, but they spent lavishly.
   The couple lived the high life in New York and Europe, and they spent lavishly.

7. Fitzgerald's works seemed on their way to obscurity after he died at the age of 44.
   After Fitzgerald died at the age of 44, his works seemed on their way to obscurity.

Two-Word Completions

Circle the pair of words that best complete the meaning of each of the following passages.

See pages T38–T48 for explanations of answers.

1. Disgruntled army officers and other _____ elements in the society engineered the bloody _____ that toppled the duly elected government a few months after it had taken office.
   a. contrite . . . nostrum
   b. restive . . . moratorium
   c. visionary . . . pittance
   d. dissident . . . coup

2. Behind the courtier's outward _____ of decorous sloth there lurked the _____ imagination of an inveterate opportunist, eager to capitalize on any windfall that came his way.
   a. aperture . . . incongruous
   b. facade . . . febrile
   c. cynosure . . . nascent
   d. chicanery . . . improvident

3. Any official who is genuinely concerned about the _____ of his or her behavior while in public office will think twice before engaging in the kinds of political _____ and backroom shenanigans that sometimes go on when a juicy government contract is up for grabs.
   a. rectitude . . . chicanery
   b. imminence . . . blandishments
   c. progeny . . . machinations
   d. iniquity . . . cognizance

4. Once the news broke, the public heaped so much _____ on the head of the hapless city official that he soon found himself a veritable political _____, even in his own party.
   a. euphemism . . . canard
   b. dissidence . . . amenity
   c. opprobrium . . . pariah
   d. efficacy . . . ghoul

5. As soon as the famous movie star walked into my shop, she became the _____ of all eyes. Customers stopped what they were doing to stare at her as if _____ by the spell of her celebrity.
   a. aperture . . . engendered
   b. cynosure . . . mesmerized
   c. moratorium . . . subsisted
   d. pillory . . . promulgated

6. The characters in Jane Austen novels display _____ manners, obeying the _____ of social conventions that range from how many consecutive waltzes a couple may dance to the type of tea that should be served to guests.
   a. abstruse . . . canards
   b. ethereal . . .pariahs
   c. decorous . . . minutiae
   d. beatific . . . recriminations

Choosing the Right Meaning

Read each sentence carefully. Then circle the item that best completes the statement below the sentence.

See pages T38–T48 for explanations of answers.

The bill sparked controversy when it was introduced. There was even a tug-of-war between chairpersons over which congressional committee was properly cognizant. (2)

1. The word **cognizant** in line 2 is used to mean
a. knowledgeable   b. informed   (c. having jurisdiction) d. aware

Only a historian of great imaginative power could extract from the desiccated figures of dusty old ledger books the drama of a great family's decline. (2)

2. In line 1 the word **desiccated** most nearly means
a. complicated   b. shriveled   c. dried out   (d. uninteresting)

Ralph Waldo Emerson, the guiding light of American transcendentalism, counted among his progeny such distinguished contemporaries as Henry Thoreau and Margaret Fuller. (2)

3. The word **progeny** in line 2 is used to mean
a. children   (b. disciples)   c. offspring   d. descendants

"But would the honest patriot, in the full tide of successful experiment, abandon a government which has so far kept us free and firm, on the theoretic and visionary (2) fear that this government, the world's best hope, may by possibility want energy to preserve itself?" (Thomas Jefferson, "First Inaugural Address") (4)

4. In line 2 the word **visionary** is best defined as
a. utopian   (b. fantastic)   c. idealistic   d. predictable

In *The Autocrat of the Breakfast-Table*, Oliver Wendell Holmes paraphrases Plutarch's "Epicurean paradox" this way: "Give us the luxuries of life, and we will dispense with (2) its necessaries."

5. The best definition for the word **Epicurean** in line 2 is
(a. pursuing pleasure) b. discriminating   c. insoluble   d. ancient

Antonyms

*In each of the following groups, circle the word or expression that is most nearly the **opposite** of the word in **boldface** type.*

1. inviolable
a. honest
b. fundamental
(c. vulnerable)
d. sound

2. engender
(a. deter)
b. beget
c. aggravate
d. exploit

3. loath
a. unwilling
(b. eager)
c. afraid
d. unable

4. epicurean
a. hedonistic
(b. ascetic)
c. refined
d. predictable

5. cacophonous
a. modern
(b. harmonious)
c. dissonant
d. classical

6. promulgate
a. enforce
b. formulate
c. issue
(d. withdraw)

7. abstruse
a. poetic
b. foreign
(c. straightforward)
d. fallacious

8. pilloried
a. ridiculed
b. caricatured
c. censored
(d. extolled)

9. dissidence
(a. agreement)
b. opposition
c. debt
d. intrigue

11. imminent
a. looming
(b. distant)
c. sudden
d. destructive

13. desiccated
a. parched
b. polluted
(c. sodden)
d. hardened

15. improvident
a. incompetent
b. inexperienced
c. shortsighted
(d. cautious)

10. panegyric
a. obituary
b. tribute
c. introduction
(d. diatribe)

12. contrite
a. apologetic
(b. unrepentant)
c. repeat
d. accused

14. incongruous
a. complex
(b. compatible)
c. jarring
d. vivid

16. iniquity
a. daring
b. wickedness
(c. rectitude)
d. skill

A. *On the line provided, write the word you have learned in Units 13–15 that is related to each of the following nouns.*
EXAMPLE: manifestation—**manifest**

1. cacophony — cacophonous
2. subsistence, subsister — subsist
3. consignment, consigner, consignation — consign
4. desiccation, desiccant — desiccated
5. mesmerism, mesmerizer — mesmerize
6. imminence, imminency — imminent
7. promulgation, promulgator — promulgate
8. incongruence, incongruity, incongruousness — incongruous
9. cognizance — cognizant
10. ghoul, ghoulishness — ghoulish
11. contrition, contriteness — contrite
12. decorousness, decorum — decorous
13. mutability — mutable
14. improvidence — improvident

B. *On the line provided, write the word you have learned in Units 13–15 that is related to each of the following verbs.*
EXAMPLE: dissent—**dissidence**

15. provide — improvident
16. mutate — mutable
17. wizen — wizened
18. machinate — machination
19. envision — visionary
20. violate — inviolable

Word Associations

In each of the following groups, circle the word that is best defined or suggested by the given phrase.

1. someone who is the center of attention
a. machination   (b. cynosure)   c. presage   d. coup

2. pulled some strings to get a contract
a. pillory   b. panegyric   (c. chicanery)   d. canard

3. an air-conditioned room with color TV and private bath
(a. amenities)   b. facades   c. efficacies   d. pittance

4. a charming person who behaves with outstanding propriety
a. captious   (b. decorous)   c. abstruse   d. mutable

5. a remark made deliberately to cause offense
a. blandishment   b. minutiae   c. iniquity   (d. affront)

6. an attitude of respect and awe upon meeting a world-famous writer
a. affront   b. efficacy   (c. obeisance)   d. coup

7. "I rise to dispute the accuracy of the statements made by the last speaker."
(a. gainsay)   b. affront   c. manifest   d. engender

8. barely enough to make ends meet
a. canard   (b. pittance)   c. amenity   d. coup

9. how you might characterize an instinct
a. epicurean   b. ghoulish   (c. innate)   d. captious

10. shipped the equipment to the buyer by parcel post
(a. consign)   b. presage   c. subsist   d. engender

11. "underprivileged" instead of "poor"
a. pariah   (b. euphemism)   c. canard   d. facade

12. "Flattery will get you nowhere!"
a. manifests   b. canards   c. facades   (d. blandishments)

13. a brilliant oratorical style that left the audience spellbound
a. engender   (b. mesmerize)   c. subsist   d. pillory

14. relies on chicken soup as a remedy for all disorders of body and mind
(a. nostrum)   b. aperture   c. coup   d. visionary

15. unshakable moral integrity
a. efficacy   (b. rectitude)   c. nostrum   d. opprobrium

16. obvious enough to be readily perceived by all
(a. manifest)   b. incongruous   c. cognizant   d. beatific

17. the first faint stirrings of an idea
a. desiccated   (b. nascent)   c. wizened   d. ethereal

18. "The weird story about me has absolutely no basis in fact."
a. amenity   b. panegyric   (c. canard)   d. moratorium

19. an "untouchable" in the caste system
(a. pariah)   b. recrimination   c. obeisance   d. facade

20. a battleship next to a rowboat
a. manifest   b. pariah   c. pillory   (d. behemoth)

Building with Classical Roots

vid, vis—to look, see

This root appears in **visionary** (page 159), which means "lacking in practicality" or, as a noun, "a dreamer or seer." Some other words based on this same root are listed below.

advisement	providence	proviso	visitation
envisage	provident	visage	vista

From the list of words above, choose the one that corresponds to each of the brief definitions below. Write the word in the blank space in the illustrative sentence below the definition.

1. a face, countenance, appearance, look, aspect (*"that which is seen"*)

The links of chains he carried, which signified his sins, gave Jacob Marley a frightening _____**visage**_____.

2. divine guidance or care; a manifestation of such guidance

Despite hard times, or perhaps especially during hard times, people of faith put their trust in _____**providence**_____.

3. a distinct view or prospect through an opening; an extensive mental view

As we rounded the bend, we suddenly beheld the most breathtaking _____**vista**_____ of our trip.

4. a conditional stipulation; an article or clause in a contract that introduces a condition (*"that which is foreseen"*)

They agreed to sign the deal, with the _____**proviso**_____ that we serve as witnesses.

5. a visit for the purpose of making an official inspection; an act of visiting; a severe punishment or affliction

Health specialists are meeting to discuss the possibility of a new _____**visitation**_____ of tuberculosis.

6. to picture to oneself (*"see into"*); conceive of, especially as a future possibility

It is hard to _____**envisage**_____ a modern America made up entirely of small farmers.

7. providing for future needs or contingencies; thrifty, economical

It is our agency's mission to explore the most _____**provident**_____ use of our natural resources.

8. a careful consideration (*"act of seeing to"*)

The committee has agreed to take your most recent request under _____**advisement**_____.

From the list of words on page 178, choose the one that best completes each of the following sentences. Write the word in the blank space provided.

1. From the summit of the mountain, a dramatic _____ vista _____ of lush pastures and rolling hills spreads out in every direction as far as the eye can see.

2. An old maxim says that luck is merely a nickname for _____ providence _____.

3. Is it possible for you to _____ envisage _____ a world free of poverty, famine, hatred, and war?

4. She agreed to chair this year's prom committee with the _____ proviso _____ that six other class members act as her assistants.

5. The scholarship committee has the application under _____ advisement _____ and has promised a decision by the end of the week.

6. It was only after I saw his gaunt eyes and haggard _____ visage _____ that I began to realize just how intense an ordeal he had experienced.

7. That old mansion is reputedly inhabited by some fiendish spirit, whose nocturnal _____ visitations _____ have frightened away anyone who has tried to live in the place.

8. "If you'd learn to be a bit more _____ provident _____ with your allowance," he scolded, "you wouldn't constantly need to borrow money from others."

---

*Circle the **boldface** word that more satisfactorily completes each of the following sentences.*

1. A good education can expose open-minded people to new (**vistas,** advisements) for the future.

2. We had few prospects of obtaining a legal remedy for our problem until a new attorney agreed to take our case under (**advisement,** vista).

3. The normal (providence, **visitation**) hours at the hospital are 2:00 PM to 8:00 PM, except for patients who are in the intensive-care unit.

4. We tried to (advise, **envisage**) the creation of the Hoover Dam by studying detailed architectural drawings chronicling its erection.

5. It must have been an act of (**providence,** visage) that the boy was rescued from the well.

6. Photographic portraits of Abraham Lincoln provide the first modern record of the deteriorating effects of constant political stress on the presidential (**visage,** proviso).

7. Our agreement with the cable company includes a (visage, **proviso**) that we must return the converter box when we move, or we will lose our security deposit.

8. It was thanks to the (**provident,** envisaged) planning of frugal pioneer women that many homesteading families were able to endure some of their unexpected hardships.

Analogies

In each of the following, circle the item that best completes the comparison.

See pages T38–T48 for explanations of answers.

1. pariah is to **opprobrium** as
a. aesthete is to ignominy
b. celebrity is to acclamation
c. victor is to animadversion
d. saint is to improvident

2. penitent is to **contrite** as
a. unwonted is to nefarious
b. sumptuous is to depraved
c. visionary is to utopian
d. pecuniary is to cacophonous

3. desiccate is to **heat** as
a. saturate is to liquid
b. mesmerize is to air
c. rebuff is to wax
d. burnish is to fire

4. captious is to **cavil** as
a. disgruntled is to grouse
b. avid is to demur
c. febrile is to importune
d. chary is to allege

5. loath is to **reluctance** as
a. insatiable is to boredom
b. blasé is to concern
c. avid is to enthusiasm
d. fervent is to apathy

6. stratagem is to **crafty** as
a. chicanery is to overt
b. peregrination is to coherent
c. juggernaut is to picayune
d. machination is to devious

7. encomium is to **panegyric** as
a. diatribe is to harangue
b. facade is to cynosure
c. canard is to verity
d. eulogy is to philippic

8. amenity is to **asperity** as
a. complicity is to collusion
b. rectitude is to iniquity
c. aesthetic is to euphemism
d. moratorium is to hiatus

9. myopic is to **discernment** as
a. pertinacious is to determination
b. imperturbable is to composure
c. improvident is to foresight
d. cognizant is to awareness

10. misanthrope is to **gregarious** as
a. pickpocket is to furtive
b. liar is to mendacious
c. lackey is to obsequious
d. hero is to pusillanimous

 Choosing the Right Meaning

Read each sentence carefully. Then circle the item that best completes the statement below the sentence.

See pages T38–T48 for explanations of answers.

"All the choir of heaven and furniture of earth . . . have not subsistence without a mind."   (Bishop Berkeley, *Principles of Human Knowledge*)   (2)

1. In line 1 the word **subsistence** most nearly means
a. persistence   b. sustenance   c. existence   d. continuance

Archaeologists could only wonder that objects so ethereal had survived intact the rude treatment of the grave robbers.   (2)

2. The best definition for the word **ethereal** in line 1 is
a. heavenly   b. airy   c. celestial   d. delicate

Of all the celestial bodies that crowd the night sky none is a more faithful and steadfast cynosure to the navigator than the North Star.   (2)

3. In line 2 the word **cynosure** is used to mean

a. center of attraction

(b. guiding light)

c. object of beauty

d. focal point

"The sumptuous feast the careworn king consumes,

Though served on gold or plate or china fine, (2)

Ofttimes tastes not so wholesome or so sweet

As lowly cotter's porridge, set out plain (4)

In sylvan trencher carved by his own hand

Of mighty oak or aspen quaking or tall pine." (6)

(A. E. Glug, "Runes," 6–11)

4. The word **sylvan** in line 5 most nearly means

(a. made of wood)

b. pertaining to woods

c. living in the forest

d. mythical

Two-Word Completions

Circle the pair of words that best complete the meaning of each of the following sentences.

See pages T38–T48 for explanations of answers.

1. A century ago it may have been possible to _____ on pennies a day, but I don't see how you expect a person to live on the mere _____ you are proposing to pay me.

a. calumniate . . . nostrum

b. accost . . . talisman

(c. subsist . . . pittance)

d. deign . . . figment

2. The straitlaced Victorians, who were concerned about the _____ of a person's behavior, would have looked _____ at the casualness of modern social conventions.

a. propinquity . . . summarily

b. celerity . . . reputedly

(c. propriety . . . askance)

d. sophistry . . . indubitably

3. If the government provides only _____ quick-fixes to complicated international problems, it runs the risk of _____ rather than solving them.

(a. ephemeral . . . exacerbating)

b. unwonted . . . countermanding

c. tenable . . . engendering

d. peremptory . . . requiting

4. A _____ should stick to the _____ of a sport and leave its finer points to the experts.

a. pedant . . . exigencies

(b. neophyte . . . rudiments)

c. dilettante . . . idiosyncrasies

d. tyro . . . minutiae

5. As soon as they received the appropriate order from the court, the local cemetery workers began the somewhat _____ business of _____ the victim's body and delivering it to the coroner for reexamination.

a. nefarious . . . interpolating

b. macabre . . . interpolating

c. abject . . . promulgating

(d. ghoulish . . . exhuming)

Enriching Your Vocabulary

Read the passage below. Then complete the exercise at the bottom of the page.

A Linguistic Rendezvous with the French

In 1066 William the Conqueror, a powerful invader from Normandy (in what is now France), overtook King Harold II and his English forces at the Battle of Hastings. From that moment onward, the sound of the English language changed forever. Norman French supplanted English in the court and in the church. For at least the next hundred years, the kings of England and the English elite spoke French rather than English! French words flooded English. Over time, their spellings and pronunciations evolved to the point where some words of French origin, such as *coupon, fanfare, iodine, liter,* and *velour,* sound like they might always have had English roots.

Modern English has embraced an extensive store of words and phrases that have been borrowed more or less unchanged from the French. One such word, *coup* (Unit 14), a highly successful plan, act, or stratagem, is pronounced as the French would pronounce it: kü. The ordinary English pronunciation of the words and phrases that follow generally observe the rules of French diction.

Baguettes, a word and food borrowed from the French, are long, thin loaves of bread.

In Column A below are 8 more words and phrases that come from the French. With or without a dictionary, match each word or phrase with its meaning in Column B.

Column A

__f__	**1.** avant-garde
__e__	**2.** communiqué
__g__	**3.** de rigueur
__b__	**4.** ensemble
__h__	**5.** joie de vivre
__d__	**6.** nom de plume
__a__	**7.** tête-à-tête
__c__	**8.** vis-à-vis

Column B

a. something private, between two persons only; a private conversation between two persons (from the French for "head-to-head")

b. a group composed of complementary elements or parts that contribute to a single effect ("together")

c. face-to-face with; in relation to; as compared with

d. a pseudonym used by an author ("pen name")

e. a bulletin; an official announcement

f. a group that develops experimental or innovative techniques; an intelligentsia ("vanguard")

g. required by the prevailing fashion or custom; socially obligatory ("indispensable")

h. a keen or carefree enjoyment of life ("joy of living")

Selecting Word Meanings

*In each of the following groups, circle the word or expression that is **most nearly the same** in meaning as the word in **boldface** type in the given phrase.*

1. the **nadir** of my fortunes
   a. twist
   (b. bottom)
   c. irony
   d. pinnacle

2. a **moratorium** on the sale of arms
   a. emphasis
   (b. suspension)
   c. penalty
   d. symposium

3. countermand the decision
   a. elucidate
   b. exonerate
   c. inundate
   (d. repudiate)

4. cognizant of the facts
   (a. informed of)
   b. ignorant of
   c. indifferent to
   d. indignant about

5. drew water from a **brackish** stream
   a. muddy
   (b. salty)
   c. fast-moving
   d. quiet

6. raze the tenements
   a. renovate
   b. appraise
   (c. demolish)
   d. condemn

7. avid advocates of democracy
   a. cynical
   b. lukewarm
   (c. enthusiastic)
   d. famous

8. the **asperities** of life
   a. rewards
   (b. severities)
   c. uncertainties
   d. pastimes

9. resented their **mordant** remarks
   (a. harsh)
   b. offhand
   c. contemptuous
   d. irrelevant

10. the **flotsam** of a big city
   a. skyscrapers
   b. frenzy
   (c. debris)
   d. exploiters

11. cleared up the **discrepancy**
   a. motive
   b. negligence
   (c. inconsistency)
   d. mess

12. yielded **paltry** results
   a. overwhelming
   (b. insignificant)
   c. ruinous
   d. beneficial

13. composed the **eulogy**
   a. critique
   (b. tribute)
   c. concerto
   d. satire

14. the only member to **demur**
   a. accept
   b. volunteer
   (c. object)
   d. applaud

15. rule by **fiat**
   a. consent
   b. democracy
   c. whim
   (d. decree)

16. disappointed by their **myopic** outlook
   a. nasty
   b. insincere
   c. pessimistic
   (d. shortsighted)

17. an **abject** beggar
   a. carefree
   b. fearless
   (c. wretched)
   d. wandering

18. substantiate a statement
   a. reveal
   (b. verify)
   c. deny
   d. amplify

19. had the **effrontery** to laugh
   a. desire
   (b. gall)
   c. sense
   d. humor

20. their **picayune** criticisms
(a. trifling)   b. humorous   c. irrelevant   d. vicious

21. **portend** a life-or-death struggle
a. overcome   b. prevent   (c. foreshadow)   d. decide

22. delivered a **panegyric**
a. explanation   b. rebuke   c. apology   (d. encomium)

23. the **mandate** of the people
a. betrayal   b. objection   c. folly   (d. authorization)

24. **deign** to acknowledge my presence
a. seem   (b. stoop)   c. refuse   d. attempt

25. **deprecate** such behavior
a. approve   (b. deplore)   c. analyze   d. improve

Word Pairs

In the space before each of the following pairs of words write:

S—if the words are synonyms or near-synonyms;
O—if the words are antonyms or near-antonyms;
N—if the words are unrelated in meaning.

26. __S__ saturnine—morose   **34.** __S__ ubiquitous—omnipresent

27. __O__ arrogate—renounce   **35.** __O__ moribund—thriving

28. __O__ moot—indisputable   **36.** __N__ ambient—pejorative

29. __N__ fecund—fatuous   **37.** __N__ detritus—gambit

30. __O__ feckless—effective   **38.** __O__ frenetic—calm

31. __S__ laconic—terse   **39.** __O__ flatter—calumniate

32. __N__ chicanery—flaccid   **40.** __S__ relentless—inexorable

33. __S__ shortcoming—foible

Words That Describe People

In the space before each word in Column A, write the letter of the item in Column B that best defines it.

	Column A	Column B
__i__	**41.** agnostic	a. one who hates all people
__k__	**42.** penitent	b. a person given to impractical schemes
__e__	**43.** charlatan	c. an extremely patriotic person
__b__	**44.** visionary	d. a rank beginner
__h__	**45.** incumbent	e. a faker
__g__	**46.** suppliant	f. a sorcerer
__a__	**47.** misanthrope	g. one who implores
__f__	**48.** necromancer	h. a current officeholder
__d__	**49.** tyro	i. a homeless wanderer
__i__	**50.** derelict	j. a religious skeptic
		k. one who regrets misdeeds

Words That Describe Physical Qualities

Some words that describe physical qualities are listed below. In the space before each word in Column A, write the letter of the item in Column B that best defines it.

	Column A	Column B
k	**51.** oscillate	a. dried out
a	**52.** desiccated	b. unpleasant to the ear
d	**53.** refulgent	c. a delicate gradation
h	**54.** piquant	d. shining brightly
g	**55.** viscous	e. to raise to a greater height
l	**56.** congeal	f. lacking clarity
c	**57.** nuance	g. thick and gluey
j	**58.** propinquity	h. having a sharp, savory taste
b	**59.** cacophonous	i. blocking out light
f	**60.** murky	j. nearness
		k. to swing back and forth
		l. to thicken or coagulate

Words of Evaluation

Some words that indicate favorable or unfavorable evaluations are listed below. They may apply to people, things, language, etc. Write the appropriate word on the line next to each of the following descriptive sentences.

Group A

acquisitive	ethereal	overweening	pedantry
dilettante	garish	sylvan	sacrilege
decorous	carping	felicitous	ebullient
banal	perspicacity	wizened	pariah

61. Even in casual conversation, his language seems to provide exactly the right words for any purpose or situation.   **felicitous**

62. She is a brilliant executive because she sees through surface appearances and gets right down to the heart of a problem.   **perspicacity**

63. The plot of the soap opera was so familiar, stale, and predictable that we soon stopped watching it.   **banal**

64. She is terribly overdressed—too many jewels, too many bright colors, too many fancy frills.   **garish**

65. Her unfailingly lively and high-spirited personality makes her delightful company.   **ebullient**

66. Because he has an exaggerated idea of his own importance, he assumes an arrogant attitude in dealing with other people.   **overweening**

67. Don't you realize that you will discourage and antagonize people with that constant, petty criticism?   <u>carping</u>

68. Her poetry seems to carry beyond the gross substance of this world into the realm of pure spirit.   <u>ethereal</u>

69. He keeps bringing literary allusions into his conversation even though he knows most people won't understand them.   <u>pedantry</u>

70. He has considerable talent as a painter, but since he is unwilling to work at that profession seriously, he will never accomplish much.   <u>dilettante</u>

Group B

lackadaisical	bestial	benign	pusillanimous
redolent	incendiary	sophistry	taciturn
pertinacious	mundane	inane	mendacious
vituperative	incongruous	mutable	ephemeral

71. His greatest weakness is that he does everything in a half-hearted way, without drive or enthusiasm.   <u>lackadaisical</u>

72. I tried at great length to elicit an opinion from the child, but to no avail.   <u>taciturn</u>

73. Telling lies is not just an occasional thing with him but a way of life.   <u>mendacious</u>

74. The arguments presented in the editorial look good at first, but they are full of deceptive half-truths and clever fallacies.   <u>sophistry</u>

75. Their behavior was so devoid of all moral standards that it seemed subhuman.   <u>bestial</u>

76. Once Tom begins something, he sticks to it until it's completed.   <u>pertinacious</u>

77. His remarks seemed calculated to ignite the heated feelings of his audience.   <u>incendiary</u>

78. Don't you think that a high-rise office tower would look out of place in that residential neighborhood?   <u>incongruous</u>

79. In their efforts to be amusing, they succeed only in being silly and vapid.   <u>inane</u>

80. Their policy of "peace at any price" was denounced by the opposition as craven appeasement.   <u>pusillanimous</u>

Word Associations

*In each of the following, circle the word or expression that best completes the meaning of the sentence or answers the question, with particular reference to the meaning of the word in **boldface** type.*

81. An example of a **euphemism** is
a. "old man" for "father"
b. "boob tube" for "television"
c. "liberate" for "steal"
d. "indeterminate" for "unsettled"

82. An **agnostic** will likely say
a. "I believe."
b. "I don't know."
c. "I'm running late."
d. "My socks are always missing."

83. Typical **amenities** of urban life might include
a. air pollution and litter
b. muggings on the street
c. traffic jams
d. museums and concerts

84. one's **progeny** might include
a. trophies and awards
b. fame and fortune
c. sons and daughters
d. assets and liabilities

85. Which advice would be most suitable for a person who is **recumbent**?
a. "Keep your eye on the ball."
b. "Rise and shine!"
c. "Turn left at the first light."
d. "Grin and bear it."

86. A **figment** usually develops in
a. a factory
b. an orchard
c. the human mind
d. the wild blue yonder

87. A taxi driver who takes you to your destination by a **devious** route may be
a. trying to build up the fare
b. getting rid of you quickly
c. showing off his driving skill
d. saving you money

88. If you **temporize** when a decision is called for, you are
a. acting decisively
b. stalling for time
c. misjudging the situation
d. losing your temper

89. The **motif** of a play refers to its
a. financial backing
b. adaptation for television
c. basic theme
d. cast of characters

90. Which would be a **coup** for a diplomat?
a. arranging an advantageous treaty
b. being sent home
c. taking a vacation
d. retiring after 40 years of service

91. The wisest course of action when confronted by a **juggernaut** is to
a. get out of its way
b. take its picture
c. stand your ground
d. make up your mind

92. **Histrionic** behavior is best suited to
a. the stage
b. the laboratory
c. the classroom
d. the museum

93. A remark you might expect to hear from someone who is **impecunious** is
a. "Let me pay for it."
b. "Keep the change."
c. "Can you change a fifty?"
d. "Why am I always broke?"

94. One generally hopes to **espouse**
a. accidents
b. charlatans
c. specious reasoning
d. good ideas

95. Primordial times occurred
a. in Ancient Greece
b. first
c. as a result of negligence
d. during WWII

96. To **allege** that someone is guilty of a crime means that
a. the person is clearly guilty
b. the charge remains to be proved
c. the charge is malicious
d. an indictment will be handed down

97. Which of the following can be **abrogated**?
a. mother and child
b. tonsils and adenoids
c. the ups and downs of life
d. contracts and treaties

98. In a **convivial** atmosphere, people may be expected to
a. suffer from boredom
b. enjoy themselves
c. go into shock
d. show off their erudition

99. You would be well advised not to give **credence** to
a. your friends
b. your creditors
c. a reliable witness
d. a habitual liar

100. Plaintive tones may issue from you if you
a. get a good night's sleep
b. receive a compliment
c. do well on this Final Mastery Test
d. do poorly on this Final Mastery Test

The following tabulation lists all the basic words taught in the various units of this book, as well as those introduced in the *Vocabulary of Vocabulary, Working with Analogies, Building with Classical Roots,* and *Enriching Your Vocabulary* sections. Words taught in the units are printed in **boldface** type. The number following each entry indicates the page on which the word is first introduced. Exercises and review materials in which the word also appears are not cited.